Landmarks in Rhetoric and Public Address

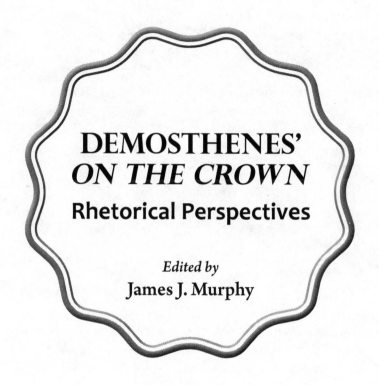

DEMOSTHENES'
ON THE CROWN
Rhetorical Perspectives

Edited by
James J. Murphy

Southern Illinois University Press

CARBONDALE

Southern Illinois University Press
www.siupress.com

Cover illustration: Artemis temple columns. iStock.com / Ahmad
    Atwah

Library of Congress Cataloging-in-Publication Data
Names: Murphy, James Jerome, editor. | Demosthenes. On the crown.
    English.
Title: Demosthenes' "on the crown" : rhetorical perspectives / edited
    by James J. Murphy.
Description: Carbondale : Southern Illinois University Press, 2016.
    | Series: Landmarks in Rhetoric and Public Address | Includes
    bibliographical references and index. | "This book is a revised
    version of *Demosthenes' "On the Crown": A Critical Case Study of a
    Masterpiece of Ancient Oratory*, published by Hermagoras Press in
    1983."
Identifiers: LCCN 2016012977 | ISBN 9780809335107 (paperback) |
    ISBN 9780809335114 (e-book)
Subjects: LCSH: Demosthenes. On the crown. | Rhetoric, Ancient—
    History and criticism. | Oratory, Ancient | BISAC: LANGUAGE
    ARTS & DISCIPLINES / Rhetoric. | LANGUAGE ARTS & DISCIPLINES
    / Speech. | LANGUAGE ARTS & DISCIPLINES / Communication
    Studies.
Classification: LCC PA3950.C6 D4 2016 | DDC 885/.01—dc23 LC
    record available at http://lccn.loc.gov/2016012977

CONTENTS

v

CONTENTS

DEMOSTHENES' *ON THE CROWN*

INTRODUCTION

James J. Murphy

> Next comes the vast army of orators—so vast that a single age produced
> ten of them at Athens. Of these, Demosthenes was by far the greatest,
> almost a law of oratory in himself: such is his force, the concentration of
> his thought, his muscular firmness, his economy, his control—one feels
> that there is nothing lacking and nothing superfluous.
>
> —Quintilian, *Institutio oratoria*, 10.1.76

THE RENOWN OF DEMOSTHENES

This praise of Demosthenes by the Roman rhetorician and educator Marcus
Fabius Quintilianus about the year 95 in the first Christian century[1] is typical of Demosthenes' reputation in the more than two thousand years since
he delivered his most famous oration, *On the Crown*, in 330 BCE.

Even his opponent on that occasion, Aeschines, who went into exile following his defeat in this famous case, later praised his speech to the students
he was instructing on the island of Rhodes. The story is told that Aeschines
had been declaiming his own crown speech to the students, who marveled
that such a fine performance could still have failed to gain one-fifth of the
votes—the minimum necessary under Athenian law to avoid a fine in such
cases. "But oh," Aeschines said, "if only you had heard Demosthenes!"

The Roman orator Cicero was so entranced by the speech that he translated
it into Latin together with that of Aeschines. Unfortunately the translations

have not survived, but in his introduction to the translations (*De optimo genere oratorum*—*On the Best Kind of Orators*) he declares that "nothing can be more inspired than the orator Demosthenes."[2]

Later scholars so admired the oration *On the Crown* that they attempted to fill gaps in the text where Demosthenes refers to long-lost decrees and letters by inserting their own versions of these documents.

The speech was first printed in 1504 and has never been out of print since. In early modern times it was esteemed by such educators as Philip Melanchthon. In fact the English scholar Roger Ascham met regularly with Queen Elizabeth to read aloud the works of Demosthenes. Later Lord Brougham, a prominent English rhetorical critic, made the orator a prime example of successful oratory. In 1742 the philosopher and historian David Hume argued in *Of Eloquence* that Demosthenes, with his force and energy, set the standard for true taste. The Edinburgh professor Hugh Blair, whose *Lectures on Rhetoric and Belles Lettres* (1783) was to have immense influence in the United States, placed Demosthenes above Cicero as an orator and ranked both of them as superior to any modern orator. Demosthenes was also heralded in the United States by such men as Chauncey Goodrich in his Yale lectures from 1822 onward.[3]

During the early part of the twentieth century the stresses of World War I spurred still another type of interest in Demosthenes. Admired by the French for his staunch resistance to the invading Macedonians, Demosthenes was eulogized as a patriot by Premier Georges Clemenceau. On the other hand, some German writers criticized Demosthenes for pursuing the petty interests of lawyers against the great Macedonian King Philip.

As the bibliography shows, scores of writers have studied Demosthenes over the past two centuries. In recent years there has been a resurgence of scholarly interest in Demosthenes, marked by a spate of books about him. These include *Demosthenes: Statesman and Orator*, edited by Ian .*mosthenes the Orator* (Oxford: Oxford University Press, 2009); Cecil W. Wooten, *Cicero's Philippics and Their Demosthenic Model: The Rhetoric of Crisis* (Chapel Hill: University of North Carolina Press, 1983); Craig A. Gibson, *Interpreting a Classic: Demosthenes and His Ancient Commentators* (Berkeley: University of California Press, 2002); and Ian Worthington, *Demosthenes of Athens and the Fall of Classical Greece* (Oxford: Oxford University Press, 2013).

Meanwhile the University of Texas Press has undertaken the translation of all of Demosthenes' speeches in a series edited by Michael Gagarin.

Demosthenes' *On the Crown* (speech 18) is translated by Harvey Yunis in *Demosthenes, Speeches 18 and 19* (Austin: University of Texas Press, 2005).

Clearly, interest remains strong for what Charles Rann Kennedy has called "the greatest speech of the greatest orator in the world."[4] And a speech that has been renowned for twenty-four centuries can surely tell us much about our own approach to the use of persuasion.

THE GOAL OF THIS VOLUME

It is our intention to make Demosthenes' *On the Crown* come alive by recreating the circumstances of his speech, presenting a translation, and then offering detailed rhetorical evaluations, employing the four analytic approaches suggested by Demosthenes' famous contemporary, Aristotle (384–322 BCE), whose *Rhetoric* was the first comprehensive attempt to understand the elements of persuasive speech.

Aristotle states flatly that "there are two parts of a speech; for it is necessary [first] to state the subject, and [then], to demonstrate it" (*Rhetoric* 3.1).[5] Consequently a large portion of his *Rhetoric* is concerned with methods of demonstration or proof—that is, ways in which a speaker can lead ("persuade") an audience to agree with his position. Aristotle says that there are two kinds of proof, first what he calls "nonartistic" or preexisting proofs, which lie outside the control of the speaker; examples are laws, witness testimony, and contracts. But it is to the second type, "artistic" proofs—that is, proofs artistically created by the speaker—that he devotes his greatest attention.

Aristotle names three types of artistic proofs derived respectively from the speaker, the audience, and the speech.

> There is persuasion through character (<u>ethos</u>) of the speaker whenever the speech is spoken in such a way as to make the speaker worthy of credence. (*Rhetoric* 1.2.4)

> There is persuasion through the hearers when they are led to feel emotion (<u>pathos</u>) by the speech. (*Rhetoric* 1.2.5)

> There is persuasion through the arguments (<u>logoi</u>) when we show the truth or apparent truth from whatever is persuasive in each case. (*Rhetoric* 1.2.6)

In addition to these three types of proof, Aristotle notes the importance of what he calls *lexis*, or the value of language: "for it is not enough to have a supply of things to say, but it is also necessary to say it in the right way" (*Rhetoric* 3.1.2).

A reader might well wonder why we have chosen to use these four particular elements as bases for rhetorical evaluation of *On the Crown*. It is not simply because Aristotle and Demosthenes were contemporaries. They moved in two parallel but separate worlds. Aristotle was not an Athenian citizen, while Demosthenes was an active public figure—and they had radically different worldviews. Aristotle taught a few students quietly, while Demosthenes spoke to many thousands over a long oratorical career. In any case, Aristotle's ideas on rhetoric were not "published"—i.e. widely distributed—until after the deaths of both men. Aristotle's ideas therefore could not have been a "cause" of Demosthenes' success, though it is intriguing to consider on the other hand that the speeches of Demosthenes were so well known in Athens that they may well have supplied some of the observational data that Aristotle used to adduce his principles of persuasive behavior.

Our choice is based, rather, on the intrinsic value of Aristotle's empirical observations of human behavior. We see in Aristotle for the first time a conception of rhetoric that is based on the entire range of human behavior—social, logical, ethical, and psychological—using methods of inquiry that today we might call sociological and anthropological. His thirty-five surviving works display a remarkable range of knowledge. The son of a physician, he applied systematic research methods to a variety of fields; for example he collected copies of constitutions of other city-states in preparing *Politics,* his own book on governance. In respect to rhetoric we know that Aristotle compiled a collection of rhetoric handbooks (*synagoge technon*), now lost, though he says of them that they only "worked on a small part of the subject" (*Rhetoric* 1.1.3). His lifelong observation of human behavior leads him to the conclusion that in addition to learning about mental processes such as logic, one needs to understand the social complexities of what happens when people use language to try to persuade other people. In other words, he concludes that a separate study of rhetoric is necessary in human affairs, and his *Rhetoric* is an attempt to answer that need.

It is important to remember, though, that Aristotle apparently never finished this work. (What we have is a compilation produced by editors after his death.) It seems highly significant that a man of Aristotle's manifest genius was unable to bring the same kind of thorough taxonomy to the subject of rhetoric that he did to so many other works. Rhetoric was perhaps too complex even for him to master.

Nevertheless, Aristotle's *Rhetoric* remains to this day one of the most exacting explanations of the mechanics of persuasion. It is for this reason that we choose his four elements to identify what is "rhetorical" in Demosthenes' famous oration *On the Crown*.

One final caution should be noted: that is, that all these four elements in a speech are *simultaneous*. To look carefully at one is not to deny the others, and often one strategy of a speaker will have several aspects to consider at the same time. This is part of artistic mastery.

THE STRUCTURE OF THIS VOLUME

Part 1, "Demosthenes and His Greatest Speech" offers an overview of Demosthenes' life and oratorical career by Lois P. Agnew. Then Donovan Ochs provides an abstract of the speech of Aeschines, Demosthenes' opponent, which is followed by the text of Demosthenes' speech in a translation by John J. Keaney.[6]

Part 2, "Rhetorical Evaluations," begins with a structural analysis of *On the Crown* by Francis P. Donnelly, SJ, followed by four chapters analyzing the roles of ethical, pathetic, and logical proof in the speech, including an examination of the role of language in its success. David C. Mirhady discusses the character of *On the Crown*, including the role of invective. Richard A. Katula treats Demosthenes and emotional proof in *On the Crown*, noting the value of nostalgia as an appeal. Jeffrey Walker describes the impact of cumulative argument leading to a stunning climax in his "On the *Deinos Logos* of Demosthenes' *On the Crown*." And Richard Leo Enos concludes in his "Demosthenes and the Style of *On the Crown*" that style was "the force that made *On the Crown* endure."

All this is offered to the reader in the hope that, as with Aristotle, observation can lead to a personal synthesis of what it takes to be successful in persuasion. It is, after all, nearly the definition of a masterpiece that new readers will eternally find in it fresh insights.

With this many-faceted approach, then, the reader may come to understand why *On the Crown* has been justly called a tour de force of the art of oratory.

NOTES

1. Donald A. Russell, ed. and trans., *Quintilian: The Orator's Education*, 5 vols., Loeb Classical Library (Cambridge: Harvard University Press, 2001), 10.1.76.

2. Cicero, *De inventione. De optimo genere oratorum. Topica*, trans. H. M. Hubbell, Loeb Classical Library (Cambridge: Harvard University Press; London: William Heineman Ltd., 1968). *De optimo* 6.17. For cautionary observations

see also Craig Cooper, "Demosthenes' Rhetorical Reputation in Antiquity," in *Demosthenes: Statesman and Orator,* ed. Ian Worthington (London: Routledge, 2000), 225–45.

3. Phillip Harding has some further evidence of later influence in "Demosthenes in the Underworld: A Chapter in the *Nachleben of a rhetor*" in Worthington, *Demosthenes,* 256–71.

4. Charles Rann Kennedy, trans., *The Orations of Demosthenes: "On the Crown" and "On the Embassy,"* Bohn's Classical Library (London: Bell, 1884), 1.

5. Citations will be to George A. Kennedy, trans., *Aristotle: A Theory of Civic Discourse: On Rhetoric* (New York: Oxford University Press, 2006). References are to book, chapter, and numbered section within a chapter.

6. Some segments—Ochs, Donnelly, Keaney—are reprinted with permission from James J. Murphy, ed., *Demosthenes' "On the Crown": A Critical Case Study of a Masterpiece of Ancient Oratory* (Davis, CA: Hermagoras Press, 1983).

Demosthenes and His Greatest Speech

1. DEMOSTHENES AND HIS TIMES

Lois P. Agnew

The oration *On the Crown* arises from the life of a man who has for many centuries represented the power and complexity of Greek oratory. The abiding interest among western rhetoricians in the oratorical achievement of Demosthenes has created a biography whose outlines are a combination of fact and legend; at the same time, the scarcity of primary documents providing reliable information about that life ensure that the lines between the two have always been difficult to define. This biographical essay offers an overview of Demosthenes' life for nonspecialist readers, for the purpose of providing context for their reading of the speech and the critical essays that follow.

This overview uses a range of secondary sources—present-day historians along with Plutarch (120?–46? BCE)—to highlight the varying interpretations of Demosthenes' life and significance. As is well known, Plutarch's *Lives* lacks both the factual reliability it might have had if the biographies had been written contemporaneously; at the same time, its distance from our own time creates a critical distance from the principles of modern historiography that we value. Plutarch's writing reflects not only the limited sources that were available to him, but also the moral and political aims his biographies served. D. A. Russell insists on the recognition of these aims as necessary to using Plutarch's work even as he emphasizes Plutarch's potential value as a source. Russell notes that the information Plutarch presents reflects his educational mission to offer "a repertoire of *exempla* for public men of Plutarch's own day" and to uplift "humanity and magnanimity, the essentials (to Plutarch as to us) of civilized life."[1] While he acknowledges that Plutarch's vision goes beyond presenting material objectively, he argues that "the *naïveté* of the *Lives*, which is real enough, and of which it is so easy to give a damning picture, lies much more in their initial conception and plan than in the execution."[2] Russell shares the generally accepted view that Plutarch's *Lives* lack features essential to modern critical biography, but also asserts that Plutarch's "attempt to reduce motives to the philosophically and morally familiar in no way destroys the magnificence of the background against which the heroes move, the greatness of the events in which they took part, or the grandeur of their struggle with destiny."[3] The discussion of Demosthenes' life in this essay relies in part on Plutarch as a source for capturing the legendary significance of Demosthenes as an important representative of Greek oratory and political leadership. Plutarch's particular view of the qualities that define excellence and his aim of presenting the glories of Greek heroism to an imperial audience cannot be detached from his depiction of Demosthenes' life.

The difficulty of accurately depicting Demosthenes' life goes beyond the limitations inherent in using Plutarch as a source. In fact, the life and career of Demosthenes embody many of the questions that persistently emerge in classical history. Perhaps it is only fitting that the figure represented across many centuries as the western oratorical ideal should also represent the tensions that have surrounded the construction of that ideal. Questions about Demosthenes' character carry forward Plato's early argument concerning the ethical dangers surrounding any art focused on mass persuasion. Debates about the relative merits of Demosthenes' oratorical prowess illustrate diverse views of the features of style and delivery worthy of emulation and emphasize the subjective qualities and cultural biases shaping those judgments. The descriptions of Demosthenes' heroic efforts to overcome his physical weaknesses in order to attain rhetorical proficiency connect with ancient controversies about the role of natural aptitude, study, and practice in the formation of the true orator. And the fact that many biographical particulars are available only through the content of the speeches of Demosthenes and his political rivals underscores the relationship, always tenuous, between questions of fact and rhetorical aims pursued through ethical and ad hominem appeals. These features of Demosthenes' biography support the present-day emphasis on history writing itself as a rhetorical enterprise, providing those arguments with particular focus as we encounter ways in which limited biographical information has been assembled into different forms in response to particular value systems and rhetorical aims of subsequent time periods. All of these questions underscore the problematic nature of the search to understand the individual behind Demosthenes' oratory while highlighting the value of critical reflection about the intriguing interplay between Demosthenes' life, oratorical and political achievements, and legacy.

The centrality of oratory to Demosthenes' identity itself provides a means of tracking major developments in his life, thought, and career as they are situated in the broader contours of Athenian political life. Peter Hunt's study of politics in fourth-century Athens draws heavily on the speeches of prominent orators, notwithstanding "the occasional inaccuracy and even the self-serving mendacity of assembly speakers," to illuminate the processes and guiding principles undergirding the determination of policy.[4] If the oratorical career of a major figure such as Demosthenes can shed light on Athenian political life more generally, it can certainly assist in understanding who Demosthenes was.

EARLY LIFE

Demosthenes was born around 384 BCE. His father, Demosthenes of Paiania, was a wealthy manufacturer, described by Plutarch as a sword maker with a large shop employing many skilled servants.[5] His mother, Cleobule, was the daughter of Gylon of Kerameis, who was banished from Attica under a cloud of allegations of treason and then married a wealthy Scythian woman. Demosthenes acknowledged that his grandfather owed the state money at one time but insisted that this debt had been repaid. Aeschines attempted to use Demosthenes' maternal lineage against him, but it is not likely that such calumny would have had much traction with Athenians. As E. Badian points out, Demosthenes' grandparents were likely married during the Peloponnesian War, when Pericles' law requiring both parents to be citizens was suspended; Demosthenes' mother would have counted as a citizen since her father was Athenian.[6]

Demosthenes' father died when he was seven and left his sizable estate in the hands of two nephews and a friend. Unfortunately, these trustees embezzled funds and mismanaged the estate, diminishing greatly the wealth that could be drawn on for Demosthenes' support. This, plus Demosthenes' fragile health, may account for the fact that he did not attend the gymnasium. Demosthenes' physical frailty was also noted by his contemporaries;

his classmates, according to Plutarch, gave him the nickname Batalus, the name of an "effeminate flute-player" in a play by Antiphanes, as well as a term connoting a writer of drinking songs and a crude word for body parts.[7] Thus from an early age Demosthenes' life story includes obstacles and limited possibilities.

EARLY EDUCATION AND ORATORICAL INTERESTS

Demosthenes' mother reportedly did assist him in his education, with both school and occasional private tutoring.[8] Plutarch cites Hermippus's reference to anonymous memoirs suggesting that Demosthenes was a student of Plato at one time, and reports Ctesibus's statement that Demosthenes "secretly obtained the rhetorical systems of Isocrates and Alcidamas, and mastered them."[9] Demosthenes' particular interest in oratory was apparently sparked by an opportunity to hear Callistratus's advocacy for Oropus in a highly visible trial. His excitement at Callistratus's power with language encouraged him to prepare himself for an oratorical career, and soon afterward he began practicing declamation under the orator Isaeus, whose tutelage would have assisted Demosthenes in achieving his practical aims.[10] Demosthenes' interest in relating theory to rhetorical practice is a persistent feature of his life as an orator.

Demosthenes was probably admitted to the *deme*, the organizational unit that offered access to Athenian political life, as a full citizen around 366 BCE. By the time he came of age, Demosthenes was aware of his guardians' perfidy and was determined to prosecute them to recover the lost funds. Although his preparation of his case was interrupted by the required military training and service, he was able to initiate formal arguments as early as the age of twenty.[11] The guardians' powerful connections and command of legal intricacies put Demosthenes at a disadvantage in spite of the prima facie strength of his case; Badian notes that "it proved easier for Demosthenes to obtain verdicts than to obtain redress."[12] However, in spite of the lack of material benefit from the case, Demosthenes' experience with the law provided a foundation for his later pursuit of a career in oratory. Although there is uncertainty about which of the speeches prepared for the case were actually composed by Demosthenes, Werner Jaeger judges that Demosthenes' experience with the case can be seen as the start of his career, demonstrating immersion in legal and oratorical principles that would only have been available through intensive study from a very young age.[13]

Demosthenes' ability to assemble an effective case provided him with a valuable starting point for beginning a career in speech writing and advocacy. He quickly became known as a logographer (speechwriter), a career path available to him as a result of his detailed knowledge of civil law and his aptitude in navigating legal procedures.[14] David C. Mirhady adds that the increasing stability of the law in the late fifth century led to a concomitant shift toward the primacy of the written word, which Demosthenes used effectively, reading from written documents to provide a "roadmap" of evidence woven into his narrative of the case.[15] Although only a few speeches are available from the period when Demosthenes worked as a logographer, it is evident that his several years in this role were profitable, in view of the impressive sum he claimed to have invested in public service through the *leitourgiai*.[16] Harvey Yunis suggests that Demosthenes had a significant role in removing the stigma that had at one time been connected with speaking from written texts, noting that Demosthenes was certainly the first person to use his career as a speechwriter as the foundation of a successful political career.[17]

One of Demosthenes' earliest public assignments came in 360 BCE, when he served as trierarch of a vessel that traveled through the Hellespont region. This experience came at a moment of relative stability for Athens, but it demonstrates Demosthenes' attention to the potential for strengthening Athens's economic and military position through alliances securing the clear passage of merchant vessels through the ports along the northern shores of the Aegean to Byzantium.[18] The vision of the world Demosthenes received from his naval tour added to his experience in producing persuasive arguments and distinguished him further as speechwriter and orator. He continued to apply his skills to writing speeches for delivery in civic trials, many of which advanced charges of unconstitutionality in the actions of individuals, a common strategy employed in efforts to gain political advantage and discredit one's rivals. In 355 BCE, Demosthenes supported arguments against the crown that had been awarded to Androtion's boule on the grounds that this action failed to adhere strictly to the law stipulating the requirements for shipbuilding. Badian argues against using this speech for insight into Demosthenes' political perspective; rather, he declares, Demosthenes was guided primarily by the interests of his clients, as well as by personal grudges he might have held in connection with the lawsuit against his guardians.[19]

EMERGING POLITICAL CAREER

Demosthenes' increasing public presence, including leadership in the popular assembly, required the further development of his oratorical skills. Plutarch's well-known recital of the obstacles Demosthenes faced at this point in his career includes his awkward and overly formal manner of argumentation, but gives greater attention to the effect of physical limitations on Demosthenes' delivery. According to Plutarch, Demosthenes had a weak voice, spoke with a peculiar hesitation, and was plagued by shortness of breath. Demosthenes did receive encouragement from a chance encounter with an elderly stranger who counseled persistence, as well as from an impromptu tutoring session with Satyrus the actor, who offered pointers after observing Demosthenes' poor performance in the assembly.[20] Demosthenes' own efforts to overcome his weaknesses, also detailed in Plutarch, have circulated widely and become established features of the common story of Demosthenes that Adams refers to as "mingled fact and fiction": that he practiced speaking with a mouth full of pebbles to improve his enunciation; that he constructed an underground dwelling where he worked on speaking and delivery in isolation; that he shaved half his head to motivate himself to continue training instead of returning to the distractions of public life; that he practiced declaiming while running and climbing stairs in order to improve his breath control; and that he practiced gestures in front of a mirror.[21] Badian acknowledges the legendary nature of these stories but accepts their existence as supporting the view that Demosthenes put a great deal of focused effort into his pursuit of oratorical aptitude.[22]

These features of Demosthenes' training have led to varying assessments of his merits as an orator. To modern ears they underscore the value of hard work and perseverance, while in the ancient world Demosthenes' diligent training program was initially advanced by Peripatetic philosophers to demonstrate his inferiority to those Attic orators who came by their skills naturally.[23] Plutarch acknowledges and to some extent supports this interpretation, declaring Demades' extemporaneous eloquence more excellent than "the studied preparations of Demosthenes" and distinguishing the favorable reception of Demosthenes by "most men" from the critical attitudes of the educated.[24] At the same time, Plutarch allows that Demosthenes could speak with forceful eloquence in the immediacy of a legal proceeding. Yunis goes further, calling into question the entire notion of Demosthenes' deficiencies in extemporaneous speaking and arguing that his use of written speeches does not at all preclude skill at spontaneous delivery: "since debate in the Assembly required speaking, Demosthenes' success makes it necessary to assume that he could do what he needed to do."[25] Anne Duncan further complicates the issue by noting that some of Demosthenes' apparently unscripted moments may actually have been carefully planned, adding that the historic debate about his proficiency with extempore delivery is in itself part of the construction of his identity as an orator: "Demosthenes' supposed inability (or unwillingness) to speak off the cuff is a fascinating aspect of his biographical tradition. We could read it as a defensive maneuver, akin to his abuse of Aeschines for having been an actor; refusing to speak on the spur of the moment could be a way of protecting himself from seeming 'histrionic.' Conversely, we could read it as a tacit admission that his speeches were studiously worked up to seem spontaneous, instead of being spontaneous, that he could not perform without a script."[26]

Whatever the reality of Demosthenes' strengths and limitations, it is clear that his oratorical performances had a strong positive effect on his audiences. He appeared to be transported by emotion in his most powerful speeches, a tactic that Plutarch suggests might have been enhanced by the fact that Demosthenes used it sparingly.[27] Plutarch also acknowledges that Demosthenes' time-consuming, painstaking preparation was a positive feature of his oratory. Demosthenes conceived of thoughtful engagement as a sign of his respect for his fellow citizens, reflecting a desire not to be the type of speaker who "relies on force rather than on persuasion."[28] Aesion's view, as reported by Plutarch referencing Hermippus, acknowledges both studiousness and spontaneity as factors making Demosthenes' speeches structurally superior and emotionally more persuasive than even those orators of a previous generation who spoke with great elegance but did not achieve Demosthenes' power.[29] In assessing Demosthenes alongside Cicero, Plutarch advances a role for both talent and diligence in the success of Demosthenes' speeches.[30]

This unusual mixture of life challenges, ability, study, practice, and logographic experience constituted Demosthenes' "way station to politics."[31] R. D. Milns notes that written copies of Demosthenes' orations were circulated during his rise for the purpose of promoting his political career and are likely to have closely resembled his actual spoken words, in view of his penchant for careful advance preparation.[32] His ability to use words was his main recommendation, in contrast to many politicians who could rely more heavily on personal wealth, family connections, or military achieve-ments to recommend them as leaders. According to Yunis, Demosthenes continued to be "forced to rely, more so than Pericles, on purely rhetori-cal means to exert leadership. Demosthenes was a politician, with all that implies, but he was a serious politician; that is, using the rhetorical means at his disposal and operating within the limits of the Athenian political world, he attempted to lead the *demos* to make the decisions that, in his view, would be best for the *polis*."[33] Oratory was necessary to Demosthenes' rise to public influence, and it continued to be the foundation of his ability to lead throughout his career.

DEMOSTHENES, ORATORY, AND POLITICS

The early speeches of Demosthenes' public oratorical career focused on varied causes, from internal corruption to external threats to Athens and its allies, generally posed by two longstanding rivals, Sparta and Thebes. In a short time, however, diplomatic and military concerns from a different direction began to predominate, as Demosthenes and other Athenians took account of the rise of Macedon under its brilliant king, Philip II. Philip's in-novative battlefield tactics and skillful diplomacy, playing the Greek states against each other, enabled him in a few years' time not only to consolidate power within Macedon, but also to establish his kingdom as a formidable power. Demosthenes and other Athenian leaders debated various ways of responding to Philip, and by the end of the decade Demosthenes emerged as the leading advocate of forceful opposition. In giving voice to this policy in his *First Philippic*, delivered in 351 when he was thirty-three years old, Demosthenes also demonstrated the sharpening of his oratorical skills in the weaving of evidence into narrative and articulating the urgency of Athens's situation.[34]

Scholars differ in describing Demosthenes' profile in opposing Macedon up to this point. Charles Darwin Adams offers a view similar to Plutarch's, that Demosthenes was involved in drawing attention to Macedonian ag-gression at an early stage.

His personal knowledge of the northern coasts and his appreciation of their vital relation to Athenian commerce, as well as his pride in the tra-ditional sea-power of Athens, impelled him to urge vigorous resistance to the new Macedonian power. He early recognized Philip as a man who would not be content with the mere restoration of Macedon to its old local power. Demosthenes saw that Philip had ambition and ability which would threaten the peace of all northern Greece, and he threw himself into the struggle to arouse the Athenians to a realization of the gravity of the situation.[35]

Badian, on the other hand, emphasizes the length of time it took Demosthenes to respond to Philip.[36] T. T. B. Ryder offers a similar view, pointing to *On the Symmories*, a speech about the threat posed to Athens by Persia, as evidence that Demosthenes was still not fully focused on Philip as late as 353 BCE.[37]

Nevertheless, it is clear that Demosthenes was the leading voice of opposition to Macedon by 351 and 336 BCE, and "from 346 to 324 Athenian policy was virtually Demosthenes' policy."[38] Yunis notes that Demosthenes faced a particular rhetorical challenge, as his determination to provide a clear, forceful statement about the danger at hand ran the risk of creating a barrier between himself and his audience.[39] However, even before the *First Philippic*, Athenians were not blind to the Macedonian threat. Athens fought alongside Sparta and Achaea at Thermopylae in 352, stopping Philip's incursion into central Greece. During this period Athens established additional alliances meant to counter Philip: Cersobleptes granted Athens's claim to the Chersonese, a move that points toward growing recognition of the danger Philip posed to the region, and the Olynthians also broke their ties with Philip and pursued peace with Athens in the same year.[40] However, Athens was unable to prevent Philip's march through Thrace to the Propontis, endangering the passage of Athenian corn supplies from the Black Sea area. It was after this, Jaeger suggests, that Demosthenes saw clearly the scope of Philip's ambition and made resistance "a single objective which put all others in the shade."[41]

Demosthenes' increasingly urgent responses to Philip's military activity continued from that point. In 349 Philip began a campaign against Olynthus, which issued three appeals to Athens for help. Demosthenes' Olynthiac orations offer strong arguments for Athenian intervention. The *First* and *Second Olynthiacs* argue that immediate action supporting Olynthus is in Athens's own interest; although Demosthenes did not get as much support as he had hoped for, the Athenian vote to provide some help may have caused Philip to delay his attack.[42] The *Third Olynthiac* (349–348 BCE) presented an even more forceful argument for Athenian action, including a proposal, ultimately unsuccessful, to draw from the theoric fund for this purpose. In keeping with his generally critical view of Demosthenes,

Cawkwell offers a negative assessment of these speeches, stating that Demosthenes "never said exactly what he wanted" and suggests that any specific courses of action Demosthenes did offer would not have been enough to stop Philip's advances. He concludes: "The unpalatable strategic fact was that the Chalcidians could not be saved and the Athenians were fortunate that no large number of their citizens was ever landed to attempt the impossible. The only hope for Athens was that they could unite the Greeks in defence of Greece itself, and Demosthenes was here as elsewhere without the true statesman's strategic sense."[43] Although Cawkwell's judgment of Demosthenes during this period is debatable, there is no question that Philip was well positioned to achieve rapid victory in Olynthus, which fell in 348.

Even in the midst of his military campaigns during this period, Philip expressed an interest in peace with Athens through Euboean envoys. John Buckler states that Athenian skepticism toward the proposal lessened following Athenian orator Ctesiphon's successful visit to Macedon to request the return of the ransom paid by Phryno of Rhamnus, who had been captured by Macedonian pirates.[44] Philocrates was elected to negotiate the peace, but the effort to pursue this goal was delayed by the fall of Olynthus, which included the capture of a number of Athenian prisoners. An embassy from Athens proposed by Eubulus, which included Aeschines, traveled to Megalopolis to discuss military action against Philip, but was unsuccessful, due at least in part to the smaller states' longstanding reluctance to work with Athens and Sparta. These developments, Buckler argues, strengthened Aeschines' sense of the importance of pursuing peace with Philip. The failure of the Athenians to reach agreement with other Greek states showed the limits of Athens's ability to garner support, and the sight of Olynthians enslaved by Philip on the return trip to Athens made clear the dangers that could come about from Philip's enmity. Moreover, Aeschines may have believed that Philip had no real designs against Athens.[45]

Meanwhile, Demosthenes' desire for a more assertive stance against Macedon led to a widening of the gulf between Demosthenes and conservative leaders such as Phocion and Eubulus as well as Aeschines. The increasing personal rancor between proponents of the two points of view was evident in an incident at the 348 Dionysiac festival, when Meidias, a friend of Eubulus, struck Demosthenes in the face. Demosthenes' subsequent preparation of a legal case concerning this incident is documented in *Against Meidias*, but a settlement was reached before the trial took place.[46]

At this point Philip indicated interest in coming to terms with Athens. This move was welcomed by both sides, and Demosthenes, Philocrates, and Aeschines were among the delegation of ten citizens who met with Philip in 346 to negotiate a treaty. There are differing interpretations of how Demosthenes represented himself in these negotiations. Jaeger repeats Aeschines' claim that Demosthenes' contribution to the discussion at the first meeting with Philip was limited, as he faltered after delivering the first part of his speech.[47] Raphael Sealey, however, questions the reliability of this report, noting that uncorroborated statements made by rivals must be viewed with suspicion.[48] According to Plutarch, Philip's court respected Demosthenes as a formidable adversary and took pains to respond to his statements carefully on the occasions when Philip and Demosthenes met, though his refusal to flatter Philip resulted in less hospitable treatment than that given to his fellow ambassadors.[49] During the first meeting with Philip, Aeschines argued that Macedon should restore Amphipolis to Athens, a position Demosthenes later criticized. At a subsequent meeting, Philip responded to the Athenian presentation, agreeing to send an embassy to Athens to finalize the terms, and promised to avoid intervention in the Chersonese while the treaty was pending.[50]

Following the meeting Demosthenes expressed his dissatisfaction with several terms of the treaty and charged Aeschines with having been a primary supporter of Philocrates, but Ryder notes that Demosthenes was as fully connected with the negotiations as other members of the embassy.[51] However, Demosthenes' attitude changed, particularly as a second embassy was sent to Macedon to secure Philip's oath on the final agreement. Philip was away when the ambassadors arrived, and the Athenians encountered embassies from a number of other Greek states also awaiting an audience with the king. According to Cawkwell, this situation made Demosthenes restless and led to fissures in his relationship with Philocrates as well as Aeschines. Buckler notes that in the end both Demosthenes and Aeschines acknowledged flaws in the treaty, but the Peace of Philocrates was enacted in 346.[52] By the time the assembly returned to Athens, Philip had attacked the region of Phocis, which had requested Athenian assistance. In subsequent assembly sessions considering the Phocian appeal, Demosthenes' break with Philocrates and Aeschines was solidified, as Demosthenes argued against Philocrates' proposal to reaffirm the peace even to the extent of going to war against the Phocians.[53] Philip's conquest of Phocis solidified his leadership in the Amphictyonic League (a loose confederation of

Greek city-states), to whom he assigned the responsibility of determining the appropriate punishment for the Phocians. In spite of his opposition to Philip, Demosthenes' *On the Peace*, delivered in 346, argued in favor of Philip's election to the Amphictyonic Council. At the same time, Philip's position on the council gave him license to take action in Greek affairs without technically violating the terms of the treaty.[54]

The sharpening of Demosthenes' opposition to Philip contributed to his growing personal enmity with Aeschines, who had become the leading advocate for preserving the agreement with Philip.[55] In 346, Demosthenes and Timarchus began planning a charge of treason against Aeschines, which Aeschines countered by attacking the characters of his opponents. Aeschines' trial against Timarchus was successful, and Buckler identifies this as a significant moment in the development of the feud between Demosthenes and Aeschines.[56] Demosthenes believed that his rivals were entangled with Macedonian interests, and he reiterated this charge with increasing boldness during the years following the treaty's enactment. Demosthenes' rivalry with Aeschines developed beyond their policy differences into a quarrel "that was generally unseemly and often vicious."[57] Sealey emphasizes the role of temperament in the division: "The experiences of 346 taught Demosthenes the task to which he had to devote his life; pursuing it, he became for a few years the leading man in Athens. Aeschines never appears in his speeches as a man with a mission. He had a more agreeable voice than Demosthenes, and he valued the privilege of abstaining from political activity."[58] The view that Demosthenes and Aeschines differed in the strength of their political commitments has colored many modern-day portraits of the two men, Duncan says, but she detects similarities in them as well. "In their disputes about diplomatic embassies and civic honors, Demosthenes and Aeschines both call attention to the fine line between oratory and acting by contrasting themselves with each other. Each suggests that his opponent is a dissembling actor who manipulates the audience. Demosthenes warns the audience not to be swept away by Aeschines' fine voice and empty phrases; Aeschines makes it seem that the weak-voiced Demosthenes is jealous of his natural talent."[59] Buckler notes that this animosity creates a challenge for historians seeking to discern in their speeches the facts of Athenian political life or even the intellectual underpinnings of their positions. "Neither Demosthenes nor Aeschines was a high-minded man whose ideals transcended the political cause that he espoused at the moment. Both men were mean, meretricious, and scurrilous."[60]

This makes it a particularly complicated challenge to identify and trace the course of the facts in the shifting political landscape during this period. Demosthenes repeatedly links the themes of bribery and accommodation to Macedonian interests as part of his effort to distinguish himself from his political opponents. Aeschines' image was damaged after he supported Philip's effort to amend the treaty through enlisting Pytho of Byzantium as an envoy. In 345, Demosthenes and Timarchus accused Aeschines of having accepted bribes from Philip in an attempt to connect Aeschines with Hyperides' charge that Philocrates had taken such bribes; however, while Philocrates fled, Aeschines remained to fight the charge and continued to maintain the value of pursuing peace as the best policy.[61] Demosthenes renewed his attacks in 343 with the delivery of *On the False Embassy*, charging that bribery accounted for a shift in Aeschines' views of Philip and the peace. Cawkwell notes that there is little evidence supporting Demosthenes' charges of bribery, and adds that reasonable people might have perceived peace with Macedon as desirable in its own right.[62] Sealey shares this view and charges that the emphasis on bribery obscures the opinions of Demosthenes' opponents, who may well have been less accommodating toward Philip than Demosthenes' charges made them seem. "The literature springing from the assembly and the courts does not provide adequate evidence of the existence of a pro-Macedonian party or of a party of advocates of peace with Philip."[63] Aeschines responded to Demosthenes' political charges and personal attacks with his own strong criticisms of his rival. Aeschines' argument achieved his acquittal, but at the same time Athenians' fears of Macedon were growing, leading to a decline in Aeschines' political fortunes while Demosthenes' position grew stronger.[64]

Philip's unceasing military action following the ratification of the Peace of Philocrates established a pattern that continued for the next five years. While technically upholding the treaty's terms, Philip acted in ways that solidified and expanded his power in the region.[65] During this time Demosthenes began to construct a more active opposition to Macedonian imperialism. After the Messenians and Argives solicited Philip's protection against Sparta in 344, Demosthenes launched a mission to argue against allowing Philip's involvement in the Peloponnese.[66] When Philip and his Peloponnesian allies sent an embassy to Athens to protest, Demosthenes delivered the *Second Philippic*, which catalogues the military action Philip had taken since the treaty was negotiated and urges distrust on the part of the state toward an unjust and ambitious ruler.

Cawkwell identifies this moment as a turning point. "From 344 onwards Demosthenes and his associates were relentless in arousing hostility to Philip."[67] Demosthenes, in Cawkwell's view, strategically misrepresented the extent to which Philip's conduct violated the peace, which reflected his determination to reject negotiations with Philip that might have better served Athenian interests.[68] Cawkwell acknowledges the difficulty of predicting what would have happened if Demosthenes' position had not prevailed, but his view at the very least offers an alternative to the positive readings of Demosthenes' political acumen that characterize many depictions of Demosthenes' career.

Demosthenes persisted in his efforts to marshal Athenian resistance as Macedon became entangled in situations where Athens had its own longstanding interests.[69] In 342, a force led by Diopeithes was sent to the Thracian Chersonese, where they violated the terms of the treaty by attacking Philip's holdings. Pro-Macedonian Athenian leaders argued that Diopeithes should be recalled, a claim Demosthenes countered in *On the Affairs in the Chersonese*, delivered in 341. Demosthenes' effort to shift the focus to Philip's own militaristic acts succeeded to the extent that Diopeithes was not recalled, although Athens did not send additional forces to the area.[70] Cawkwell challenges the veracity of Demosthenes' charge that Philip was breaking the peace, arguing that Philip had no need to do so since many Greek cities considered themselves to be profiting through their alliance with him.[71] Nevertheless, Demosthenes' view succeeded in enlisting the support of many Athenian leaders. In his *Third Philippic* (delivered in 341), Demosthenes argued passionately that Athens must mobilize for war to fulfill its rightful role as a leader in promoting liberty throughout Greece. Jaeger contrasts this vision of Greek unity through solidarity against the Macedonian enemy with Isocrates' Panhellenism in which Philip would lead the Greek states in their longstanding struggle with Persia. "*His* [Demosthenes'] Panhellenism was the outgrowth of a resolute will for national self-assertiveness, deliberately opposed to the national self-surrender called for by Isocrates—for that was what Isocrates' program had really meant, despite its being expressed romantically as a plan for a Persian war under Macedonian leadership."[72] The authenticity of Demosthenes' *Fourth Philippic* (341 BCE) is questioned by many scholars, but Sealey notes that the speech extends Demosthenes' earlier arguments in which he questions the value of sending envoys to request help from the Persian king.[73]

Demosthenes' appeals in the *Third Philippic* were at least partly responsible for a crystallization of Athenian sentiment during this period. The Assembly endorsed Demosthenes' motion to establish an alliance with Chalcis in Euboea, which set the stage for its first significant military action to challenge Philip's influence since the Peace of Philocrates, a joint mission to free the town of Oreus from the rule of the tyrant Philistides. Demosthenes continued his efforts by leading an embassy through Greece to form a league of Greek city-states willing to oppose Philip, including an alliance with Byzantium. Demosthenes was awarded a crown in 340 in recognition of his leadership. Meanwhile, Philip's actions continued to encroach on Athenian interests. His attacks on the north shore of the Propontis endangered the Athenian corn-supply route, which had been an ongoing concern of the Athenians through Philip's various initiatives in the region. Philip's strong letter protesting Athens's failure to observe the terms of the peace treaty may have been responsible for the lack of Athenian support for Perinthus, but Philip's subsequent attack on Byzantium and seizing of the fleet of corn ships was a provocation the Athenians could not ignore.[74] Following a letter in which Philip declared war against Athens in September 340, Demosthenes secured a decree of war against Macedon, and "the stone recording the Peace of Philocrates was destroyed."[75]

In 340, Philip used a dispute in the Amphictyonic Council as an excuse to move troops into central Greece on the road to Athens. Because Aeschines had made the argument against the Locrian cultivation of sacred land that had set the stage for the declaration of a Sacred War led by Philip, Demosthenes accused Aeschines of accepting bribes that had shaped his position on the attack against the Locrians. According to Ryder, Demosthenes' argument—that Athenian representatives should not attend the council meeting to discuss the issues leading to the Sacred War—was prompted by his desire to avoid further bad will between Athens and Thebes, a strategy that soon had a positive outcome. Although many Athenians expected Thebes to facilitate Philip's effort to march toward Attica, Demosthenes and a team of envoys traveled to Thebes in 339 to propose an alliance. This was perhaps the greatest diplomatic challenge Demosthenes had faced in building a league of Greek city-states, given the Thebans' history of friendly relations with Philip and their longstanding hostility toward Athens. Philip attempted to counter Demosthenes by sending his own envoys to pursue a peaceful settlement.[76] Although the Thebans feared war, Plutarch credits Demosthenes with convincing them to join the alliance.[77]

Demosthenes reportedly played an important role in both the Theban and Athenian assemblies and was respected by both. Plutarch asserts that Demosthenes achieved his influence "not illegally nor unworthily, as Theopompus declares," but instead prevailed through the persuasiveness of his patriotic vision of Greek unity.[78] The Athenians and Thebans joined forces to defend western Boeotia and prevent Amphissa from being invaded. Demosthenes was awarded a crown at Great Dionysia in March of 338, demonstrating his continued influence during this period.[79]

But in spite of the efforts of the alliance of Greek city-states forged through Demosthenes' diplomacy, the Athenians and their allies were unable to stop Philip's army. Philip conquered Amphissa, then offered to negotiate another peace with Athens and Thebes; the rejection of this initiative reflected Demosthenes' fear that such an agreement would only perpetuate the pattern of giving Philip unlimited power to determine the nature of the relationship.[80]

Athens's rejection of Philip's overture set the stage for the devastating battle of Chaeronea, "one of the most decisive battles in history,"[81] in August 338. The armies of Athens and Thebes were routed, and Greek military opposition to Macedon effectively came to an end. Plutarch expresses disapproval of Demosthenes' lack of prudence and courage in his conduct; not only did he foolishly refuse to heed the warnings of defeat given by the oracles, but he also threw aside his weapons and fled the field during the battle.[82] Following up on this complete victory, Philip consolidated his authority over all of southern Greece, treating Athens with greater magnanimity than Thebes.[83] He released Athenian prisoners without ransom, did not establish military outposts in Athens, maintained Athens's democratic institutions, and agreed to a peace treaty negotiated by Aeschines, Demades, and Phocion.[84]

Although Plutarch insists that Demosthenes' influence with the people was unabated after Chaeronea, he also reports that the defeat sparked a new round of criticisms by his political opponents, including the filing of indictments against him. Demosthenes became less active for a time and submitted decrees only under his friends' names, recognizing that his own had been damaged by the disastrous result of the policies he had advocated.[85] Yet the people of Athens did not entirely turn from Demosthenes' leadership and continued to share his distrust of Philip, notwithstanding the king's apparent magnanimity following the battle.[86] Demosthenes continued to explore the possibility of forming an alliance with Persia against Macedonia, which received the king's respectful attention, Plutarch reports, due to his regard for Demosthenes' rhetorical ability.[87] The people not only acquitted Demosthenes of the charges filed against him, but also gave him the distinction of presenting the eulogy for those who fell at Chaeronea, an honor that Duncan attributes to the widespread perception that Demosthenes embodied the feelings of the people of Athens.[88] Although Demosthenes lost the election to the synhedrion responsible for oversight of the Common Peace treaty, he was elected commissioner for walls and commissioner of the theoric fund. In 336, Ctesiphon proposed a crown honoring Demosthenes' service to the city. After the boule's vote in support of the resolution, Aeschines brought charges against Ctesiphon for proposing an illegal resolution before the Assembly could act, which led to a lengthy delay in the final decision.

Philip's murder in October of 336 reinvigorated Demosthenes' public profile. Demosthenes appeared in festive garments and gave thank-offerings immediately after hearing the news, in spite of the fact that his own daughter had died only a week before. Aeschines pointedly questioned Demosthenes' propriety in this action, but Plutarch defends Demosthenes' conduct both personally, arguing that private grief can be appropriately present even when the outward signs are missing, and politically, in that it was appropriate for Demosthenes to provide Athenians with an opportunity to rejoice over Philip's death.[89] Soon after Alexander's accession to the throne, Demosthenes again summoned the league to rise up in arms, but the Athenians lost courage when Alexander brought his army into Boeotia. The Thebans fought, but they were defeated and their city was razed, a dramatic indication that Macedonian power did not end with Philip's life. Although the Athenians selected Demosthenes as an ambassador to meet with Alexander, he "abandoned" the embassy, which Plutarch attributes to fear of the "wrath of the king." Soon afterward, Alexander demanded that Athens surrender its most important orators, including Demosthenes, for trial; Demades interceded and issued a plea for the pardon of the orators and reconciliation between Athens and Alexander.[90] Alexander's agreement to this request established a temporary rapprochement with Athens.

Aeschines' indictment against Ctesiphon finally came to trial in 330, six years after Ctesiphon had originally put forward the motion to award Demosthenes a crown for his public service. Aeschines' rationale for the charge against Ctesiphon was threefold: it was illegal to honor an official still in office; the state of Demosthenes' accounts had not yet been determined; and Demosthenes' service to the city was questionable in view of the harm that had come to Athens from following his advice.[91] Although the first two points were technically valid, scholars agree that the crux of the matter for Aeschines rested in the third, and it was this point that allowed him to shift the focus of the trial toward a general attack on Demosthenes' career. Aeschines' argument against Demosthenes' leadership included a return to the details of his parentage and citizenship, and his lack of integrity, wisdom, and courage.[92]

Demosthenes' stirring response to Aeschines is described by Adams as "one of the supreme triumphs of rhetorical strategy of arrangement and treatment." Demosthenes treats the technical features of the indictment in a cursory manner and distances himself from the Peace of Philocrates, focusing the jury's attention instead on a portrait of true patriotism defined by his persistent resistance to Macedonian domination. The speech gains force from Demosthenes' fierce counterattack against Aeschines, whom he portrays as having damaged Athenian interests through acting as Philip's agent. Demosthenes represents his own actions as guided by his desire to uphold Athenian ideals, the only course of action the city could follow with integrity, notwithstanding the ultimate unsuccessful outcome. His speech was an overwhelming success; Aeschines' case against Ctesiphon was defeated. Aeschines left the city immediately after the trial and spent the rest of his life teaching rhetoric in Rhodes, while Demosthenes continued his life and public service in Athens.[93]

Plutarch describes the trial as holding remarkable public interest due to the renown of the participants and the courage of the judges who voted to support Ctesiphon in the face of the prosecutors who "were then at the height of power and acting in the interests of Macedonia."[94] While Aeschines' charge merely claimed that Ctesiphon's motion was inappropriate for the time and place, the debates in the trial covered the entire scope of Demosthenes' career and therefore provided Demosthenes with a rare opportunity for public vindication. This successful outcome was possible because of Demosthenes' remarkable oratorical skill and ability to connect his defense with the needs of his audience. Yunis points out that Demosthenes

> offered his audience a noble version of their reasons for adopting his advice, reasons that were compelling in the face of a failure which they were forced to reckon with but not prepared to accept as final. While presenting himself as a hero, D. takes meticulous care to present his audience simultaneously as true-born Athenian heroes like the fighters of Marathon. . . . If they could not defeat Philip, at least they could save their reputation and their purpose, which is what D. managed for them while preserving his career.[95]

The brilliance of Demosthenes' defensive strategy consists of his providing his fellow citizens a framework for affirming their historic identity in the face of their recent humiliation.

Demosthenes' dramatic vindication in the trial was followed, however, by the gradual decline of his political influence from 330 to 324. Alexander's extended campaign into and far beyond Persia, beginning in 334, allowed Athenians breathing space to take up issues other than the Macedonian threat. Demosthenes appears to have resumed his work as a logographer and to have turned his attention toward issues internal to Athens. He rarely made public appearances in the twelve years after Alexander assumed power, which leads to some uncertainty about the nature of his activities during this period.[96]

Demosthenes' fortunes took a more sharply negative turn in 324. Alexander's treasurer Harpalus left his service in Babylon with a large quantity of goods and money, and came to Athens seeking refuge. Plutarch reports that many prominent Athenians favored granting Harpalus's request, but Demosthenes initially advised sending him away.[97] When Harpalus returned, Demosthenes persuaded the Athenians to imprison him and keep the seven hundred talents he had brought with him.[98] Various interpretations are offered for the events that followed. According to Plutarch, Demosthenes changed his mind when Harpalus sent him twenty talents and an exotic Persian cup that Demosthenes had admired. He recounts an incident in which Demosthenes feigned laryngitis in order to avoid speaking further against Harpalus, which sparked the outrage of Athenians after the events that followed. Harpalus subsequently escaped, and the authorities made a thorough inquiry after it was discovered that much of Harpalus's property was missing.[99]

Demosthenes was among those accused of accepting a bribe, and he was eventually tried in the Areopagus, where he was condemned and fined fifty talents. Worthington suggests that the trial's outcome was shaped by political motives, as Demosthenes was convicted on scant evidence, while others on trial were acquitted.[100] Demosthenes was unable to pay the fine, but "through the carelessness of some of his keepers and by the connivance of others" escaped from captivity and fled Athens.[101] Plutarch states that Demosthenes "bore his exile without fortitude," spending most of his time in Aegina and Troezen, "looking off towards Attica with tears in his eyes."[102] Following the trial, the orator Hyperides rose to new heights of influence as Athens returned to a more oppositional stance toward Macedon.[103]

After Alexander's death in 323, the Athenians saw an opportunity to regain independence, and prepared for war against Alexander's successor Antipater. Leosthenes took the lead in advocating war, while Pytheas and Callimedon fled Athens to seek Greek support for a continued relationship with Macedon. Demosthenes recommenced his own efforts to form an alliance of Greek states against Macedon, which prompted the Athenians to take elaborate steps to arrange payment of his fine and recall him from exile. Plutarch describes the joyful greeting the citizens provided Demosthenes when his ship arrived from Aegina. "Not an archon or a priest was missing, and all the rest of the people also met him in a body and welcomed him eagerly."[104]

But the Macedonian army quickly defeated the Greeks, and Antipater imposed new restrictions on Athens, including a measure sharply curtailing the size of the Athenian citizenry, limiting it to those of wealth and high social standing.[105] Demosthenes and other anti-Macedonian leaders fled as Antipater and Craterus marched toward the city. Upon a motion of Demades, the people passed a sentence of death, and Antipater's soldiers pursued the condemned throughout the countryside. Hyperides, Aritonicus, and Himeraeus were found in Aegina and sent to Antipater at Cleonae where they were executed. Demosthenes took sanctuary at the temple of Neptune in Calauria, where he refused to listen to Archias's pleas to return with him to see Antipater. Plutarch says that Demosthenes feigned willingness to go along with Archias, but requested time to write a letter to his family. Demosthenes bit the poison-filled reed he was using to write, bowed his head, and covered it before collapsing. Immediately after painting this vivid scene Plutarch lists other possibilities for the end of his life: the Thracians claimed that Demosthenes took the poison from a rag; the maid stated that Demosthenes had worn the poison as an amulet in his bracelet; and Eratosthenes said that the poison had been kept in a hollow piece of jewelry. Plutarch concludes that Demosthenes' manner of death is less significant than the fact, which a relative described as a divine intervention to spare Demosthenes from the fate he would otherwise have suffered. He died on the "sixteenth of the month of Pyanepsion, the most gloomy day of the Thesmophoria."[106]

DEMOSTHENES' LEGACY

The details of Demosthenes' life story have assumed varying points of significance as his reputation has developed and shifted through the centuries. Plutarch suggests that Demades' political advantage over Demosthenes was not sustained by subsequent generations, as the Athenians eventually (ca. 280) erected a brass statue in Demosthenes' honor, while Demades was put to death as a traitor in Macedonia, "whose people he had disgracefully flattered."[107] Worthington interprets the statue as a material representation of Greek nationalism as much as a tribute to Demosthenes, but acknowledges that it helped to form Demosthenes' public image as "statesman and diplomat *par excellence*."[108] The Peripatetics favored other Attic orators and considered Demosthenes' speeches to be examples illustrating the dangerous affectations denigrated by Aristotle, but Dionysius of Halicarnassus, Cicero, and Quintilian later praised Demosthenes' forceful delivery, language use, and powerful connection with the audience.[109] Cooper adds that Demosthenes' reputation in the ancient world tended to be lower among philosophers but very high among rhetoricians who perceived that Demosthenes "showed rhetoric can be taught (and sold)."[110] Demosthenes' reputation in the ancient world is evident in Plutarch's choice to compare his life, accomplishments, and legacy alongside the career of Cicero in the parallel *Lives*. Demosthenes' modern reputation has experienced similar ebbs and flows, rising in periods when eloquent political rhetoric was in vogue.[111] Clearly Demosthenes' very identity has also been conceived in multiple ways by biographers and historians. Although interpretations of Demosthenes vary significantly in their emphasis and focus, no one disputes his central position in the Athenian resistance to Macedonian imperialism. Moreover, the attention he has received across centuries itself affirms his historical significance.

Demosthenes has, across centuries of Western rhetorical history, served as a symbol of the power and civic vision available through oratory. Yunis notes that the pronounced attention to Demosthenes' rhetoric began early. "In the postclassical ancient world that revered prose eloquence and made the formal study of Attic literature into an industry, the artistry of D.'s work became a topic of immense, some would say obsessive, proportions."[112] Cooper notes that "by the first century, he was regarded as the greatest of Attic orators,"[113] and his reputation for exceptional oratorical skill has been sustained, with many adjustments, ever since. This element of Demosthenes' reputation is based at least in part on what Harding describes as his "inimitable" style.[114] Terry Papillon notes that "it is now, as it was in the ancient world, a commonplace that the great contribution to oratory by Demosthenes was his ability to mix styles appropriately and effectively within a single speech."[115] Jaeger also asserts that "the style of Demosthenes' speeches, both forensic and political, may be characterized as giving voice to the whole range of temperaments and manners of expression to be met with in actual life, in conscious reaction to the even monotony of Isocrates' academic platform rhetoric."[116]

The enduring interest in Demosthenes has included the perception that his rhetorical proficiency was consistently directed toward the enactment of a broader political vision. Yunis places Demosthenes with Thucydides and Plato as influential practitioners of "rhetoric as a mode of discourse capable of civic tasks higher and more potent than mediating conflict—such tasks, for example, as instructing mature, autonomous citizens in the real choices, problems, and best interests of the *polis*; establishing the authority of rationality in the public realm; or even summoning the *polis* into actuality as a community." Yunis goes on to say that Demosthenes' vision of rhetoric and its role in civic life, like that of Thucydides and Plato, is not merely instrumental. "All three adopt ideal criteria when they propose their models of political rhetoric. All are well versed in the uses of language; none countenances the use of charisma or a mystical kind of persuasion to conjure an end to political conflict and create a community sustained by emotion or faith. All three seek a rational, instructive political discourse, a discourse that applies human intelligence and will to make the citizen-community wiser, and therefore better." Yunis suggests that Demosthenes' speeches reflect not only his determined pursuit of immediate political goals, but also his awareness and cultivation of the deliberative process surrounding those speeches, "shap[ing] the mature, responsible, attentive audience that is asked to respond favorably to his candid, demanding, reasoned argument." Thus, Demosthenes unites skillful speech with consistent political action and instruction aimed at forming an informed populace prepared to take action that is in their best interest.[117]

While Demosthenes' political focus has contributed to his perceived significance, it has at the same time complicated his historical reputation. Critics as well as defenders acknowledge that he is a central figure in Athenian political history and in subsequent interpretations of that history. Cawkwell emphasizes the way in which Demosthenes' forceful speeches shaped the historical perception of Philip and the conflict between Athens and Macedon. "Generally speaking, the Demosthenic view prevailed. At Rome the speeches of Demosthenes were studied and imitated; histories had less appeal.... Thus Demosthenes the orator had his way in antiquity."[118] Not surprisingly, however, there are diverse assessments of Demosthenes' political wisdom. Jaeger notes that the fluctuations in Demosthenes' reputation largely correspond to changing values assigned to political events and systems at different points in time. For example, the nineteenth-century decline in Demosthenes' reputation reflected that period's confidence in progress and nation-building based on triumphant, self-assured modernity; in this view, Demosthenes was a "tiny obstacle in the path of an irresistible historical process;"[119] his insistence on Athenian independence stood in the way of a broader vision of Greek unity under Macedonian hegemony.

Cawkwell offers a sharper critique of Demosthenes' policy toward Macedon, arguing that his influence was largely responsible for the disastrous consequences that Athens faced for opposing Philip.[120] Sealey concurs with a bleakly negative assessment. "The career of Demosthenes ended in failure. It was the failure not only of the statesman but of his city."[121] Jaeger acknowledges Demosthenes' role in Athens's downfall, but insists that there is nevertheless ample cause to be interested in Demosthenes' political and oratorical career, since Macedon's triumph "does not diminish our interest in the spirit which made him resist the forces of his time."[122]

This spirit of resistance is a particularly appropriate focus for scholars in rhetoric. In spite of the significant arguments for and against the strengths of Demosthenes' political position and contributions, the fact of the political influence he acquired through his determined pursuit of oratorical excellence is itself worth noting. Much contemporary scholarship demonstrates Jaeger's judgment that "it is impossible for the modern observer not to take sides when he contemplates the struggle in which Demosthenes consumes himself."[123] Rhetoricians, however, can acknowledge the ambiguities surrounding the particular outcomes of Demosthenes' efforts while also noting that his life and vision are embodied in remarkable oratorical performance. Demosthenes is an enduring exemplar of the power and possibility of eloquence across centuries of rhetorical history. He is compelling not only because of the strength of his determined resistance, but also because that resistance was so fully manifest in language setting forth the ancient ideal of rhetoric's power to establish an informed and committed citizenry.

NOTES

1. D. A. Russell, "On Reading *Plutarch's Lives*," *Greece and Rome* 13, no. 2 (October, 1966), 141, JSTOR, retrieved 01/19/15, http://jstor.org/stable/642595.

2. Ibid., 143.

3. Ibid.

4. Peter Hunt, *War, Peace, and Alliance in Demosthenes' Athens* (Cambridge: Cambridge University Press, 2010), 8.

5. Plutarch, *Plutarch's Lives*, vol. 7, *Demosthenes and Cicero*, trans. Bernadotte Perrin (Cambridge: Harvard University Press, 1918), 1.

6. E. Badian, "The Road to Prominence," in *Demosthenes: Statesman and Orator*, ed. Ian Worthington (London: Routledge, 2000), 14.

7. Plutarch, *Demosthenes*, 4.4.

8. Badian, "Road to Prominence," 15.

9. Plutarch, *Demosthenes*, 5.5.

10. Ibid., 4.

11. Badian, "Road to Prominence," 16; Werner Jaeger, *Demosthenes: The Origin and Growth of His Policy* (Berkeley: University of California Press, 1938), 26.

12. Badian, "Road to Prominence," 18.

13. Badian, "Road to Prominence," 16–17; Jaeger, *Demosthenes*, 27.

14. Charles Darwin Adams, *Demosthenes and His Influence* (New York: Longmans, Green, 1927), 5.

15. David C. Mirhady, "Demosthenes as Advocate: The Private Speeches," in Worthington, *Demosthenes: Statesman and Orator*, 182–85.

16. Badian, "Road to Prominence," 19.

17. Harvey Yunis, *Taming Democracy: Models of Political Rhetoric in Classical Athens* (Ithaca: Cornell University Press, 1996), 242–43.

18. Adams, *Demosthenes*, 11.

19. Badian, "Road to Prominence," 21.

20. Plutarch, *Demosthenes*, 7.1–4.

21. Adams, *Demosthenes*, 4; Plutarch, *Demosthenes*, 7.3; 8.1; 9.1–2.

22. Badian, "Road to Prominence," 16.

23. Craig Cooper, "Philosophers, Politics, Academics: Demosthenes' Rhetorical Reputation in Antiquity," in Worthington, *Demosthenes: Statesman and Orator*, 226–27.

24. Plutarch, *Demosthenes*, 10.1; 11.3.

25. Yunis, *Taming Democracy*, 245.

26. Anne Duncan, "Demosthenes versus Aeschines: The Rhetoric of Sincerity," in *Performance and Identity in the Classical World* (Cambridge: Cambridge University Press, 2006), 85.

27. Plutarch, *Demosthenes*, 9.3–4.

28. Ibid., 8.4.

29. Ibid., 11.4.

30. Ibid., 1.1.

31. Badian, "Road to Prominence," 30.

32. R. D. Milns, "The Public Speeches of Demosthenes," in Worthington, *Demosthenes: Statesman and Orator,* 207–9.

33. Yunis, *Taming Democracy,* 239.

34. Milns, "Public Speeches," 211.

35. Adams, *Demosthenes,* 14.

36. Badian, "Road to Prominence," 35.

37. T. T. B. Ryder, "Demosthenes and Philip II," in Worthington, *Demosthenes: Statesman and Orator,* 46.

38. Ryder, "Demosthenes," 45; Worthington, "Introduction: Demosthenes, Then and Now," in Worthington, *Demosthenes: Statesman and Orator,* 1.

39. Yunis, *Taming Democracy,* 261.

40. George Cawkwell, *Philip of Macedon* (London: Faber and Faber, 1978), 76.

41. Jaeger, *Demosthenes,* 108.

42. Ryder, "Demosthenes," 55.

43. Cawkwell, *Philip,* 87–88.

44. John Buckler, "Demosthenes and Aeschines," in Worthington, *Demosthenes: Statesman and Orator,* 117.

45. Buckler, "Demosthenes," 118–19.

46. Adams, *Demosthenes,* 20–21.

47. Jaeger, *Demosthenes,* 148.

48. Raphael Sealey, *Demosthenes and His Time: A Study in Defeat* (New York: Oxford University Press, 1993), 151.

49. Plutarch, *Demosthenes,* 16.1–2.

50. Cawkwell, *Philip,* 98.

51. Ryder, "Demosthenes," 65.

52. Buckler, "Demosthenes," 130–31.

53. Cawkwell, *Philip,* 106.

54. Buckler, "Demosthenes," 132.

55. Cawkwell, *Philip,* 120.

56. Buckler, "Demosthenes," 133.

57. Ibid., 114.

58. Sealey, *Demosthenes,* 164.

59. Duncan, "Demosthenes versus Aeschines," 60.

60. Buckler, "Demosthenes," 115.

61. Ibid., 134.

62. Cawkwell, *Philip,* 122–23.

63. Sealey, *Demosthenes,* 165.

64. Buckler, "Demosthenes," 140.

65. Adams, *Demosthenes,* 20; Buckler, "Demosthenes," 134.

66. Cawkwell, *Philip,* 119.

67. Ibid., 119.

68. Ibid., 131.

69. Adams, *Demosthenes*, 33.

70. Ryder, "Demosthenes," 78.

71. Cawkwell, *Philip*, 132.

72. Jaeger, *Demosthenes*, 173.

73. Sealey, *Demosthenes*, 182.

74. Ryder, "Demosthenes," 79.

75. Cawkwell, *Philip*, 137.

76. Ryder, "Demosthenes," 80–81.

77. Plutarch, *Demosthenes*, 17.4–18.4.

78. Plutarch, *Demosthenes*, 18.4.

79. Ryder, "Demosthenes," 81.

80. Ibid., 82.

81. Cawkwell, *Philip*, 145.

82. Plutarch, *Demosthenes*, 20.1–2.

83. Sealey, *Demosthenes*, 198.

84. Ryder, "Demosthenes," 82–83.

85. Plutarch, Demosthenes, 21.1–3; Sealey, Demosthenes, 201, 208.

86. Ryder, "Demosthenes," 83.

87. Adams, *Demosthenes*, 35; Plutarch, *Demosthenes*, 20.4.

88. Duncan, "Demosthenes versus Aeschines," 80; Plutarch, *Demosthenes*, 21.1–3.

89. Plutarch, *Demosthenes*, 22.2, 4–5.

90. Plutarch, *Demosthenes*, 23.3.

91. Buckler, "Demosthenes," 146.

92. Ibid., 146–147.

93. Adams, *Demosthenes*, 50–51.

94. Plutarch, *Demosthenes*, 24.2.

95. Harvey Yunis, "Introduction," in *Demosthenes: On the Crown*, ed. Harvey Yunis (Cambridge: Cambridge University Press, 2001), 17.

96. Ian Worthington, "Demosthenes' (In)activity during the Reign of Alexander the Great," in Worthington, *Demosthenes: Statesman and Orator*, 101.

97. Plutarch, *Demosthenes*, 25.2.

98. Worthington, "Demosthenes' (In)activity," 103.

99. Plutarch, *Demosthenes*, 25.2, 5–6.

100. Worthington, "Demosthenes' (In)activity," 105.

101. Plutarch, *Demosthenes*, 26.2.

102. Ibid., 26.4.

103. Worthington, "Demosthenes' (In)activity," 106.

104. Plutarch, *Demosthenes*, 27.5.

105. Worthington, "Demosthenes' (In)activity," 106.

106. Plutarch, *Demosthenes*, 29.3–5, 30.1–4.

107. Ibid., 30.5, 31.3.

108. Worthington, "Demosthenes' (In)activity," 3.

109. Cooper, "Philosophers, Politics, Academics," 229–34.

110. Ibid., 238.

111. Philip Harding, "Demosthenes in the Underworld: A Chapter in the *Nachleben* of a Rhetor," in Worthington, *Demosthenes: Statesman and Orator*, 246–71.

112. Yunis, "Introduction," 18.

113. Cooper, "Philosophers, Politics, Academics," 224.

114. Harding, "Demosthenes in the Underworld," 248.

115. Terry L. Papillon, *Rhetorical Studies in the Aristocratea of Demosthenes* (New York: Peter Lang, 1998), 14.

116. Jaeger, *Demosthenes*, 32.

117. Yunis, *Taming Democracy*, 23–29, 257, 275.

118. Cawkwell, *Philip*, 18.

119. Jaeger, *Demosthenes*, 1.

120. Cawkwell, *Philip*, 82.

121. Sealey, *Demosthenes*, 219.

122. Jaeger, *Demosthenes*, 5.

123. Ibid., 190.

2. AESCHINES' SPEECH *AGAINST CTESIPHON*: AN ABSTRACT

Donovan J. Ochs

THE CAREER OF AESCHINES

The sources of biographical data for Aeschines are essentially restricted to his three extant speeches *Against Timarchus, On the Embassy,* and *Against Ctesiphon*—and the orations of his rival, Demosthenes. From these sources we know that of the two men Aeschines was older. His birth is placed between 403 and 390 BCE. Demosthenes was born in 384 BCE.[1] When the Crown speeches were given, therefore, Demosthenes was fifty-four years old, Aeschines well over sixty. The careers of both orators are curiously similar, and their bitter encounters may be explained, in part, by this similarity.

Demosthenes' father, a member of the Athenian aristocracy, owned an armament industry. He died when Demosthenes was seven. The court-appointed trustees squandered the youth's inheritance, so Demosthenes' yearly education was seriously restricted by lack of funds and by poor health. In 367 BCE, we are told, after hearing the orator Callistratus successfully argue a lawsuit, Demosthenes became enamored of the power of oratory. Resolving to recover his patrimony, Demosthenes studied the art of speechmaking with Isaeus, a sophist whose specialty was testamentary law. Demosthenes won a series of five lawsuits and did regain a portion of his inheritance. His feeble voice, labored breathing, ungainly gestures, and confusing sentence structure were ridiculed when Demosthenes first spoke to the Athenian Assembly. Enlisting the aid of Satyrus, an actor, and subjecting himself to severe self-discipline,[2] he perfected his delivery, re-entered the political arena, and, as Philip's major opponent, became famous as the greatest speaker the Greek nation ever produced.

Aeschines' father returned to Athens, after suffering financial ruin in the Peloponnesian War and subsequent exile, to open a school. Aeschines taught for some years with his father, then served as a soldier in the war with Thebes. In a later campaign at Tamynae he was cited for bravery. By profession, however, Aeschines was a tragic actor of no mean ability.[3] After leaving the stage he became a court clerk and, when Philip destroyed Olynthus (348 BCE), Aeschines was elected ambassador to Arcadia.

Shortly afterward, Aeschines—politically a conservative and, therefore, an advocate of peace with Philip—traveled with Demosthenes, then leader of the war faction. The purpose of their mission was to negotiate a treaty with Philip. Although the machinations and intrigue that surround the events of this first embassy, the Macedonian mission to Athens, and the ratification of the Peace of Philocrates are still disputed,[4] the following account seems most probable.

On the first proposal to Philip, Aeschines did side with Demosthenes in opposition to the terms of Philocrates' peace negotiations. A day later both orators reversed their commitments, endorsed Philocrates' proposal, and returned to Athens believing that Philip would attack Thebes, then an enemy of Athens. Both men were, of course, woefully deceived. Philip captured Phocis, an enemy of Thebes, and negotiated a treaty of unification between Thebes and Macedonia thereby creating a balance of power unfavorable to Athens.

Amid the subsequent deliberations of the Amphictyonic Council, a loosely organized group of Greek states, Aeschines successfully argued that revenge against the Phocians be mitigated. The Phocians had desecrated the temple at Delphi, and it is a tribute to Aeschines' oratorical ability that he was able to allay the indignation of the council. At the conclusion of this meeting, Philip, one of the council members, held a celebration attended by Aeschines and other Athenians. Aeschines was, therefore, implicated as a traitor for his attendance and indicted as such by Timarchus at the prompting of Demosthenes. Only by delaying the trial and successfully arguing a counterindictment against the youthful profligacy of Timarchus was Aeschines able to regain partial support from the Athenians.

In 343 BCE Demosthenes himself charged Aeschines with treason in the trial, *On the Embassy*. Neither orator won. Demosthenes lost the case, Aeschines much of his popular support. Four years later Aeschines, acting as an unofficial delegate to the Amphictyonic Council, advocated a holy war against Amphissa on the grounds that the Amphisseans were living on and cultivating cursed soil. Demosthenes opposed Aeschines' policy, realizing that such a war would provide Philip an opportunity to split central Greece. The council voted for war. Shortly thereafter Athens and Thebes confronted Philip at Chaeronea in 338 BCE. The Macedonian won.

In 336 Aeschines indicted Ctesiphon who had proposed that Athens honor Demosthenes with a golden crown for his service to the state. Immediately after the battle at Chaeronea the Athenians had decided to rebuild and strengthen the city's walls. Demosthenes was elected by his deme [district] to oversee the repairs on their portion of the city's fortifications. Approximately ten talents from the state treasury were entrusted to Demosthenes to which sum Demosthenes added funds of his own.

While the project was under way in 336, Ctesiphon, as a gesture of friendship and admiration, proposed that Demosthenes be granted a gold crown in recognition of his services.

Martin and Bude have reconstructed Ctesiphon's proposal to read as follows:

> Since Demosthenes, in the capacity of an inspector of fortifications, has conscientiously had ditches dug along the wall and has contributed for this work a sum of 100 minae from his own means, the people resolve to award him praise and to crown him with a gold crown. The herald will proclaim at the Athenian festival of Dionysius that the people of Athens crown Demosthenes for his virtue and goodwill, because he continues to act and to speak for the greatest good of the people and because he has shown himself zealous in doing all the good he can.[5]

Similar proposals had been successfully made for other Athenian leaders in 340 and 338 BCE; therefore, precedents did exist. Ctesiphon's bill was first presented to the Athenian Council and was approved. When the draft of the proposal reached the popular Assembly in 336, Aeschines declared it to be illegal and stated that he would indict Ctesiphon on the basis of three illegalities in the decree.

First, Aeschines charged that Ctesiphon proposed to crown Demosthenes before Demosthenes' magistracy had been audited. Athenian law did prohibit granting of honors to an accountable magistrate. Second, the location for the proclamation contradicted a law that specified that crowns conferred by the people be proclaimed only in the Assembly. Finally, Aeschines claimed that the proposal was contrary to the truth, specifically, that Demosthenes had not always acted for the public good.

From a legal point of view Aeschines had the letter of the law on his side for the first two accusations. These laws, however, were infrequently invoked and numerous precedents authorized or at least excused Ctesiphon's proposal. Demosthenes himself had twice received a crown at the theater as a result of decrees similar to Ctesiphon's. The third accusation, that Demosthenes had not always acted for the public good, was, in fact, the central issue. If the jury concurred with Aeschines, then part of the odium surrounding the embassy trial would be removed and Aeschines would be revenged.

Six years elapsed before the trial was held. In this period (336–330 BCE) Philip was assassinated, Alexander took command of the Macedonian forces, and, by destroying Thebes, the young king secured a fearful respect from the Greek states.

Those who attended the crown trial, either as jurors or mere listeners, had probably heard rumors about Alexander's defeat of Darius and the Persians. In short, Demosthenes had the difficult task of defending his unsuccessful anti-Macedonian policy when Macedonian influence encompassed most of the world.

No record remains to indicate the number of jurors who decided the crown trial. We surmise that at least several hundred dicasts (jurors) were involved. Both speakers address themselves to the "Athenians," the formula used in the popular Assembly. The two orators undoubtedly spoke as much for the crowd of listeners outside the court as for the tribunal itself. Aeschines, since he was the accuser, spoke first.

ABSTRACT OF AESCHINES' SPEECH *AGAINST CTESIPHON*

In the following abstract,[6] the style of the first person narrative
is retained to heighten the immediacy and urgency that
seem to typify the speech. The abbreviations D. and Ct. are
used to signify Demosthenes and Ctesiphon, respectively.

Athenians, we can and have seen attempts made to halt this trial. I, however, rely upon the gods, the laws, and you judges. The old legal procedures would be helpful now, but the old ways have been abolished by intrigue and intimidation; therefore, restraint of public speakers is no longer possible. Nevertheless, we do retain the right to prosecute for violation of laws.

Of the forms of government democracy alone depends upon upholding established laws. If, therefore, you prosecute a violation of the law, you are upholding democracy. Be ashamed, therefore, to desert your station as defenders of democracy. If you convict *Ct.* for making an illegal proposal, you will decree what is just, what is consistent with your oaths, and advantageous to you and the entire state.

I wish to speak about the laws concerning accountable persons. A law exists forbidding anyone to crown a state official before he is audited. This law can be circumvented by appending the clause, "after he is examined by the magistrates," to their proposal. But *Ct.* transgresses the law, dispenses with the circumvention, and proposes a crown for *D.* before the audit.

D. will argue that he was a commissioner and not a magistrate, and, therefore, not accountable. But your law reads that inspectors are to be considered magistrates, and *D.* was an inspector. Therefore, *D.* is a magistrate and falls under the law. The more ingeniously anyone may speak proposing illegal measures, so let him incur greater resentment.

D. will argue that he is guilty only of giving generously of his own funds. But in our state any public servant must make an accounting, in short, anyone who receives or spends or interferes with public affairs must be audited. Consequently, *D.* must follow the law and be audited if we wish to maintain our democracy.

Was *D.* in fact accountable? The Senate calendar shows him to be the magistrate over the theatrical funds when the crown was proposed. *D.* was also inspector of public works at the time of the proposal. In this capacity he managed the public funds, fined other magistrates, and had the privilege of the courts; consequently, he is accountable.

D. will argue that he was neither appointed by lot nor chosen by the people. Yet the law states that any person appointed by a deme shall be considered a magistrate and the Pandionian deme appointed *D.* magistrate and inspector in addition to giving him ten talents of gold. Our law prohibits such a person from receiving a crown without an audit.

The proclamation of the crown is also illegal. The law clearly states that if the senate awards a crown to anyone, the proclamation must take place in the senate. If the people award a crown, the proclamation shall be made in the Assembly, because anyone so honored should not be pompously displayed to foreigners. *Ct.*, however, desires that the proclamation take place in the theater before the entire Greek nation.

D. will argue that contradictory laws exist on this question. But the Thesmothetae annually check the laws to eliminate contradictions. If we examine the so-called contradictory law, we find, in fact, that it refers to those persons crowned without a decree by their own demes. Such a proclamation is illegal in the theater.

Since it is also illegal, to insert falsehoods into decrees, I now turn to *D.*'s pretense for being crowned.

Consider the life of *D.* He is the man who attacked his own kinsman, Demomelas; he prosecuted his general and friend, Cephisodotus; and he is the man who lost the case to Meidias for thirty minae. I will consider his life in four periods: from the war with Philip to the Peace of Philocrates; the Peace; the resumption of the war to the battle of Chaeronea; and the present.

In the first period *D.* and Philocrates flattered Philip and betrayed the king of Thrace to Philip. When Philocrates was impeached, *D.* successfully defended the culprit. On the peace mission to Philip, *D.* argued and won the provision that each Greek state should conclude a separate alliance with Philip. On his return to Athens, *D.* so hurried the Assembly into ratifying his proposal, that when the decree was approved, Thrace was absent; and therefore, Thrace was excluded from the negotiations. Then when Philip's ambassadors came to Athens, *D.* gave these enemies cushions, carpets, and front seats in the theater, and he subsequently escorted the Macedonian embassy to Thebes. Shortly afterwards *D.* pretended to see visions of Philip's death. Another example of his questionable character is that he also is guilty of offering sacrifices before performing the funeral rites for his own daughter.

During the Peace of Philocrates, as Philip moved to Phocia and Thebes, the people became angry with Philocrates and *D.*, in an attempt to be on the winning side, betrayed and turned on his fellow ministers. Then, *D.* caused our alliance with Euboea and Thebes, with the Calcidians, and with Callias. We have suffered from each of these alliances; *D.* has profited.

In the third period, prior to the battle at Chaeronea, *D.* destroyed the interests of the Greeks and of the state. He offended the gods by refusing to punish the Amphisseans who farmed the cursed land in the Cirrhaean plain. Therefore *D.* rejects our oaths and imprecations and the oracle which decreed that anyone farming the Cirrhaean plain shall be punished. As a result of his immorality our forces, land and sea and whole cities, have been utterly destroyed because of this man's administration.

None of our best orators could persuade Thebes to join an alliance with us. Thebes was in danger, Athens was able to ally with that nation; but it was the crisis of affairs and terror, not D., that brought Athens to Thebes.

Let me consider D.'s offenses against you, Athenians. After pretending that the alliance with Thebes was his doing, he allowed the financial burden of the war to fall on Athens. Rather than seek peace with Philip, D. sent the Thebans to fight, and they were killed. Imagine his coronation ceremony in the sight of the orphans whose parents he urged to their death.

In the fourth period D. abandoned his post in the field and took money from the state and from the Greeks. He then attempted to insinuate himself to Alexander. If D. was hostilely disposed toward Alexander, he should have urged an alliance with Persia, or capitalized on Darius's military successes, or advocated engagement of the enemy when the Macedonians were cut off at Corragus. D. did nothing.

Consider also the life of Demosthenes. A true friend of freedom will have freeborn parents, ancestors who served the people, temperate and moderate habits, the ability to speak powerfully, and manliness of spirit. However, D.'s mother was the granddaughter of Gylo, a traitor, and a Scythian woman; therefore, D. is not actually a native Greek. D. squandered his paternal inheritance and now supports his life, not from his own revenues, but from dangers you risk. He is powerful in speaking, profligate in his life. Recall that Solon decreed that men who leave their posts are criminals, and recall also that cowards are legally prohibited from being crowned and taking part in public sacrifices. Therefore, when D. refutes my charges, consider not his words, but his actions.

You must not award crowns excessively. Honors were rare in the days of our ancestors, today they are plentiful. Should you give crowns to athletes who please you, few will compete. Therefore, grant honors to only a few worthy persons of true political merit. Great leaders of the past—Themistocles, Miltiades, Aristides—neither sought nor received crowns since they did not think it necessary to be honored in the public records. D. will claim that my analogy is false, but one seeking honor contests against virtue, not another person.

In the past those proposing illegal measures were strictly censured, but today a defendant is concerned only with precedents of acquittal. Remember that anyone who enables a defendant to propose illegal measures destroys the constitution.

When *Ct.* comes up to speak, force him to dwell on the indictment. If you call for *D.*, you do so against the laws and the constitution. If you do call *D.*, have him use the same order I used—namely, have him discuss the laws prohibiting accountable persons from being crowned, for I have shown that *Ct.* proposed *D.*'s crown while *D.* was still accountable. Then make *D.* discuss the illegality of the people crowning a person outside the Assembly. Then insist that *D.* discuss his private and public acts of injustice. If *D.* uses any other arrangement, he will do so only to baffle you.

If *D.* argues that such a procedure is unfair, remind him that our democracy was founded on the type of fairness that *I* ask. If he argues that he is truthful merely because he has taken an oath, remind him that an habitual perjurer requires either new gods or a new audience to gain credibility. If *D.* argues that he ought not to be banished because he has nowhere to go, ask him where Athens can go, now that he has ruined the state. Do not be moved to tears by his tears or his threats of suicide; if he were sincere, he would decline the crown.

Ct. is not to be trusted either. You know him to go about the forum saying that he will probably be freed because of inexperience, but that he worries about the corruption of *D*. *D.*, however, says that he is confident of himself, but fears *Ct.*'s iniquity.

All the calumnies that *D.* will hurl at me are false. He will say that the woes of the state resulted from my speeches, but I would deliver the same speeches again. Or, he will say I was silent, but moderation caused my silence. He will say I indicted him just to please Alexander, but I did so when Philip was still alive. He will say I should have censured each act of his administration, but I speak at intervals because it is a principle of democracy to do so and such is the characteristic of men who speak only when it is expedient. He will say that like a good doctor, he prescribed what he could to save the state, but his lies and treacherous acts prevented others from speaking when the state might have been saved. And yet such a man demands honors.

On what basis should *D.* be crowned? He fortified the walls by demolishing the public tombs, he was corrupt in his dealings with regard to the Amphisseans and Euboeans, he frequently took bribes, and now his only means of defense is self-praise. If you honor *D.*, you disgrace yourselves and those who have died for our country. Public proclamations serve to instruct our youth. If you honor *D.*, you present an example of corruption to our youth. Therefore, punish *Ct.* and our youth are instructed.

When D. concludes his speech, imagine Solon and Aristides asking how it is that you condemned Arthmius, a man who did comparatively little wrong, and yet you consider honoring D.

Be ye my witnesses, O Earth and Sun, and Virtue, and Conscience, and Education, by which we distinguish the honorable and the base, that I have heard my country's call, and have spoken. If I have presented the accusations well and in a manner commensurate with the crime, I have spoken according to my desire; if insufficiently, according to my ability. It remains for you, fellow citizens, in view both of what has been spoken and what is left unsaid, yourselves to give the verdict that is just and for the city's good.[7]

NOTES

1. Another primary, though less trustworthy source for the life of Aeschines is the dual biography in Plutarch's *Lives of the Ten Orators*. An account of Demosthenes' life can be read in chapter 1 of this book. Among modern digests which treat of Aeschines' life I suggest George Kennedy, *The Art of Persuasion in Greece* (Princeton: Princeton University Press, 1963), 236–45; and *The Speeches of Aeschines*, translated by Charles Darwin Adams (Cambridge: Harvard University Press, 1919), vii–xxiii. Essentially the same material can be found in Thalheim, "Aischines," in *Paulys Realencyclopaedie der classischen Altertumwissenschaft* (Stuttgart: Alfred Druckenmueller Verlag, rpt. 1959), 1.1.1050–62; and Victor Martin and Guy de Bude, eds. and trans., *Discourse [par] Eschines* (Paris: Les Belles Lettres, rpt. 1962). Cf. Friedrich Blass, *Die Attische Beredsamkeit* (Hildesheim: Georg Olms Verlagsbuchhandlung, 1962), and Arnold Schaefer, *Demosthenes und seine Zeit* (Leipzig: Teubner, 1858).

2. The accounts of Demetrius, Phalcreus, and Plutarch are possible exaggerations. Nonetheless, it is conceivable that Demosthenes may have rehearsed with pebbles in his mouth to correct his enunciation, or rehearsed before a mirror to improve his gestures, or declaimed while running up steps to increase his lung capacity, or spoken against the crashing waves to reinforce his concentration. Quite probably Demosthenes did copy and declaim the speeches in Thucydides, since numerous stylistic similarities exist. To a modem reader, however, such concern with delivery may seem overzealous, if not pathological. Parallels, however, can be found in the aberrations of the nineteenth-century elocutionists.

3. Insufficient attention has been given to the implications of Aeschines' dramatic training. Adams remarks that, "as an actor he fell just short of the highest attainments." Thalheim refers briefly to Aeschines' "schoenen und

volltoenenden Stimme." Kennedy, however, does admit that "as an actor he probably knew more about delivery than most." Fourth-century actors endured a physical regimen not unlike our best professional athletes. The demands on their voice and movement were, by our standards, incredibly severe. Cf. Peter D. Arnott, *An Introduction to the Greek Theatre* (Bloomington: Indiana University Press, 1959), chapter 3.

4. Cf. G. L. Cawkwell, "Demosthenes' Policy after the Peace of Philocrates," *Classical Quarterly*, 13 (1963), 120–38. Also, A. W. Pickard-Cambridge, *Demosthenes and the Last Days of Greek Freedom* (New York: G. P. Putnam's Sons, 1914), chapter 8.

5. Martin and Bude, *Discourse [par] Eschines*, 9.

6. The abstract is based on Martin and Bude's edition of the text.

7. Aeschines, *Speeches*, trans. Charles Darwin Adams, section 260.

3. DEMOSTHENES' ORATION *ON THE CROWN*: A TRANSLATION

John J. Keaney

This translation is based on the editions of the speech by S. H. Butcher, Demosthenis Orationes 1 *(Oxford, 1903) and, with commentary, by W. W. Goodwin,* Demosthenes, De Corona *(Cambridge, 1901). Where the texts differ, I have usually preferred the readings chosen by Goodwin. The medieval manuscripts of this and other speeches by Demosthenes also contain documents to which Demosthenes refers in the course of his argument—e.g., decrees, letters of Philip, the epigram of section 289—which were read aloud in court. It has long been recognized, however, that these documents, in the form in which they have been transmitted, are ancient forgeries (and many of them, to use Goodwin's phrase, ignorant forgeries) that were inserted into the text when the original documents had been lost. They have been omitted from the text and replaced by headings that tell what the original documents contained and where they stood in the delivered speech.*

(1)* My first words, men of Athens, are a prayer to all our gods and goddesses that in this trial I may depend on as much good will from you as I have continually maintained toward our city and toward all of you; secondly— something which concerns your piety and your reputation to the highest degree—I pray the gods to implant in your minds the thought that you

---

* Numbers in parentheses refer to the traditional divisions of the text of the speech. Later references to the speech will use these section numbers as guides to the reader. (Editor's note.)

46

should not let my opponent advise you of the manner in which you should listen to me (for that would be harsh) (2) but that you be guided by the laws and your oath, which imposes the special obligation upon you to listen to both parties in the same manner. This means not only that you should make no prejudgment, nor even that you should give both parties an equal share of your good will; it means that you should allow each party in the trial to use the type of defense he has chosen and to arrange his defense as he wishes.

(3) In this trial, Aeschines has many advantages over me, but there are two important ones, men of Athens. The first is that the result of the trial cannot have the same meaning to both of us, for it is not the same thing for me to fail to achieve your good will and for him to fail in his prosecution, while for me—I don't wish to say anything offensive at the beginning of my speech, but he accuses me from a superior position. Secondly, it is a natural characteristic of all men to enjoy listening to insults and accusations, but to be offended when they hear men praising themselves. (4) The pleasurable side is given to Aeschines, the part which irritates nearly everybody is left for me. If, to prevent this, I do not mention my achievements, I will seem to have no way of acquitting myself of the charges nor of pointing out the grounds for my claim that I deserve to be honored. But if I take up my actions and public policies, I will necessarily have to talk about myself frequently. I will attempt to do so as moderately as possible, but it is fair that Aeschines, who instituted this trial, bear the responsibility for whatever the situation itself compels me to say.

(5) I think all of you would agree that Ctesiphon and I are equally involved in this trial, and that it requires no less concern on my part. For it is a painful and cruel experience to be deprived of anything, especially if one's enemy is responsible; but it is particularly so to be deprived of your good will and affection, as to obtain these is the highest blessing. Since these are the issues in the trial, (6) I expect and ask to receive a fair hearing from all of you alike when I defend myself against the accusations, as indeed the laws require. It was Solon, a benevolent supporter of popular government, who was the original author of these laws, and he thought their validity should lie not only in the fact that they were enacted but also in that an oath was imposed on the jurors; his motive was not, it seems to me, mistrust of you, (7) but he saw that it was not possible for a defendant to avoid false and slanderous accusations—a strong advantage the prosecutor has since he addresses you first—unless each of you jurors, by preserving your piety toward the gods, would receive with good will the just arguments of the

second speaker and would make your decision about the entire case on the basis of an equal and impartial hearing of both speakers.

(8) Since I am about to give an account of the whole of my personal life, it seems, today, as well as of my public policies, I wish again to invoke the gods and, in your presence, to pray, first, that in this trial I may depend on as much good will from you as I have continually maintained toward our city and toward all of you; secondly, that the gods may implant in you the ability to make a decision about this indictment which will prove to be conducive to the good reputation of all of you and the religious piety of each.

(9) If Aeschines had limited his accusations to the items contained in his indictment, I, too, would begin my defense with the Council's decree. But since he has spent at least as much of his time in discussing other matters, and mostly in lies about me, I think it at once necessary and fair that I speak briefly about these matters first, so that none of you be induced by arguments extraneous to the indictment to give an unfavorable hearing to the justice of my answer to it.

(10) See how simple and fair is my reply to the abusive slanders he has voiced at my personal life. If you know me to be the type of man he has accused me of being (for I have never lived anywhere but among you), do not tolerate the sound of my voice, not even if my statesmanship has been brilliantly successful, but stand up and condemn me now. But if you have always assumed and have personal knowledge that I (and my family) are far better, and better born, than he and inferior to none of our respectable citizens—to avoid an invidious term—do not trust what he says about other matters (clearly it is all woven from the same fabric) but grant me today also the same good will you have shown me in many previous trials.

(11) The duplicity of your character, Aeschines, has led you to the thoroughly simple notion that I would have to reply to your abuse and neglect to discuss my public actions and policies. I shall not do it; I am not so demented. I will review my policies, the subject of your abusive falsehoods, and will take up later your loose insults—language worthy of peasant women at a comic festival—if these jurors are willing to listen to them.

(12) I have been accused of many crimes, for some of which the laws provide grave and extreme penalties. But his purpose in this trial is not that: it is to allow an enemy to heap upon me spite, malice, abuse, dirt, and everything of the kind. The city cannot come close to exacting a penalty of the sort demanded by his charges and accusations, if they were, in fact, true. (13) To prevent me from appearing before the people and obtaining

a hearing from them—and this because of his spite and his envy—is, by the gods, not right or constitutional or just, men of Athens. If he saw me committing crimes against our city which were as enormous as he has just described them in his theatrical style, he had an obligation to use the penalties which the laws provide when the crimes were being committed; if he saw that my actions deserved impeachment, by impeaching me and using this procedure for settling the matter in your courts; if I was proposing illegal measures, by indicting me on these grounds. For surely it cannot be that he is prosecuting Ctesiphon through me, but that he would not have indicted me, if he thought he could convict me. (14) Furthermore, if he saw me doing any of the other things with which he has now slandered me or any crime whatsoever against you, there are laws and punishments for all of them; there are processes and suits which carry grave and severe penalties, and all of these he could have used; if he had ever clearly done this and had taken advantage of such possible measures against me, his accusation now would be consistent with his behavior in the past. (15) As it is, he has stepped off the path of right and justice and avoided investigating my actions at the time they were done; he is playing a stage part, piling up charges and jokes and abuse much after the events. In the second place, he accuses me, but brings Ctesiphon to trial; his enmity toward me is the preeminent feature of this whole trial but, never daring to meet me on that ground, he clearly seeks to deprive another man of his civic rights. (16) Yet, men of Athens, beside all the other arguments one could cite in support of Ctesiphon, it seems to me that one could say with much justice that it was fair for Aeschines and me to settle our personal feuds by ourselves, not to dismiss a personal confrontation and look for a third party to cause trouble to. This is the height of injustice.

(17) All of his accusations alike, one may see, are neither just nor based on the truth. I wish to examine them one by one, and especially the lies he has told about me in the matter of the Peace and the embassy, attributing to me what he himself did in conjunction with Philocrates. It is necessary, men of Athens, and fitting as well that I remind you of the chronology of the events so that you may observe each event in its temporal context.

(18) When the Phocian War broke out (I was not to blame for this; at that time I had not entered public life), your first reaction was to desire the safety of the Phocians, although you saw that some of their actions were unjust, and to enjoy whatever trouble came to the Thebans—your anger against them was neither unreasonable nor unfair, since they had made immoderate use

of their successes at Leuktra. Further, the whole of the Peloponnese was in dissension, the most bitter enemies of the Spartans were not strong enough to destroy them, those who formerly ruled through the influence of the Spartans were not in control of their cities, but there was a kind of strife-ridden confusion among these peoples and among the rest of the Greeks which did not admit of settlement. (19) When Philip saw the situation (it wasn't hard to see), he embroiled and stirred them up against each other by lavishing bribes on the traitors in each city. He prepared himself to take advantage of others' blunders and errors of judgment and was becoming a threat to all. Exhausted by the length of the war, the Thebans—once overbearing, now luckless—were clearly being forced to have recourse to you; Philip, to prevent this and to prevent our cities joining together, offered peace to you and assistance to them. (20) What ally did he have to trap you almost into deceiving yourselves? It was—shall I call it the cowardice or the ignorance or both of the rest of the Greeks, who did not provide men or money or anything to help you although you were fighting a long and drawn-out war, and this for the benefit of all of them, as later experience made clear. Your anger at them was just and deserved, and you were ready to listen to Philip. And so we acquiesced in the Peace for these reasons—not because of me, as Aeschines has falsely charged—and it was made. If one examines fairly the crimes and venalities of these men in the matter of the Peace, he will find that they are responsible for the present state of affairs. (21) It is for the sake of the truth that I go through all these facts in detail. For if it should become evident that there was wrongdoing, it has, of course, nothing to do with me. The first to mention and suggest the Peace was Aristodemos, the tragic actor; Philocrates of Hagnous, who took up the cue, proposed the peace and hired himself for this purpose—your associate, Aeschines, not mine—not even if you burst a blood vessel lying about it; the ones who joined this proposal (for whatever motives, I omit this for the present) were Euboulos and Kephisophon. I had nothing to do with any of it.

(22) Although these are facts and are supported by the truth, Aeschines reached the limit of shamelessness when he dared to say that, in addition to being responsible for the Peace, I also prevented the city from making the Peace in consultation with the rest of Greece. Then, you—what is the proper word to describe you? When was it that you, with your own eyes, saw me depriving Athens of so important an enterprise, so beneficial an alliance as you have described it, when was it that you became indignant or came forward and revealed in detail what you are now accusing me of?

(23) If I had sold out to Philip the means to prevent Greece uniting, it was your duty not to be silent, but to cry aloud, to protest, to reveal it to these citizens. You never did this, no one heard you say this. No embassy was visiting any Greek state at the time, but all states had been canvassed long before, and nothing Aeschines has said on the matter is sound. (24) Apart from this, it is the city which is the chief victim of his false slanders. For if you were summoning the Greeks to war, while at the same time you were sending ambassadors to discuss peace with Philip, that was an act worthy of Eurybatos, not of a city, nor of honorable men. It simply is not so. What purpose could you have had in sending ambassadors at that stage of the crisis? Peace? It was available to everybody. War? The topic of your own deliberations was peace. Clearly I was not the author of the Peace in the beginning, nor responsible for it, nor are any of his other accusations against me shown to be true.

(25) When the city agreed to the Peace, consider again the policies each of us chose. From these you will learn who was Philip's ally in all areas of the struggle, and who acted in your behalf and sought the advantage of Athens. As a member of the Council, I introduced a motion that the ambassadors should find out where Philip was and sail there as quickly as possible to administer the oath. They were unwilling to do this, even when I had the motion approved. (26) What did this mean, men of Athens? I will tell you. It was to Philip's advantage that the longest possible time should intervene before the oath was administered, but to your interest that the time be the shortest possible. Why? Because you broke off all your preparations for war not only from the day on which you swore the oath but from the day on which you expected that there would be peace; for all this time, he was busy preparing for war, believing—as was true—that whatever possessions of the city he could acquire before the oath was administered would be firmly in his control. No one, he thought, would abrogate the Peace for the sake of these places. (27) I foresaw this result, men of Athens, and this was the reasoning behind my motion of the decree that they should sail to wherever Philip was and administer the oath as quickly as possible, so that the oath would take effect while the Thracians, your allies, still held the places which Aeschines was ridiculing just now, Serrion and Myrtenon and Ergiske; so that Philip would not establish control of Thrace by seizing strategic areas; and so that he would not, with the large supply of money and soldiery so gained, interfere in our future affairs. (28) Aeschines does not discuss this motion nor does he have it read to you; rather he attempts

to defame me with the charge that, as a member of the Council, I thought that the ambassadors should be introduced to your Assembly. How should I have acted? Should I not have motioned that they be brought to negotiate the peace with you, when this was their purpose in coming? Or, should I not have instructed the manager to give them seats at the dramatic festival? But they would have watched from the inexpensive seats, if this motion was not made. Should I have guarded the minor interests of the state and sold out, as these did, its main interest? Of course not. Read, please, this decree, which Aeschines has passed over, although he clearly knows of its existence.

DECREE (29)

(30) Although I proposed this decree then and sought the city's benefit, not Philip's, our noble ambassadors, who couldn't have cared less, sat in Macedonia for three whole months until Philip returned after subjugating all of Thrace; it was possible for them to have arrived at the Hellespont and save those places within ten days, perhaps within three or four, by administering the oaths before they were seized by Philip. For, if our representatives were there, he would not have laid a hand on the places; else, we would not have administered the oath, with the result that he would have failed to gain the Peace, and would not now have both, the Peace and the territory.

(31) It was in the embassy, then, that Philip played his first trick and these unjust men took their first bribe. In this matter, I avow that I am opposed to them and at war with them, then and now and in the future. But look at another act, still more criminal than this, which took place right afterwards. (32) When Philip swore to the Peace, after he had already taken Thrace through the reluctance of the ambassadors to obey my proposal, he bribed them again, not to leave Macedonia until he had completed preparations for an expedition against the Phocians; his purpose was that, while we were reporting here his intention and preparations to march, you would not sail to Pylae with warships and close off the area, as you had done before, but that, at the same time you were listening to our report, you would hear that he was inside Pylae and there was nothing you could do. (33) Although he had already seized the places he had, so fearful and anxious was Philip that control of events might escape him if you should decide to send aid before Phocis was lost, that he hired this contemptible Aeschines, not now in union with the rest of the ambassadors but singly, by himself, to make the kind of reports to you which caused the loss of everything. (34) I think you should—I beg you—remember throughout this trial, men of Athens, that

if Aeschines had not charged me with matters not contained in the indictment, I would not be answering in kind. But, since he has made all sorts of
defamatory charges, I also must make a brief reply to each of his accusations.
(35) What did he say in the speeches delivered by him at the time, speeches
through which everything was lost? "That there is no need to be disturbed
by Philip's arrival at Pylae; everything will work out to your desire; you
will hear in two or three days that Philip has proved to be a friend of those
to whom he came as an enemy, and an enemy of those to whom he came
as a friend. It is not words," he said, "which cement relationships—how
exalted his language!—but mutual interest; it is in Philip's interest and in
the Phocians' and in yours, all alike to free yourselves of the oppressive
brutality of the Thebans." (36) These words had a pleasant sound to some,
because of the hatred of the Thebans which then existed. What happened
shortly, almost immediately, after this? The Phocians were destroyed and
their cities razed; you kept quiet and believed him; a little later, you moved
your possessions in from the country-districts; Aeschines got his money;
finally, the city received the hatred of the Thebans and Thessalians, Philip
received the gratitude for the outcome of the events. (37) To prove that
these are the facts, read, please, the decree of Kallisthenes and the letter of
Philip; from both, all I have stated will be clear.

DECREE (38)

Were these the expectations with which you made the Peace? Were these
the promises which this hireling made to you?

(39) Read the letter which Philip sent afterwards.

LETTER

(40) You hear how clearly and precisely he defines matters to his allies in the
letter he wrote to you. "My action was against the wishes and to the distress
of the Athenians; consequently, if you are prudent, Thebans and Thessalians,
you will take the Athenians to be your enemies and put your trust in me."
He does not write this in so many words, but this is what he wants to make
clear. Afterward, he transported them to such a peak of insensibility about
any future results of his actions that they even allowed him to control all
their affairs. The result is that his wretched allies enjoy their present miserable condition. (41) His assistant in this persuasion and his comrade, the
one who made those false reports here and tricked you, it is he who now
bewails the sufferings of the Thebans and has given us such a pitiful catalogue

of them and of what the Phocians suffered and of all the other troubles of the Greeks; yet he himself is responsible for all of them. Of course you feel sorrow at what has happened, Aeschines, and pity the Thebans; you have an estate in Boeotia and farm Boeotians' land; of course I rejoice, whose person was demanded immediately by the destroyer of Thebes.

(42) But I have slipped into matters which it is, perhaps, more fitting to mention a little later. I return to my exposition of how the crimes of these men have proved to be responsible for the present state of affairs.

When you were deceived by Philip, because of his agents who had sold themselves in the embassies and reported nothing true to you, and the miserable Phocians were deceived and their towns destroyed, what ensued? (43) The contemptible Thessalians and the brutal Thebans thought Philip their friend, their benefactor, their saviour; he was everything to them, nor did they hear the voice of anyone who would say otherwise. Suspicious and offended by what had happened, you kept the Peace nevertheless; you had no other choice. The rest of the Greeks, like you, deceived and cheated of their hopes, kept the Peace, although they had, in a certain sense, been warred against for a long time. (44) For when Philip was in the territory of the Illyrians and Triballoi, he subjugated some of the Greeks also and put under his control many large forces. Even some from our cities went there with the freedom of travel gained by the Peace and were corrupted; Aeschines was one of them. At that time, all against whom Philip was directing these preparations were in fact at war. If they were unaware of it, that is another matter and has nothing to do with me. (45) For I made solemn and public forewarnings to you, on every occasion, and wherever I was sent as ambassador. But the cities were diseased; their political leaders *were* corrupting themselves by taking bribes; their citizens—the majority—partly had no foresight, partly were ensnared by the indolent leisure of daily life. All alike were the victims of a similar delusion, each thinking that disaster would strike everywhere except upon himself, and that they could safeguard, whenever they wished, their own possessions because the danger would be to others. (46) Then, I think, it turned out that the citizens lost their freedom in return for their great and untimely indolence, and their leaders, who thought that they had sold out everything except themselves, found that they had sold themselves first. Instead of "friend" and "guest," the names they had when they were taking bribes, they now hear themselves called "flunkies" and "hated of the gods" and every other name which fits them. (47) For no one, men of Athens, seeks to benefit the traitor when he spends money, nor, when he has got control of what he has bought, does he use the traitor to advise him in the rest of his affairs. If it were not so, no one would lead a more blessed life than the traitor. But it is not so. How could it be? When one who desires to rule establishes control over the situation and is master of those who sold out, it is then that he recognizes their baseness, then that he hates and mistrusts and insults them. (48) Look at it in this way. Even if the opportunity to affect events has passed, the prudent always have open to them the opportunity to understand them. Lasthenes was called "friend" up to the time he betrayed Olynthus; Timolaos, up to the time he destroyed Thebes; Eudikos and Simos of Larisa, up to the time they put Thessaly in Philip's control. Then the whole world came to be filled with men like these, exiled and rootless, insulted and exposed to every calamity. What about Aristratos in Sicyon and Perillos in Megara? Were they not thrown out? (49) From such examples it is clear to see that the statesman who best guards his homeland and offers the most opposition to men like these is the one, Aeschines, who provides the opportunity to traitors and hirelings to take their bribes; it is through the majority of the citizens here and those who resisted your plans that you are safe and can earn your wages, since you would long ago have ruined yourselves, if left to your own efforts.

(50) Although I still have much to say about the events surrounding the Peace, I think what I have said is more than enough. This man is to blame, who has spewed at me the garbage of his own villainy. I must defend myself to those of you who are too young to have witnessed the events; others of you were, perhaps, irritated at my remarks, I mean those of you who knew that he had been bribed, before I said anything about it. (51) And yet he calls this bribery an act of "friendship" and just now, somewhere in his speech, referred to him "who reproaches me with the friendship of Alexander." I reproach you with the friendship of Alexander? Where did you get it from? How did you deserve it? I would not call you—I am not insane—the guest of Philip or the friend of Alexander, unless one should also call farmhands or any other kind of hireling guests and friends of their employers. (52) Before, I called you the hireling of Philip and now, the hireling of Alexander, as do all of these here. If you don't believe me, ask them, or, rather, I will do it for you. Does Aeschines seem to you, men of Athens, to be the hireling or the friend of Alexander? You hear what they say.

(53) Finally, I wish to make my defense against the indictment itself, and to discuss my activities in detail so that Aeschines, although he already knows them, will hear my reasons for saying that I have a just claim on the

rewards mentioned in the Council's resolution and much greater rewards than these. Please read the indictment.

INDICTMENT (54–55)

(56) These are the details of Ctesiphon's decree, men of Athens, on which he bases his prosecution. In the first place, I think I will make clear to you, from these very details, that my whole defense will be fair. For I will use the same order of the items in the indictment as he; I will speak to each of these in order; and I will omit nothing willingly. (57) The words of Ctesiphon's proposal are that I "spoke and acted continually for the best interests of the people and was eager to do whatever good I was capable of and that I be praised for this." I believe that your judgment on the proposal should be based on my political actions. When these are examined, it will be found whether the items of Ctesiphon's proposal which concern me are true and deserved or whether they are in fact false. (58) As to the fact that Ctesiphon did not add the clause "when I pass the audit," and bade the crown to be proclaimed in the theater, I think that this too is connected with my political actions, that is, whether I deserve the crown and the public proclamation or not. Further, I think that I should specify the legal basis of Ctesiphon's proposal. This is the simple and fair defense I have decided to make, and I will now proceed to my actions. (59) But let no one think that my remarks are irrelevant to the indictment, if I happen to discuss foreign policy. For the prosecutor, who has called untrue that part of the proposal which states that my actions and speeches were for the best, is the same man who has made a discussion of all my policies relevant and necessary to the charge. Secondly, of the many areas of government which were open to me, I chose the one which deals with foreign policy, so that I can fairly begin my exposition in this sphere.

(60) I will pass over what Philip seized and held before I began to make speeches on public policy. None of this, I think, has anything to do with me. I will mention and give a full account of what he was prevented from doing, beginning with the day on which I involved myself in this sphere, promising only this much. Philip had one large advantage, men of Athens. (61) For among the Greeks, not some but all alike, there grew a crop of traitors and hirelings and men hateful to the gods, the like of which no one can ever recall before. With these as his assistants and accomplices, he worsened the relations between the Greeks, which even before this were bad and faction-ridden. Some he deceived, others he bribed, others he thoroughly corrupted; he split the Greeks into many factions, although they all had

a single interest, to prevent him from becoming powerful. **(62)** When all the Greeks were in this state and ignorant of the growing and gathering danger, you, men of Athens, should consider what was the proper course of action for our city to have chosen and expect an account of this from me. For I took my position in this area of government. **(63)** Should Athens, Aeschines, denying her pride and her dignity, have taken a position with the Thessalians and Dolopians, by this act obtaining the rule of Greece for Philip and nullifying the just and glorious deeds of our forefathers? That was not the proper course—it is truly unthinkable—but was it proper for Athens to allow acts to go on, which she knew long before would take place, if no one prevented them? **(64)** I would now like to ask the severest critic of our actions, on which side he would have wanted Athens to be: on that which shares the responsibility for the shameful and ugly results which befell Greece (here were the Thessalians and their followers) or on the side which overlooked what was going on in the hope of personal aggrandizement (here we would put the Arcadians, Messenians, and Argives)? **(65)** But even many of these, rather all of them, fared worse than we. If Philip, after gaining control, had departed, kept peace afterward and harmed none of his own allies or the rest of the Greeks, there might be some grounds for accusing and blaming those who opposed his actions. But if he has taken away, from all alike, reputation, leadership, and freedom—and even the free governments of as many as he could—how could the decision you took at my urging fail to be most glorious?

(66) I return to my question. What was the right course for Athens, Aeschines, when it saw Philip attempting to gain for himself tyrannical rule over Greece? What was the only policy for a statesman at Athens—for this makes all the difference—to advise or propose, a statesman who knew that our country, throughout its history up to the day he himself ascended the speaker's platform, always fought for the first rank in honor and reputation, and had spent more men and money for the honor and benefit of all than the rest of the Greeks had spent in their own behalf, **(67)** a statesman who saw that Philip, with whom was our struggle, had had his eye knocked out, his collarbone broken, his hand and his leg maimed for the sake of preserving his rule, and was ready to sacrifice any part of his body which fortune would take, so that he could live the rest of his life in honor and glory? **(68)** Indeed no one, I suppose, would have the nerve to say that a person born in Pella, a small and graceless place in those days at least, could fittingly have born in him such greatness of spirit as to let a desire to rule Greece come into his mind, while it was proper for you, who are Athenians, who have before you every day of your lives, in everything you see and hear, memorials of the courage of your forefathers, to have such cowardice as to become eager volunteers in yielding your freedom to Philip. Not a single person would say this. **(69)** Therefore the only choice, and the necessary choice, left to you was justly to oppose all his unjust actions against you. This course you took from the beginning, naturally and fittingly, this course I proposed and advised in the time of my political activity. I admit it. What should I have done? Now I ask you, Aeschines, omitting everything else, Amphipolis, Pydna, Potidrea, Halonnesos. I mention none of these. **(70)** Serrion, Doriskos, the sacking of Peparethos, the other injustices of which our city was victim—I don't even know if they happened. Yet it was you who said that I brought Athens into the quarrel by talking about these places, although the decrees were proposed by Euboulos and Aristophon and Diopeithes, not by me—how easily you say whatever you please! But I will not talk of this now. **(71)** Philip, who appropriated Euboea, who prepared to make it a fortress against Attica, who attempted to get control of Megara, who seized Oreos, who razed Porthmos, who set up the tyrants Philistides in Oreos and Kleitarchos in Eretria, who subjugated the Hellespont, who besieged Byzantium, who destroyed some Greek cities and restored exiles to others; in these actions was Philip doing wrong, and breaking treaties, and disrupting the Peace or not? Was there a need for someone to rise among the Greeks and put a stop to these actions or not? **(72)** If not, if Greece was to present the spectacle of Mysian booty—a prey to everyone—while there were still Athenians alive, I have wasted my efforts in talking; the city, in following my advice, has wasted its efforts; let all the actions we took be my crimes, my blunders. But if there was a need for someone to rise and put a stop to Philip, who more fittingly than the Athenian people? This was my policy: I opposed Philip when I saw him enslaving all mankind; continually I spoke out and my clear advice was, "Do not surrender!" Finally, it was Philip, not the city, Aeschines, who broke the Peace by seizing the merchant ships.

(73) Bring the decrees and the letter of Philip and read them in order. It will become clear from these documents who is responsible for what.

DECREE **(74)**

(75) Euboulos proposed this decree, not I, Aristophon the one after this, then Hegesippos, then Aristophon again, then Philokrates, then Kephisophon, then all together. I had nothing to do with them. Read the decrees.

DECREES

(76) As I point to these decrees, Aeschines, so you point to what decree of mine makes me responsible for the war. You won't be able to. If you could, there is nothing else you would have produced first. Even Philip does not impute any blame for the war to me, although he censures others. Read the letter of Philip.

LETTER (77–78)

(79) Nowhere in this letter does he indict Demosthenes, or attach any blame to me. When he censures others, why does he not mention my actions? Because he would have to mention his own crimes, which I watched closely and opposed. First, I proposed an embassy to the Peloponnese, as soon as he slipped into the Peloponnese, then an embassy to Euboea, when he laid his hands on Euboea, then a military expedition—no longer an embassy—to Oreos and one to Eretria, when he set up tyrants in those cities. (80) Afterwards, I was responsible for sending out all the naval expeditions which saved the Chersonese, Byzantium, and the rest of our allies. As a result of these actions, you received the noblest rewards from those who received your help: praise, glory, honors, crowns, gratitude. Some of the victims of his injustice—those who were persuaded by you—were rescued; the rest, who consistently depreciated your warnings, now remember them and believe not only that you had their interests at heart but were also prudent men and even prophets. For everything turned out as you predicted. (81) Everyone knows that Philistides would have spent a great deal of money to keep Oreos, Kleitarchos a great deal to keep Eretria, and Philip himself a great deal to have these two places to depend upon against Athens, to avoid exposure of the rest of his intrigues, and to prevent any general investigation of his unjust actions; everyone knows this, you most of all. (82) For when the ambassadors from Kleitarchos and Philistides came here then, they stayed with you, Aeschines, and you were their official host. They were your friends, whom the city rejected as enemies and as making proposals which were neither just nor beneficial. Nothing of the kind was successful with me, although you defame me and say that I am silent, when I have taken a bribe, and start screaming, when I have spent it. But not you. You scream all the time, and never will stop unless these jurors stop you by voting against you today. (83) On that occasion, you Athenians voted me a crown for this policy; Aristonikos, who proposed this crown, used the very same words

in his proposal that Ctesiphon has now used; the crown was proclaimed in the theater—that was the second proclamation for me; Aeschines was in the assembly, but he did not speak against the proposal nor indict the proposer. Read, please, this decree too.

DECREE (84)

(85) Is there any one of you who knows of any shame or mockery or ridicule the city suffered because of this decree? These are the results he now predicts, if I am voted a crown. Yet, it is when the situation is fresh in everybody's mind that the adviser is rewarded with gratitude, if things go well, and is punished, if not. At the time, I clearly was rewarded with gratitude, not with censure or punishment.

(86) Up to the time these events took place, it is agreed that everything I did was for the best interests of the city, by the fact that my advice and proposals were carried when you were deliberating, by the fact that I accomplished what I proposed and thereby brought crowns to the city, to me, and to all of you, by the fact that you had sacrifices and processions to the gods because my proposals were successful.

(87) When Philip was driven out of Euboea by you—I mean, by your weapons but as a result of my policy and decrees proposed (even if some burst a blood vessel at this) by me—he began to look for another place to be used as a fortress against Athens. He saw that we import more grain than any other people and, intending to control the grain route, he sailed to the Byzantines in Thrace, who were his allies; first, he demanded that they join him in the war against you, and, when they were reluctant to do this, saying that their alliance with him was not on these terms—as was true—he built a palisade around the city, brought up artillery, and began to besiege it. (88) I will not ask what was your proper course of action when this happened. It was quite clear. But who was it who went to the aid of the Byzantines and saved them? Who was it who prevented the Hellespont from falling into his power at that time? You, men of Athens. And when I say you, I mean our city. But who was the one who spoke and proposed and, in a word, devoted himself completely to the situation? It was I. (89) You have experienced in fact, and don't need any words of mine, how much this policy benefitted everybody. Not to consider the glorious reputation it brought you, the war which then broke upon us supplied you with all the necessities of life in greater abundance and cheaper than they are in the present peace, a peace which these noble gentlemen preserve to the detriment of their country and

in the hope of future personal gain; may they be cheated of that hope; may they share with you, who want what is best, the blessings which you seek from the gods; may they not have you share in the certain results of their policies. Read for the jury the decrees of the Byzantines and Perinthians, in which they voted you crowns.

DECREE OF THE BYZANTINES (90–91)

(92) Read also the similar decrees from the inhabitants of the Chersonese.

DECREE OF THE PEOPLE OF THE CHERSONESE

(93) The effect of my policies not only was to save the Chersonese and Byzantium, to prevent Philip from controlling the Hellespont then, and to gain distinction for our city, but it also showed to all mankind the nobility of our city and the evil of Philip. Everyone saw the ally of the people of Byzantium besieging it; what could be more shameful or more disgusting than this? (94) Although you had many just grounds of complaint for their inconsiderate conduct toward you in former times, you showed that you did not bear grudges nor abandon the victims of injustice but even saved them. As a result, you gained fame and good will from all. You know, all of you, that you have crowned many of your political leaders before now, but no one can show that it was through the efforts of anyone else—I mean as speaker and adviser—that our city was crowned, except through mine.

(95) I want to show you that the slanderous remarks he directed against the people of Euboea and Byzantium, carefully reminding you of every unpleasant act of theirs toward you in the past, were intended to be provocative, not only because they were false (I presume you know this) but because, even if they were true, the way I handled matters was beneficial to you. I will do this by discussing one or two of the glorious actions of our city in your time, but my discussion will be brief. A man, by himself, and citizens, in common, should always attempt to base their future actions on the noblest standards of their past. (96) When the Spartans ruled on land and sea, and their governors and garrisons controlled all the areas surrounding Attica, Euboea, Tanagra, all of Boeotia, Megara, Aegina, Keos, the other islands, when our city then had no walls, no ships, you, men of Athens, marched to Haliartos and a few days afterwards to Corinth, although the Athenians of that time had many bad memories of what the Corinthians and Boeotians had done to them in the Decelean War. But they did not let these memories influence them, far from it. (97) Both of these marches,

Aeschines, were not made to reward benefactors nor, as the Athenians saw, were they without danger. In spite of this, they did not sacrifice those who took refuge with them, but they were willing to face possible catastrophe in order to preserve their honor and reputation, a correct and noble decision. Death is the end of every man's life, even if, to protect himself, a man shuts himself up in a little room. Good men must always involve themselves in every noble course, holding good hope before them as a shield, and bear in a noble spirit whatever the god sends. (98) Your forefathers did this; your elders did this when they prevented the Thebans, the victors at Leuktra, from destroying Sparta, although the Spartans were not their friends and benefactors and indeed had done many grievous wrongs to our city; they did not fear the strength of the Thebans nor the military reputation they had then, nor did they take into account what wrongs they had suffered from the people for whom they would be risking themselves. (99) With these acts, you showed all of Greece that, if someone did you harm, you would preserve your anger, but for other times; if danger to their freedom or security should come upon that people, you showed that you would not bear grudges or allow a grudge to influence you. You displayed this quality not at that time alone, but again, when the Thebans were attempting to appropriate Euboea, you did not fail to respond: nor did you need reminding of the wrong done to you by Themison and Theodoros in the matter of Oropos, but you came even to their aid; this was the time the city first had volunteer trierarchs, and I was one of them (I will talk about this later). (100) Your action even in saving the island was noble, but still more noble was your action when, with the fate of their persons and their cities in your hands, you justly restored these to people who had wronged you, and you were not influenced by the injustice you suffered at a time when they trusted you. I pass over the innumerable other actions I could mention, the naval battles, the land expeditions—those of long ago and those of our own times—all of which our city engaged in for the freedom and security of the rest of Greece. (101) When I observed that our city voluntarily fought for the benefit of others in so many situations of this nature, what was I to bid or to advise her to do when she was deliberating about what was, in a certain sense, her own benefit? To remember past grievances, by God, against those who wanted to be rescued and to search for excuses to sacrifice everything. Who would not have killed me with justice, if I had attempted, even with words, to bring shame upon any of the noble traditions of our city? I know well that you would not have done any shameful action. If you wanted to, what stood in your way? Was it not possible? Didn't you have men like these advising such a course?

(102) Well, I wish to return to my policies after this. And think over what was best for Athens then. I saw that your fleet, men of Athens, was being broken up; that your wealthy citizens were failing their obligations by making small contributions and that those of your citizens who possessed a moderate or small amount of property were losing what they had; further, that our city was missing opportunities because of the financial situation. I submitted a law which compelled some citizens, the wealthy, to meet their obligations, stopped the oppression of the poor and—what was most useful to the city—made us prepared to meet any opportunity. (103) When the legality of this law was attacked, I came before you in that trial and was acquitted; the prosecutor did not receive a fifth of the votes. And yet, how much money do you think I was offered by those in the highest tax brackets not to submit this law for passage; or, if not that, at least to let it be suspended while its legality was being appealed? Men of Athens, I would hesitate to tell you how much it was. (104) But their attempt was reasonable. According to the former law, they could make their contribution in groups of sixteen, each contributing little or nothing, and crushing the poor citizens; according to my law, each had to pay a quota assessed on his property, and the man who formerly contributed one-sixteenth to the expense of a single trireme[†] now became trierarch of two. They had not even called themselves trierarchs any longer, but joint-contributors. There is nothing they would not have offered so that this law would be abrogated and they would not be compelled to meet their just obligations.

(105) Please read the decree for which I was indicted, then the list of contributors, the one from the former law and the one according to mine.

DECREE

(106) Bring up also that noble list.

LIST

Put up beside this the list according to my law.

---

†. A trireme is a ship or galley with three banks of oars. In Athens a citizen providing the funds for outfitting a trireme was known as a trierarch. (Editor's note.)

LIST

(107) Do you think that this was a small help to the poor, or that the rich were willing to spend only a small amount to avoid meeting their obligations? I pride myself not only that this practice was stopped and that I was acquitted when indicted but also that the law I had passed was beneficial and was proved so in fact. Throughout the war, when naval expeditions were sent out according to the provisions of my law, no trierarch ever made an appeal to law with the claim that he was being treated unjustly by you, no trierarch became a suppliant in Mounichia, no trierarch was imprisoned by the Naval Boards, no trireme was abandoned at sea and lost to the city, no trireme was left in the harbor because it was unfit to sail. (108) Yet all of these things used to happen under the former laws. The reason is that the trierarchic obligation was imposed on the poor: many of these obligations became impossible. I transferred the trierarchies from the poor to the rich. Everything now happened as it was supposed to. Moreover, I deserve praise for this, and I chose the policies which brought praise and honor and power to the city. No policy of mine was ever malicious, vindictive or malign, nor paltry, nor unworthy of Athens. (109) It will be clear that I preserved the same quality in internal policy as well as in foreign policy: in internal policy, I did not prefer favors from the rich to justice toward the poor; in foreign policy, I did not desire the gifts and the friendship of Philip instead of the common benefit of all Greece.

(110) It remains, I think, for me to speak about the proclamation and about the audit, for I believe that it has become sufficiently clear from what I have said that I acted for the best and that I continued to be well-minded toward you and eager to benefit you. Yet I pass over the most successful of my policies and actions, on the assumption, first, that I must speak on each of the items in the charge of illegality; secondly, that, even if I say nothing of the rest of my policies, all of you are certainly familiar with them.

(111) I think that you did not understand nor was I myself able to grasp most of the legal arguments Aeschines used; he made them thoroughly confusing by putting up details of different laws side-by-side. I will speak about the rights of the case simply and straightforwardly. I am so far from saying that I am not accountable—the gist of his slander—that I admit I am accountable throughout my life for the public monies I have handled or for my public acts. (112) As far as what I offered and gave to the people from my private resources, I claim that I am not accountable for a single

day of my life (do you hear, Aeschines?), nor is anyone else, not even if he be one of the nine archons [magistrates]. What law is so thoroughly inhuman and unjust as to cause an official who gave some of his personal property and performed a humane and generous act to be robbed of gratitude, to be exposed to malicious accusers, and to put these in control of the accounts he submitted? There is no such law. If he says there is, let him point to it. I will be satisfied and will keep silent. (113) There is no such law, men of Athens; his accusation is malicious in that, because I made personal gifts of money when I was Commissioner of the Theoric Fund, he says, "Ctesiphon praised him while he was still accountable." You mention, malicious person that you are, none of the things for which I was accountable, but only my gifts. "But you were also a member of the Commission on the City Walls." For this I was rightly praised, because the expenditures were my gift and I did not claim reimbursement. A claim for reimbursement requires audits and officials to examine it, but a free gift deserves gratitude and praise. This is why Ctesiphon made his proposal about me. (114) I will easily show with many examples that this procedure is defined in your customs as well as in your laws. In the first place, when Nausikles was a general, he was frequently crowned by you for expenditures he made from his own resources. Secondly, when Diotimos and again Charidemos contributed shields, they were crowned. Thirdly, Neoptolemos here, who was in charge of many public works, was honored for his contributions. It would be a cruel thing if a man, in any office, were not allowed to contribute to the city from his personal resources throughout his term of office or if he were subject to investigation for what he had given instead of receiving gratitude. (115) To prove that I speak the truth, please read the decrees in honor of these men.

DECREES (116)

(117) Each of these men, Aeschines, was accountable for the office he held; he was not accountable for the gifts which brought him a crown. Surely, then, I am not either. For I make the same claim as these others in the same situation. I made contributions; I am praised for these; I am not accountable for my contributions. I held office; I submitted accounts of my office, not of my contributions.

"By God (you say) you were corrupt when in office."

Why didn't you accuse me when the examiners submitted my accounts to the court? You were there.

(118) Read the whole proposal made in my honor, that you may see that Aeschines himself bears witness to the fact that I was not crowned for acts for which I was accountable. He will prove himself a malicious accuser, because he fails to include in his charges some details of the Council's decree.

DECREE

(119) These were my personal contributions; you have indicted none of them. You admit that it is legal for the city to receive gifts, but you charge that it is illegal to express gratitude for them. What kind of man, in the eyes of the gods, would be all-wicked, hated of the gods, and utterly vindictive? Would it not be a man like this?

(120) The next item is the proclamation of the crown in the theater. I pass over the innumerable times innumerable crowns were so proclaimed, and that I myself was frequently crowned in this way before. But, for heaven's sake, Aeschines, are you so imperceptive and so stupid that you cannot grasp the fact that the gift of a crown causes the same pride in its recipient wherever it is proclaimed? And that the proclamation in the theater assists the purposes of the donors? All who hear the proclamation are encouraged to serve their city, and they praise those who confer the favor more than its recipient. This is why the city has this law. Please read the law.

LAW

(121) You hear, Aeschines, the clear statement of the law: "Except in cases which the people and Council approve: let the herald proclaim these." Why then, miserable man, do you make malicious accusations? Why do you fabricate arguments? Why don't you take hellebore to cure your madness? Do you feel no shame at bringing in a suit based on envy, not on any offense, at remaking laws and omitting parts of laws when it is only right that the whole law be read to jurors who have sworn to make their decision according to the laws? (122) You act like this, and then you list the qualities a public servant should have, just like one who contracts to have a statue made and then gets it back with the contract unfulfilled, or as if public servants were known by their words and not by their actions and policies. You scream every kind of filthy name at me, like a comic reveler from a wagon, names which suit you and your family, not me. There is also this to think of, men of Athens. (123) I believe that the difference between insult and accusation lies in this, that accusation is directed at crimes for which there are penalties in the laws, while insult involves slander, which naturally involves only the

statements which personal enemies make about each other. It is my conviction that your forefathers built these courts, not so that we could collect you here to listen to men making libelous statements about each other for their own reasons, but so that we could convict anyone who has committed a crime against the city. (124) Aeschines knows this as well as I, but he has chosen to revel in slander rather than make accusations. It is not right that he should leave without getting as much as he has given. I will now take up this point, asking him this small question. Should one say, Aeschines, that you are the city's enemy or mine? Mine, clearly. When it was possible for you to seek legal satisfaction from me, if I committed a crime, for the benefit of these Athenian citizens, in the audits, in civil suits, in the other trials, you neglected to do so. (125) Have you chosen to face me where I am immune in all respects: in respect to the laws, to the time that has passed, to the statute of limitations; immune because the facts of the case have been frequently argued in court, because I have never been convicted of any wrong against you citizens, because the city must have a larger or smaller share with me in the reputation she gained from her actions? Watch out that you don't prove to be the enemy of these citizens here, while you claim to be mine.

(126) Since I have shown you the only vote which respects your oath as well as justice, it seems, because of his calumnies and not because I am fond of abuse, that I must state some bare facts about him, in return for the many lies he has told about me; and I must point out who he is and who his parents were that he can so readily break into abuse and ridicule certain expressions of mine, although he has himself used words—what decent man would not hesitate to give voice to his language—? (127) If Aiakos or Rhadamynthos or Minos were the prosecutor, and not this idle babbler, this court hack, this damned secretary, I think none of them would say what Aeschines says nor provide from his repertoire such offensive expressions, like an actor in a tragedy bawling out "O Earth and Sun and Virtue" and such phrases, and then appealing to "Education and Intelligence, by which noble and ignoble acts are distinguished." You were familiar with his performances, of course. (128) What do you and yours have to do with "Virtue," you scum? How can you distinguish the noble from the ignoble? Where did you get this knowledge? How can you claim it? What right have you to mention "Education"? No one who is truly educated would make any such claim about himself, but would blush even if another claimed it for him. People who have missed out on education, like you, but tactlessly affect it, make their listeners cringe with pain when they speak, and their pretense fails.

(129) I have no difficulty in finding things to say about you and your family; my difficulty is where to begin. Should I say that your father, Trembler, was a slave in the elementary school of Elpias near the Theseum, wearing leg-irons and a wooden collar? Or that your mother plied her trade of daylight marriages in the little shack near the statue of Kalamites, she who raised you, her pretty little doll, to be the paragon of third-rate actors? Everybody knows this, and I don't have to mention it. But should I mention that the boatswain Phormio, the slave of Dion the Phrearrian, raised her out of this noble oc-cupation? By all the gods in heaven, I hesitate to say what deserves to be said about you, lest I be thought to have chosen expressions unworthy of me. (130) I will let that be and begin from the kind of life Aeschines led. He was born of no ordinary parents; they were the type of parents solemnly cursed by the Athenian people. Late in his career—do I say late? It was yesterday or the day before that he became an Athenian citizen and an Athenian politician at the same time. By adding a syllable, he made his father Nontrembler instead of Trembler; his mother was endowed with the quite exalted name, Eyegleam, though everyone knows she was called Hobgoblin, a name derived from her occupation because she would do anything and submit to every request of her clients. How else did she get it? (131) You were elevated from slavery to freedom and from begging to riches thanks to these citizens, but you are such an ingrate and so deformed in your nature that you have no way to thank them except by selling yourself and pursuing a policy detrimental to their interests. I will not mention his speeches; some might claim they were delivered in the city's interest. But I will remind you of his actions; their results have shown that they were clearly in our enemies' interest.

(132) Who among you does not know of the case of Antiphon? He was deprived of his citizenship, but returned to Athens after promising Philip that he would burn the dockyards. I found him hiding in Peiraios and, when I brought him before your Assembly, Aeschines, that malicious man, yelled and screamed that my action was outrageous in a democratic state, that I was insulting citizens who were down on their luck, that I had entered a home without a supporting order. He obtained Antiphon's release. (133) If the Council of the Areopagus, which learned of the case and saw that your ignorance of the facts was untimely, had not ordered a further investiga-tion, arrested the man and brought him to you for trial, he would have been snatched from your grasp, avoided his penalty, and been sent on his way by this mouther of noble phrases. As it was, you tortured him and put him to death, the penalty which Aeschines should have received. (134) The

Council of the Areopagus knew of his activities in that case; and when you elected him to argue your side in the dispute about the Delphic temple, out of the same ignorance of the facts which has caused you to sacrifice many of your interests, the Council, which the Assembly had made its associate and put in control of the matter, rejected him as a traitor and instructed Hypereides to take on the task. Their votes were solemnly placed on the altar, and no vote was cast for this morally polluted man. To prove that I speak the truth, call the witnesses.

WITNESSES (135)

(136) Accordingly, when the Council rejected him as an advocate and chose another, it declared its opinion that he was a traitor and opposed to your interests.

Here was one of the typical acts of this hothead, similar—is it not?—to acts of mine he attacks? Let me remind you of another. When Philip sent Python of Byzantium and a group of ambassadors from each of his allies to put the city to shame by showing her injustice, I did not retreat before the flood of insolent rhetoric which Python spat at you, but I rose and refuted his claims. I did not play false our city's reputation for just dealings, and showed Philip to be in the wrong so convincingly that his own allies rose and agreed with me. But Aeschines here was on Philip's side and asserted that the false and inimical claims of Python were true.

(137) That was not enough. Afterwards, he was caught with Anaxinos, the spy, at Thrason's house. Whoever associates closely with, and makes plans with, an emissary of the enemy must himself be naturally presumed to be a spy and hostile to his country. To prove that I speak the truth, please summon the witnesses.

WITNESSES

(138) I omit a thousand other things I could say about him. For the situation is like this. I have many more facts to point to, which reveal that he served the enemy in that period and treated me insolently. But you don't have an accurate memory of these facts nor have they aroused the anger they deserve; rather, by a habitual weakness of yours, you have given anyone who wants it a complete license to trip up and falsely accuse him who speaks to your advantage, and you exchange the city's benefit for the joy and pleasure you get from listening to abuse. Consequently, it is always easier for a person to serve the enemy and to take bribes than to serve his city as a patriot.

(139) It was a fearful thing—Earth and the gods, how could it not have been?—to take Philip's side against our country, even before we were openly at war with him. Yet, allow him, if you want, allow him this. But when our ships had been openly seized and robbed, when the Chersonese was being plundered, when the man was marching toward Attica, the situation was no longer in dispute, war was upon us. This evil man, this writer of lampoons, cannot point out anything he did to serve you nor is there any decree in the city's favor, either of large or of small importance, which carries the name of Aeschines. If he says there is, let him specify it; he can use my speaking-time. There is none. One of two things must be the case: either he proposed no measures beyond what I proposed, because he found no fault with what I was doing, or he did not produce better measures, because he was seeking ways to help the enemy.

(140) As he made no proposals, did he also fail to speak, whenever the need to harm you arose? No one else had a chance to speak. Most of his other actions, it seems, the city was able to tolerate, and he was able to get away with them. But one accomplishment caps all his previous ones, men of Athens, and he has spent a lot of time talking about it. I refer to the details he gave us about the Amphissians' decrees in hope of distorting the truth. In fact, he cannot do it. How could he? You will never wash away the stain of those actions. You don't have enough words.

(141) In your presence, men of Athens, I invoke all the gods and goddesses who protect the land of Attica, and Pythian Apollo, our city's paternal god; if I should be speaking the truth now and spoke the truth before the people as soon as this impious man involved himself in that affair (for I knew it, I knew it immediately), I pray all of them to grant me continued and secure good fortune; but if, because of my hatred of Aeschines and my personal ambition, I am dragging in a false charge against him, I pray them to take away anything good I might have.

(142) Why have I made this solemn prayer and extended it to such lengths? Because, although I have the records which were deposited in the public archives—these will provide clear proof—and know that you will recall what happened, I fear that he may be thought incapable of the crimes he has committed. Indeed, this happened before, when he caused the poor Phocians to be destroyed by reporting false information to Athens. (143) It was Aeschines who assisted Philip in bringing on the war in Amphissa, which enabled Philip to come to Elateia, and a man to be chosen leader of the Amphictyonic Council, who completely overturned the situation in Greece;

this one man—Aeschines—is responsible for all the terrible results. When I protested right away and cried in the Assembly, "You are importing a war into Attica, Aeschines, an Amphictyonic war," some—those with whom he had packed the Assembly—would not let me go on speaking, others were surprised and thought that I was bringing an unfounded charge because of my personal hostility toward him. (144) What the true nature of that situation was, why these preparations were made, how their plans were accomplished, hear now, since you were prevented from doing so then. You will see that the plot was well organized; you will get much help for learning about public policies, and you will discern how very clever Philip was.

(145) There was no end to the war against you nor relief for Philip, unless he were to make Thebes and Thessaly hostile to our city. Although your generals were conducting a sorry and ineffective war against him, he still was suffering many setbacks from pirates and because of the mere fact of the war. He could not export any of the products of his own country nor have imported what he needed.

(146) At that time, he was no stronger than you on sea nor was he able to invade Attica without the help of his Thessalian accomplices and unless the Thebans allowed him passage. When he did begin to win out over whatever kind of generals you sent (I will not speak of these), he was still at a disadvantage because of the nature of the locality and the relative resources of each side. (147) If, to pursue his own hostility, he were to persuade either the Thessalians or the Thebans to march against you, he thought that no one would pay any attention to him. But if he were to find some grounds common to both and were elected their leader, he expected to win out more easily, partly by deception, partly by persuasion. What then? He attempts—how successfully you will see—to involve the Amphictyons in a war and create a disturbance at the meeting in Thermopylae. He supposed that they would require his immediate leadership for this war. (148) If one of his own Council delegates or one of his allies introduced this matter, he believed that the Thebans and the Thessalians would be suspicious and everybody would be on his guard. But if an Athenian did this, someone sent by you, his enemies, he would easily avoid suspicion. This is what happened. How did he accomplish it? He hired Aeschines. (149) Since no one foresaw this plot, I think, or guarded against it—this is the way things are usually handled by you—Aeschines was nominated Council delegate and was declared elected when three or four hands were raised in his favor. When he came to the meeting of the Council, attended by the prestige of our city, he

completely ignored everything else and set about the job for which he was hired. Composing some specious and fanciful tales about why the plain of Kirrha had been consecrated and relating them to men unused to hearing speeches and unable to see what was coming, (150) he persuaded them to vote an inspection of the plain which the Amphissians claimed belonged to them for cultivation but which he alleged was part of the consecrated land. The Amphissians were bringing no suit against us then nor were they doing what he now falsely claims as his excuse. The proof is here. It was not possible, of course, for the Amphissians to prepare a suit against the city without a summons being served. Who served this summons on us? On what authority? Mention someone who knows, point him out. You cannot; this was an empty and false pretext you used. (151) While the Amphictyons were making a survey of the land according to the directions of Aeschines, the Amphissians attacked and nearly killed all of them; in fact, they seized some of the delegates. Once legal charges and war were stirred up against the Amphissians, at first Kottyphos led an army of Amphictyons; but when some members did not join the expedition, others joined but didn't do anything, those with whom arrangements had been made, the longtime traitors in Thessaly and the other cities, were for putting Philip in charge of the war before the coming meeting in the autumn. (152) And they had specious reasons. Either, they claimed, the members themselves had to contribute to the support of a mercenary army and fine noncontributors, or they had to elect Philip. Need I say more? The result was the election of Philip as leader of the war. Immediately afterwards, he collected a force and started out as if toward Kirrha, but, quite ignoring the Kirrhaians and the Amphissians, he seized Elateia. (153) If the Thebans had not reversed themselves immediately upon seeing this and joined our side, the whole thing would have swept into our city like a river in torrent. As it was, they checked him, for the moment at least, thanks especially, men of Athens, to the good will of one of the gods, but, besides that, thanks to my efforts insofar as it depended on one man. Give me, please, those resolutions and the records of the times at which each of the events took place, so that you may see how much disturbance this evil man caused, without paying the penalty for it. Read the resolutions, please. (154)

RESOLUTION OF THE AMPHICTYONS SECOND RESOLUTION (155)

Read also the record of the time of these events. They took place when this man was a delegate to the Council.

RECORDS

(156) Give me the letter which Philip sent to his allies in the Peloponnese, when the Thebans would not comply, so that you may learn clearly from this too that he concealed his true reason for action, which was to harm Greece and Thebes and you, and claimed to be doing what was for the common interest and what had been resolved by the Amphictyons. It was Aeschines who provided him with a starting point and a pretext. Read the letter.

LETTER (157)

(158) You see that he avoids any personal motives, but takes refuge in reasons supplied by the Amphictyons. Who assisted him in arranging these circumstances? Who provided him with those reasons? Who is the one most responsible for the trouble which ensued? Is it not Aeschines here? But, men of Athens, do not go around saying that the troubles Greece suffered were caused by a single man, Philip. Not by a single man, but by many evil men in each city, on Earth and the gods. (159) Aeschines was one of them and, if I had to speak the truth without reserve, I would not hesitate to say that he was the accursed plague which caused the loss of everything afterwards, of men, of places, of cities. For it is the sower of the seed who is responsible for the crop of evil. I am surprised that you did not recoil from him as soon as you saw him. But a cloud of darkness, it seems, stands between you and the truth.

(160) Since I have touched upon his actions against our country, I have come around to discussing the policies I chose in opposition to his. There are many reasons why you should hear them from me; the main one is that it is a shameful thing, men of Athens, if, while I endured the actual labors in your behalf, you cannot bear to hear a review of them. (161) When I saw that, under the influence of men in both cities who were sympathetic to, and had been corrupted by, Philip, the Thebans, as well as you to a large extent, were ignoring what should have been a cause of fear to both peoples and were entirely inattentive to what required much and careful attention, namely that Philip was being permitted to grow powerful and that you were on the point of hostility and an open clash, I was continually on my guard to prevent this. It was not only my own judgment that this was the best policy, (162) but I knew that Aristophon and, after him, Euboulos wanted perpetual friendship between you; I knew also that, while they frequently disagreed on other matters, they were always of the same mind on this. When they

73

were alive, you sly beast, you were their most attentive flatterer, but now you don't see that it is dead men you are accusing. In censuring my Theban policy, you are attacking them more than me, for they approved this alliance before I did. (163) But I return to the main point, that Aeschines caused the war in Amphissa and that Aeschines and his accomplices succeeded in creating hostility against the Thebans. Then Philip marched against you, which was their purpose in setting the cities at odds. If we had not roused ourselves a little too soon, we would have been unable to recover. Their plot was that close to success. What your relations were with Thebes at that stage, you will learn from these decrees and the replies to them. Please read them.

DECREE (164)

SECOND DECREE (165)

(166) Read also his replies.

REPLY TO THE ATHENIAN PEOPLE

REPLY TO THE THEBAN PEOPLE (167)

(168) This was how Philip created dissension between the cities, and, encouraged by the decrees and replies, he came with a force and seized Elateia, feeling that it would no longer be possible for us and the Thebans to act in harmony. All of you know the confusion which then beset the city; nevertheless, listen to a few—the most essential—details.

(169) It was evening. Someone came reporting to the Prytanes that Elateia had been captured. Some of them got up immediately, in the middle of dinner, and began to drive out the merchants in the stalls around the market place and to burn the wicker booths; others had the generals summoned and called for the trumpeter. The city was filled with confusion. At dawn of the next day, the Prytanes summoned the Council to the Council chamber, while you proceeded to the Assembly. The whole people was already seated before the Council started their business and passed a motion. (170) Afterward, when the Council came and the Prytanes reported the information they had received, they brought in the messenger, and he spoke. Then the herald asked, "Who wishes to speak?" No one came forward. The herald asked the same question again and again, but no one rose, although all the generals were present, all the orators were present, and although our country was calling for someone to speak for its security. For it is right to

believe that the voice of the herald, when he speaks as the laws direct, is the common voice of our country. (171) And yet, if we only needed men to come forward who wanted our country secure, all of you, with the rest of the citizens of Athens, would have mounted the speaker's platform. For all of you, I know, wanted Athens to be saved. If we needed the wealthy to come forward, the three hundred would have; if we needed men with both these qualifications, patriotism and wealth, those who made large contributions afterward would have come forward; for this act was motivated by their patriotism and their wealth. (172) But, the crisis of that day, as it seems, called not only for the patriotic and wealthy citizen, but also for a man who had closely followed the course of events from the beginning and who had correctly reasoned why and with what intention Philip was acting. For one who did not know this and who had not carefully examined the situation for a long time, not even if he were patriotic, not even if he were wealthy, was any the more likely to know what had to be done or able to advise you. (173) That man, on that day, was I. I came forward and addressed you, and you should now attentively listen to what I said then, for two reasons: the first, that you may realize that I, alone of the advisers on public policy, did not desert the post that patriotism required in time of danger, but the record shows that I advised and proposed what had to be done for your sake in that fearful crisis; the second, that by spending a little of your time now, you may become far more experienced in the whole area of public policy for the future. (174) I said then,

I think that those who are overly disturbed because they believe that the Thebans are firmly on Philip's side are ignorant of the actual state of affairs. For I am convinced that, if this were so, we would hear, not that he is in Elateia, but that he is at our borders. I am certain, however, that he has come to prepare matters in Thebes. Hear (I said), why this is so. (175) He has prepared to receive his orders all the Thebans he could bribe or deceive. In no way can he win over those who took a stand against him originally and remain opposed to him now. What is his purpose and why has he seized Elateia? By making a show of force and displaying his armament near their city, he hopes to encourage and embolden his supporters and stun his opposition so that they will either yield through fear what they are now unwilling to or may be compelled to do so. (176) If, in the present situation, we choose to remember any trouble the Thebans caused us in the past and mistrust them because they are now on the enemy side, we will, in the first place, answer Philip's prayers, and I fear also that both Philip and the Thebans will march upon Attica, if we look at all the Thebans, those who oppose him and those who support him, in the same light. But if you accept my advice and look carefully, rather than cavil, at what I am saying, you will agree, I think, that I am advising what must be done and that I will free the city from the danger which hovers over it. (177) What do I propose? First, dismiss the fear you have now; then, turn and fear for the Thebans. They are much nearer disaster than we, and the danger will come upon them first. Secondly, those of military age and the cavalry should march to Eleusis and make it clear to everybody that you are at arms, so that the Thebans who sympathize with us may have an equal chance to speak freely about a just course when they see that, as there is a military force in Elateia to support those who are selling out their country to Philip, so you are at hand ready to help those who want to fight for their freedom, if anyone attacks them. (178) After this, I recommend that you elect ten ambassadors, and give these, with the generals, authority to decide when you should march there and the details of the march itself. How do I suggest that the ambassadors deal with the situation when they arrive at Thebes? Pay close attention to me here. They should not ask the Thebans for a thing (their crisis makes any request shameful) but promise to come to their aid, if they so instruct us, since they are now in extreme danger and we are in a better position to see what will happen than they. If they accept our proposals and advice, we may have accomplished what we wish and have done so with a motive worthy of our city; if it turns out that we fail, they may have themselves to blame for any mistake they make, while no action we took was shameful or mean. (179)

With these and similar recommendations, I stepped down. All, together, praised my advice; no one opposed it. I did not speak, but fail to propose measures; I did not propose measures, but fail to serve as ambassador; I did not serve as ambassador, but fail to persuade the Thebans; from beginning to end I persevered and faced, without reserve, the dangers threatening the city. Please read the decree which was voted then.

(180) But wait. Aeschines, how do you wish me to describe your position, and mine, on that day? Was I Battalos, your insulting and degrading nickname for me; were you—no ordinary hero, but one of the great heroes of the stage—Kresphontes or Kreon or Oinomaos, a part which you once murdered in a performance at Kollytos? In that time of crisis, I, Battalos

of Paiania, was clearly of more value to his country than you, Oinomaos of Kothokidai. You were entirely useless; I did everything the duty of a good citizen required. Read the decree, please.

DECREE OF DEMOSTHENES (181–87)

(188) This was the beginning and the first step in establishing good relations with Thebes; before this, thanks to the influence of these men, there was hatred and distrust and hostility between the two cities. This decree made the danger then hanging over our city pass by like a cloud. It was the duty of the good citizen, if he had anything better to advise, to bring it into the open then, and not be criticizing my policy now. (189) For the adviser and the malicious opportunist, who are alike in no other way, differ most in this: the one reveals his opinion before the events and makes himself responsible to those he has persuaded, to fortune, to opportunities, to all men; the other, who was silent when he should have spoken, cavils if anything unpleasant results. (190) Then, as I said, was the opportunity for one who cared about his city and about honest advice. I even go so far as to say that I acted wrongly, if he can point to a better policy now or even if there was anything else at all which could have been done, apart from the policy I recommended. If anyone sees any measure now, which would have been beneficial if acted upon then, I say that it should not have escaped me. But if there is none, if there was none, if none can be mentioned even to this day, what should the statesman have done? Should he not have chosen the best of the possible policies which revealed themselves? (191) This is what I did, when the herald asked: "Who wishes to speak?" not, "Who wishes to bring charges about events of the past?" nor, "Who wishes to guarantee what the future will bring?" In those times of crisis, you sat mute in the assemblies; I rose and spoke. You wouldn't then, tell us now. What advice, which should have been available, or what opportunity for Athens was neglected by me? What alliance, what action was there to which I should rather have persuaded these citizens?

(192) Everyone dismisses the past and no one ever proffers advice about it. It is the future or the present which requires the statesman at his post. At that moment, it seems, some danger was in the future, some was already at hand; consider the policy I chose in the circumstances; don't cavil at the outcome. For the final result of all actions depends upon the will of heaven, but the choice itself reveals the mind of the statesman. (193) Don't blame me for a crime, if it turned out that Philip was victorious in battle;

the result here rested with the gods, not with me. Show me that I did not choose everything that was possible according to human calculation, and that my actions were not just and careful and that they did not require almost superhuman strength, or that they were not noble, not worthy of the city, not necessary; show me this, and then accuse me. (194) If the lightning that struck us was too great not only for us but for the rest of Greece as well, what were we to do? It is just as if one were to blame for the shipwreck the owner who has taken every precaution, has equipped his ship with everything he believes will ensure its safety, but then the ship meets with a storm and its tackling weakens or is completely ruined. But I was not a captain of a ship, one might say (as I was not a general either), nor did I control fate; rather, fate controlled everything. (195) Look at it in this way, Aeschines. If this result was fated, although we had the Thebans fighting with us, what should we have expected if we did not have them as allies, but had let them join Philip—a policy which all the eloquence of Aeschines supported? If so much danger, so much fear surrounded Athens when the battle was three days away from Attica, what should we have expected if we had the same experience somewhere on our own territory? Aren't you aware that one and two and three days allowed us to make a stand, to compose and refresh our forces, and provided much for the security of the city? But if so—it is not right to mention something we did not have to suffer, by the good will of one of the gods and because the alliance, which you accuse, provided a shield for the city.

(196) All of this—and it has been much—I intended for you, men of the jury, and for the spectators listening outside; a brief and plain account would have been a sufficient reply to this contemptible man. If the future were clear to you alone, Aeschines, you should have spoken out when the city was deliberating. If you did not foresee the future, you have the same responsibility as others for the same ignorance; and so, why should you accuse me rather than I you? (197) I proved myself so much better a citizen than you in these particular events (I do not yet mention others) that I devoted myself to policies which all thought to be advantageous, not hesitating before, nor considering, any personal danger, while you, who had no better policy than mine (if you had, the Athenians would not have followed mine) and did not make yourself at all useful in implementing this policy, are found to be doing precisely what the worst type of man and worst enemy of the city would do after the matter is finished. Aristratos in Naxos and Aristoleus in Thasos, the outright enemies of our city, are bringing to trial the friends of

the Athenians; in Athens, at the same time, Aeschines is accusing Demosthenes. (198) And yet, a person who finds matter for personal glory in the misfortunes of Greece would more justly suffer the penalty of death than be accusing another; a person who was benefited by the same time of crisis as were the enemies of his city cannot be a patriotic citizen. You prove this from your life, from your actions, from your policies, and from your lack of policy. A measure is being discussed which the Athenians think supports their interests; Aeschines is silent. There was resistance, and something unexpected happened; Aeschines is there, like ruptures and strains which afflict the body when it is stricken by some disease.

(199) Since he concentrates his charges on the outcome of these events, I wish to make a rather paradoxical assertion. Do not be amazed, by Zeus and the gods, if I say something extreme; rather, let everyone examine what I say with good will. If the outcome was entirely clear, and everyone knew about it beforehand, and you were predicting it, Aeschines, shouting at the top of your voice—you who did not utter a word—not even in those circumstances should the city have backed off from its course, if in fact it was concerned for its reputation or its forefathers or the future. (200) As it is, it seems we have failed to achieve our material ends, a result which can happen to all men when the gods so decide. But if Athens had claimed to be the leader of the rest of Greece, and then had backed off from this claim in the face of Philip, she would have been open to the charge that she betrayed all of Greece. If she had yielded to Philip, without a fight, what our forefathers had taken every risk to preserve, who would not have spit upon you, Aeschines? Not on the city, not on me. (201) Events have turned out as they have, and Philip has been chosen absolute master of all Greece; but how could we look visitors to Athens in the face, if others apart from us had made the struggle to prevent this result, especially since our city in former times never chose an ignominious security over danger to gain a noble end. (202) Is there any Greek, any non-Greek, who does not know that Athens could have kept what was hers and received whatever she wanted from the Thebans, from the Spartans, who were even stronger than the Thebans before, and from the king of Persia—and they would have been very glad to give it—if she would do what they commanded and allow another power to be the leader of Greece? (203) For Athenians, however, to make such a choice was not something they had learned from their ancestors nor morally tolerable nor natural; from the beginning of her history, no one has ever been able to persuade our city to attach herself to those who are strong, but act unjustly,

and thus live the secure life of slavery; rather, Athens has continually fought for and taken risks for first place in honor and reputation throughout this time. (204) You should understand that these qualities are so lofty and so consistent with your character that you reserve your highest praise for those of your ancestors who followed this course. Rightly so. For who would not admire the courage of the men who endured leaving their city and their land and taking to warships to avoid obeying another's orders, who chose Themistocles, the adviser of this action, as general, who stoned Kyrsilos to death (and not only Kyrsilos; your wives slew his wife as well) because he proposed submission. (205) The Athenians of that day were not looking for an adviser or a general who would lead them to become happy slaves, but they did not even think it right to go on living, if they could not live in freedom. Each of them thought himself a child not of his parents alone but also of his country. What is the difference? One who considers himself only a child of his parents is satisfied to await the natural death which fate brings; he who is a child of his country as well will be willing to die not to see her enslaved and will believe that the insults and dishonor he must suffer in a city of slaves are more to be feared than death itself.

(206) If I were trying to say that I induced you to feel sentiments worthy of your ancestors, anyone could criticize me with justice. In fact, I am showing you that this was your own choice, and I am pointing out that the city had this spirit before me, but I do say that I contributed some service in each of the actions you took, and that Aeschines here, (207) who censures the whole of this policy and bids you to feel bitterness toward me because I am the cause of the fearful dangers which befell the city, hungers to deprive me of this immediate honor and is robbing you of the praise you deserve for all future time. If you will condemn Ctesiphon on the grounds that my policies were not for the best, you will be thought to have made a mistake, and you will make it appear that the results you suffered were not due to the harshness of fate. (208) But it cannot, it cannot be that you made a mistake, men of Athens, in taking upon yourselves the burden of danger for the freedom and security of all; I swear it by your ancestors in the front lines at Marathon, by those who stood at Plataia, by your naval men at Salamis and Artemisium and by many others who lie in public tombs, good men, all of them, whom the city buried because it thought them worthy of the same honor, not only those of them who were successful and victorious. And justly so. For they all performed the duty expected of brave men, and they accepted whatever fate heaven allotted to them. (209) But now,

you abominable clerk, in your desire to rob me of the honor and affection of these jurors, you have been talking about victory trophies and battles and deeds of old; which of them do we need in the present trial? Whose spirit should have inspired me, you third-rate actor, when I approached the speaker's platform to advise our city how to preserve her preeminence? His, whose advice would be unworthy of these citizens? They would justly have put me to death. (210) For you should not decide public and private lawsuits, men of Athens, from the same point of view: in the one case, you should examine the business contracts of daily life with reference to specific statutes and facts; in judging public policy, you should keep your eyes on the standards of your ancestors. Each of you, when he accepts his juror's staff and ticket, should realize that he is also inheriting the spirit of the city, if indeed you think that your actions should be worthy of your ancestors when you come to court to decide public cases.

(211) But I have digressed about the deeds of your ancestors, and there are decrees and actions I have omitted. I wish to return to the points I was making before my digression.

On arriving at Thebes, we found there representatives of Philip, of the Thessalians and of his other allies, and discovered that our supporters were in fear, his brashly confident. To show that my statements now are not for my own benefit, read, please, the letter which we ambassadors sent back immediately. (212) The malice of Aeschines is so deep that he claims that the opportunity, and not I, was responsible for anything successful that was done; but he blames me and my luck for everything which turned out otherwise. As it seems, I, the adviser and spokesman, seem to him responsible for none of the actions produced by discussion and deliberation; I alone am responsible for our military and strategic failures. How could a person who makes such a malicious accusation be more coarse or more contemptible? Read the letter.

LETTER

(213) When the Thebans called an assembly, they introduced the others first because of their position as allies. They came forward and delivered their harangues, with much praise of Philip, many accusations against you, and frequent reminders to the Thebans of everything you had ever done against them. In short, their claim was that the Thebans should be grateful for the favors they had received from Philip and should inflict whatever penalty they wished upon you for the wrongs they had suffered, either by allowing

Philip and his allies to march through Boeotia against you or by joining them in the invasion of Attica. They showed, as they thought, that, if Thebes followed their counsel, animals and slaves, and other possessions of yours would be moved from Attica to Boeotia, but, if Thebes accepted what they alleged we would say, everything in Boeotia would be ravaged by war. They made many additional claims, all tending to the same end. (214) While I would give my whole life to repeat each detail of the reply we made, yet I fear that, since the crisis is past and you may think that everything which took place has been obliterated as if by a flood, you might believe that a detailed discussion would be an empty pile of words. But hear how we persuaded them and how they answered us. Read this document.

REPLY OF THE THEBANS

(215) After this, they invited your help and summoned you. You marched out, you came to their aid, and—to omit the intervening steps—they received you in such a friendly manner that, with their own cavalry and infantry outside the walls, they took your army into the city and into their homes, among their wives and children and most valuable possessions. On that day, the citizens of Thebes showed all the world three qualities of yours which deserve the highest praise: the first is your bravery, the second your justice, the third your decent behavior. For in choosing to make the fight with you rather than against you, they judged that you were better and your claims more just than Philip's; by putting in your care what they and all men guard most closely, their wives and children, they revealed their confidence in your behavior. (216) In these areas, men of Athens, their judgment about you was obviously correct. When your army had entered the city, no one, even unjustly, made any complaint about you, so decently did you conduct yourselves. When they lined up alongside you in the first battles, the one at the river and the winter battle, you showed yourselves not only faultless but even admirable for your discipline, your state of preparation, and your zeal. On these grounds you received praise from other peoples, you offered sacrifices and processions to the gods. (217) I would take pleasure in asking Aeschines whether he shared your joy and joined in the sacrifices when they were being conducted and the city was filled with pride and joy and praise or did he sit at home, grieving, lamenting, sulking at our common success? If he is proved to have been there with the rest of us, is not his behavior monstrous, or even sacrilegious, if he invoked the gods as witnesses of the excellence of our policy and now thinks it right that you, who have

sworn an oath to the gods, should condemn this policy because it was bad? If he was not there, should he not justly suffer a thousand deaths, because he was aggrieved by what was a cause of joy to the rest of us? Please read these decrees as well.

SACRIFICIAL DECREES

(218) While we were engaged in sacrifices and the Thebans believed that they had been rescued by us, it turned out that we, who, it seemed, would require help as a result of the activities of these traitors, were ourselves helping others because you accepted my recommendations. Further, you will learn from the letters Philip sent to the Peloponnese what reactions he voiced and how confused he was at this turn of events. Please read them so that you may see what was accomplished by my persistence, by the journeys I made, by my labors and by the many decrees which Aeschines ridiculed just now.

(219) And yet, men of Athens, you had many great and famous advisers before me, the notable Kallistratos, Aristophon, Kephalos, Thrasyboulos, a thousand others. Nevertheless, none of these ever put his whole person entirely at the service of our city, but if one made proposals, he would not serve as an envoy; if another was an envoy, he would not make proposals. Each of them reserved for himself some enjoyment in leisure as well as some resource to fall back on, if anything went wrong. (220) What is my point? Someone might ask, "Were you so superior in forcefulness and enterprise that you did everything yourself?" I do not say this, but I so thoroughly persuaded myself that the danger which had the city in its grasp was great that there did not seem to be any room for consideration of my personal safety, but one had to be content if he did what he had to do and omitted nothing. (221) As to myself, I was persuaded—perhaps senselessly, but nevertheless I was persuaded—that, in proposing measures, no one would propose better measures than I, that in acting and in serving as an ambassador, no one could act or serve more zealously and more correctly than I. For these reasons, I was at my post in each of these spheres. Read the letters of Philip.

LETTERS

(222) This was the situation in which my policy put Philip, Aeschines. This was the language he used now, no longer the many brash threats against the city. For this I was justly voted a crown by these citizens; you were there and did not oppose the crown; Diondas, who contested it, did not receive

a minimum of the votes. Please read the decrees whose legality was vindicated and which were not contested by Aeschines.

DECREES

(223) These decrees, men of Athens, have precisely the same words and syllables as those which Aristonikos proposed before and Ctesiphon proposes now. Aeschines did not contest them himself and did not assist anyone else contesting them. Yet it would have been more reasonable for him to prosecute Demomeles, their proposer, and Hypereides, than Ctesiphon, if his present accusations are true. (224) Why? Because it is possible for Ctesiphon to refer to those men and to the decisions of the courts, to the fact that Aeschines did not accuse them when they made the same proposals as he makes now, to the fact that the laws do not allow further indictments on matters settled judicially, and to many other facts. Had Aeschines prosecuted Demomeles and Hypereides, the matter would have been decided on its own merits, before any precedents existed. (225) But in that case, I think, it would not have been possible for Aeschines to follow his present procedure; he misrepresents the facts by selecting details of many decrees from ancient history which no one knew about before the trial or thought would be mentioned today; he seems to say something to the point by rearranging chronology and substituting false grounds of action for the true ones. (226) This procedure would not have worked, but all arguments would have rested on the truth, the events were recent, you still remembered them and almost had each detail in your grasp. For this reason, avoiding an inquiry into the facts, he has come here believing that you will hold a public speaking contest, as it seems to me, and not a review of my policies, and will make it a trial of eloquence, not of which policy was beneficial to the city.

(227) Then he becomes subtle and says you should ignore the opinion about us you had when you came to court; just as you acquiesce when, thinking that someone has a surplus, you total up the accounts and find that both sides of the ledger are even and there is no surplus, so also now you should acquiesce in the plausible conclusions of his argument. But look how rotten, it seems, are the foundations supporting every plan unjustly contrived. (228) By using the clever illustration just mentioned, he has agreed that you must now be assumed to have made a decision about us, that I speak for my country, and he speaks for Philip; he would not be seeking to change your minds, unless such a decision about each of us is to be assumed. (229) Moreover, I will easily show that, in asking you to change this

opinion, his statements are unjust; I will do it not by bookkeeping (this type of reckoning is irrelevant to affairs of state) but by reminding you briefly of each detail, using you, my audience, as examiners and witnesses at the same time. Instead of the Thebans joining Philip in an invasion of our land, as all expected, my policy, which Aeschines attacks, caused the Thebans to line up with you to check Philip; (230) instead of the war being fought in Attica, it was fought eighty miles from the city at the farther borders of Boeotia; instead of pirates from Eubrea plundering and pillaging, the side of Attica on the sea enjoyed peace throughout the war; instead of Philip seizing Byzantium and holding the Hellespont, the Byzantines fought with us against him. (231) Do you think, Aeschines, that the examination of these results is like bookkeeping? Or should we erase my services from the books, and fail to consider that they will be remembered for all time? I do not add, as a credit, that it was the misfortune of others to suffer that savagery which Philip displayed once he had people entirely in his power, while it was our good fortune to reap the fruits of the clemency in which he draped himself as he schemed for the future. But I pass over this.

(232) Further, I will not hesitate to say that one who wishes to examine the record of a statesman fairly, and not maliciously, would not use the kind of accusations you have just voiced, inventing illustrations, imitating my words and gestures (the fate of the Greek world, to be sure, depended on whether I used this word and not that, or moved my hand this way and not that way), (233) but he would inquire, on the basis of the facts, what means or military resources our city had when I entered public life, what resources I gained for her afterward through my leadership, and what was the condition of our enemies. If I diminished our power, he would show that the wrong rested with me; but if I greatly increased it, he would not bring malicious charges. Since you have avoided this course, I will take it, and look to see, men of Athens, if my assertions be fair.

(234) In military resources, the city had the islanders, not all but the weakest, for Khios, Rhodes, and Corcyra were not with us. The financial subscription was forty-five talents, and this had been collected in advance. We had no infantry or cavalry except our citizen forces. What was most frightening of all and most helpful to the enemy, these traitors had brought all our neighbors, Megara, Thebes, and Euboea, closer to enmity than to friendship with us. (235) This was all the city could rely on, and no one can mention any other resource. Consider the condition of Philip, whom we were fighting. First, he had absolute rule over his followers, which is the greatest single advantage in

war. Second, his followers were armed for war all the time. Third, he was well supplied with money, and did whatever he decided, not publishing his decisions in decrees, not being constantly brought to court by malicious accusers, not defending himself against charges of illegality, not accountable to anyone, but simply ruler, leader, master of all. (236) When I took my position against him (for it is fair to examine this), of what was I master? Of nothing. For even the opportunity to speak on policy, the only privilege I had—and a shared one, at that—you extended equally to Philip's hirelings and to me, and, as often as they got the better of me (these instances were many, whatever reason there was for each of them), that often did you leave the Assembly with your enemies' advantage the result of your deliberations. (237) Although I started with disadvantages like these, I brought into alliance with you Euboea, Akhaia, Corinth, Thebes, Megara, Leukas, Corcyra, and these contributed a total of 15,000 mercenaries and 2,000 cavalry apart from their citizen armies. I effected the largest contribution of money I could. (238) If you talk about the justice of our arrangements with Thebes, Aeschines, or with Byzantium or with Euboea or about equal contributions in general, in the first place you show your ignorance of the fact that once before our city provided 200 of those famous 300 warships which fought for Greece, and did not believe itself cheated, did not put the advisers of this policy on trial, did not take offense at this burden (that would have been shameful) but was grateful to the gods that Athens contributed twice as much as the rest to secure all of Greece from the danger which threatened it. (239) In the second place, it is an empty favor you do these citizens by slandering me. Why is it now you say what I should have done, why did you not offer proposals then, since you were in Athens and were present at the meeting of the Assembly, if indeed proposals were feasible in a time of crisis when we had to accept what circumstances allowed, not what we wished? For there was one man bidding against us and ready to accept immediately the men we drove out of our city and to pay them as well.

(240) But if I am now open to criticism for my actions, what do you think these impious men would say or do, if the cities left us and attached themselves to Philip because I was quibbling about the terms of alliance, and Philip gained control of Euboea and Thebes and Byzantium at the same time? (241) Would they not say that these cities had been given up? That they had been rejected, although they wanted to join you? They would say, "Because of Byzantium, Philip has gained control of the Hellespont, and of the grain route to Greece; because of Thebes, a war between neighbors

has shifted its severe burden to Attica; because of pirates with their base in Euboea, the sea has become unsafe." Would they not say this and much more besides? (242) A worthless thing, men of Athens, a worthless thing is a person who brings malicious accusations always and everywhere, a spiteful thing, a fault-finder. This paltry man is an animal to the core, who has done nothing helpful or worthy of a free man from his birth; he is a stage monkey, a rustic Oinomaos, a counterfeit statesman. How has your eloquence helped our country? (243) Why do you speak to us now of the past? You act like a doctor who, when he visits his sick patients, does not prescribe anything to cure them of their sickness, but when one of his patients dies and funeral services are being held, follows the body to the tomb, saying, "If the man had done this and that, he would not have died." Madman, is it now you speak?

(244) If you exult at the defeat to our city which you should lament, accursed man, you will not find that it resulted from anything in my control. Look at it in this way. Wherever you sent me as ambassador, I never came back worsted by Philip's ambassadors, not from Thessaly or Ambracia, not from the Illyrians or from the kings of Thrace, not from Byzantium, not from anywhere else, not, finally, from Thebes, but wherever his ambassadors were defeated in debate, he came in with his weapons and overturned the decision. Do you make me accountable for this, (245) and feel no shame at ridiculing the same man for his cowardice, while claiming that this one man should have been stronger than the whole might of Philip? With words my only weapon? What else did I control? Not the life, not the fate of the soldiers, not the generalship, which you demand that I justify; that is how stupid you are. (246) Make a complete review of everything for which the statesman is accountable; I do not avoid it. What would this be? To see situations as they arise and to inform the rest of the citizens. This I did. To confine within the smallest possible limits, whenever they arise, hesitation, reluctance to act, ignorance, personal ambition—those necessary and inherent defects of all free governments—and to convert these qualities into concord and friendship and the impulse to do what must be done. All of this I did, and no one will ever find anything left undone, so far as it rested with me. (247) If it should be asked how Philip managed most of what he accomplished, everyone would mention his army and his bribes and his corruption of men in political life. I had no forces at my command or under my control, so that the question of what was done in this sphere does not concern me. In the matter of bribery and corruption, I was victor over Philip. For, as the offerer of a bribe is victor over the taker, if it is accepted,

so he who does not take the bribe is victor over the offerer. Thus, our city was not defeated, insofar as I am representative of it.

(248) It was these activities, and many others like them, which I provided to justify Ctesiphon's proposal in my honor; I will now mention what all of you provided. Immediately after the battle, the Athenian people, which knew and had witnessed all my actions, although it was in the middle of a terrible and fearful crisis when it was not surprising that most people would be out of sympathy with me, first voted to approve my suggestions for the security of the city and put into operation, through my decrees, everything which was done for its protection: the posting of guards, the ditches, the expenditures to fortify the city walls. Next, the people chose me from all the citizens in the election of a grain commissioner. (249) Afterward, when those whose concern it was to injure me banded together and instituted all sorts of suits and trials and impeachments against me, not in their own names at first but using persons who they thought would be quite unknown to you (you know, of course, and remember that I was in court on trial on every day of that first period and these men left nothing untried against me, not the desperation of Sosikles, not the maliciousness of Philokrates, not the madness of Diondas and Malantos) but in all these trials I was safely acquitted, thanks mainly to the gods but also through you and the rest of the citizens of Athens. And justly, for acquittal was in accordance with the truth and to the credit of jurors who rendered the only decision in keeping with the oath they had sworn. (250) In the trials of impeachment, when you voted to acquit me and did not give the minimum vote to the prosecutors, you voted that I acted in the best way; in trials of illegality, I was proved to advise and propose only legal measures; in trials when you put an official seal on my accounts, you further acknowledged that everything I handled was handled fairly and without a suspicion of venality. What name was it proper or right for Ctesiphon to attach to results effected by me? Was it not the name which he saw the Athenian people attach, which he saw the sworn jurors attach, which he saw the truth establish to the world?

(251) "Yes," he says, "but it is Kephalos's glory that he was never brought to trial." Yes, indeed, and a blessed stroke of fortune. But why should a man, who has often been prosecuted but never convicted of any crime, be subject in justice to any greater censure because of that? And yet, men of Athens, as far as Aeschines is concerned, I can claim Kephalos's glory, for he never indicted me or prosecuted me, and so he himself agrees that I am not a worse citizen than Kephalos.

(252) One might see his insensitivity and his spitefulness in every paragraph of his remarks, not least in what he had to say about luck. In general, I think, a man who, only a man himself, criticizes another man for his luck is crazy. For what right does a man, who thinks he is very fortunate and has excellent luck, yet does not know if his luck will last till evening, have to talk about his own luck or reproach another man for his. Since Aeschines, besides much else, has used very arrogant language about this subject, you should watch, men of Athens, how much more truthful and more humane will be my remarks on luck. (253) I believe that the luck of our city is good— and I see that the oracle of Zeus at Dodona declares this to you—but that the luck which now prevails for mankind in general is hard and cruel. What Greek, what non-Greek, has not experienced many evils in these times? (254) I count it part of the good luck of our city that it chose the noblest course of action and fares better than those Greeks who thought they would live in blessed prosperity by abandoning us. Our disaster and the fact that everything did not turn out as we wished is, I believe, our share of the luck of the rest of mankind. (255) I think an examination of one's personal luck, my own and that of each one of us, should be restricted to his private affairs. This is what I believe about luck, a correct and fair judgment, it seems to me, and to you also, I think. Aeschines says that my own luck is more decisive than the luck of the whole city, that something small and insignificant is more decisive than something excellent and great. How is this possible?

(256) If you wish to examine my luck fully, Aeschines, compare it with your own; and if you find mine to be better than yours, stop reviling it. Compare them from the beginning. And, by Zeus, let no one condemn me for lack of feeling. I don't think a person has sense if he reproaches someone for his poverty or if he prides himself on being raised in wealth. But I am compelled by the cruel and malicious insults of this abusive man to mention things like this, although I will be as moderate as circumstances permit.

(257) When I was a boy, Aeschines, I was privileged to attend the proper schools and my financial advantages were such that I was not compelled to do anything shameful through need; when I left boyhood, my actions were consistent with my antecedents—I was choregus, trierarch, a financial contributor to the city, I was deficient in no area of private or public munificence but was useful to my city and to my friends; when I decided to enter public life, I chose the type of policies which brought me frequent crowns of honor from my own country and from other Greeks, such policies which not even you, my enemies, dare to say were dishonorable. (258) This

is the good luck I have enjoyed in my life and, although I could mention many other aspects of it, I pass over them to avoid offending any of you by magnifying myself. You, Aeschines, a man haughty and contemptuous of others, compare your luck with mine, luck which saw you raised in deepest poverty, assisting your father in the schoolroom, grinding ink, swabbing benches, sweeping the room, doing the chores of a servant, not of a free man's son; (259) when you became a man, you read the holy books for your mother's rituals and organized the other details: at night wearing a fawn skin, mixing the wine, cleansing the initiates by wiping them with mud and bran, and, after the purification, instructing them to say, "I have escaped the bad, I have found the better," priding yourself that no one ever could howl as loudly as you (and I believe it; (260) don't think that he can speak so loudly here without being absolutely brilliant at howling); in the daytime, you led your noble bands through the streets wearing garlands of fennel and poplar, squeezing puffed-cheeked adders and waving them over your head, crying "Euoi Saboi" and dancing to the rhythm of "Hyes Attes Attes Hyes," the leader of the dance, the ivy-wreathed leader of the band, the bearer of the winnowing-fan, and addressed with these titles by the little old ladies, taking your pay in the form of sops and cakes and pastry (what glorious rewards! who would not think himself and his luck most truly blessed to receive them?); (261) when you were enrolled in your deme by some trick (I won't go into that), when you were enrolled, you immediately chose the most honorable of professions, that of a clerk and a flunky to minor officials. When you somehow escaped this career, after committing in it all those acts which you accuse in others, (262) you brought no shame, by Zeus, on any of your former occupations by your life afterwards, but hired yourself out to the actors Simukas and Sokrates, the famous "Groaners," and played your small roles collecting from the audience, like a fruit seller from other people's farms, figs and grapes and olives, getting more from this source than from your dramatic contests, in which your troupe engaged at the risk of its life. For there was a truceless and never-ending war between you and the spectators, who inflicted upon you so many wounds that you naturally ridicule as cowards those who never faced such risks. (263) But, passing over actions which one can attribute to poverty, I will proceed to faults in his way of life which deserve accusation. When somehow it occurred to you to enter public life, you chose the kind of policy which, when our country enjoyed success, made you lead the life of a rabbit, fearing, trembling, always expecting people to strike you for the crimes you knew you were guilty of, but put on a show of boldness when the rest of us had unfortunate luck. (264) What is the just reward a man should get from those living, when his spirit is emboldened by the death of a thousand citizens? I omit many other details about his character. For it is not every ugly and shameful reproach which attaches itself to him that I can scrupulously mention, but only those whose mention brings no disgrace to me.

(265) Compare the kind of lives each of us lived, calmly, Aeschines, not bitterly. Then ask these jurors whose luck each of them would choose. You taught school, I attended school. You initiated people, I was an initiate. You were a minor clerk, I was a member of the Assembly. You were a minor actor, I was a spectator. You were hissed off the stage, I joined in the hissing. Your policies supported our enemy, mine, our country. (266) I pass over the rest, but now, today, my qualifications to receive a crown of honor are under examination, it is agreed that I have done no wrong; the reputation you have as a malicious accuser is set, you are in constant danger, whether you must continue to behave like this or whether you will soon be stopped, by failing to receive a minimum of the votes. Good luck has marked your life—good, indeed!—and you accuse my luck.

(267) Bring here the evidence which deals with my voluntary services and let me read them to you. Alongside these, Aeschines, you read the verses you murdered, "I am come to the crypt of the dead and the gates of darkness" and "Be assured I have no wish to bring evil tidings" and "evil man, evilly" may you be destroyed, first by the gods and then by all of these jurors, bad citizen and bad actor alike.

Read the evidence.

EVIDENCE

(268) This is the way I was in public matters. In my private life,—if all of you do not know that I was at the service of all, humane and generous to those in need, I am silent; I would not mention a thing; I would not even provide evidence for my actions, whether ransoming some citizens from the enemy, whether assisting others with dowries for their daughters, nothing like this. (269) For I have this conviction. I believe that one who receives a favor should remember it all his life, but that he who does the favor should put it out of his mind immediately, if he is to behave like a man of honor, not of mean spirit. To be reminding people and to keep talking about one's personal favors is nearly the same as reproaching them. I will do nothing like this, nor will I be induced to, it is enough for me that you know how I feel in such matters.

(270) Leaving the topic of my private life, I wish to add a few remarks about political matters. If you can say, Aeschines, that there is any man under the sun, Greek or non-Greek, who has escaped harm from the tyranny of Philip before, and of Alexander now, all right, I grant that my—whether you prefer to call it luck or bad luck—has been entirely responsible. (271) But if many, who never saw me or heard my voice, have suffered many and harsh troubles—not only individuals but also whole cities and peoples— how much truer and fairer is it to believe that the general luck, as it seems, of all mankind and the cruel and inescapable rush of events is responsible. (272) You dismiss this and blame me, whose political career has been spent among these citizens, although you know that part at least, if not the whole, of your abuse falls upon all the citizens and especially upon you. For if I had absolute control of our deliberations in my hands, it would be possible for you other speakers to blame me. (273) But if you were at all the meetings of the Assembly, on each occasion when the city put forward for consideration the question of correct policy, and if my policies seemed to all to be the best, and especially to you, Aeschines (for it was not out of good will toward me that you yielded your hopes for the pride and honor which attended the results produced through me, but clearly you were defeated by the truth and had nothing better to advise), how can your words fail to be unjust, fail to be cruel, when you now censure these citizens for policies you could not improve on then? (274) I see that certain principles are defined and settled by all men in this way. A man commits a crime voluntarily; the result is anger and punishment of him; a man made a mistake involuntarily; punishment is replaced by sympathy. A man commits no crime, makes no mistake, devotes himself entirely to a policy which all think beneficial but, in common with all, fails of success; it is not just to reproach or revile such a man, it is just to share his grief. (275) Not only will all these principles appear in our laws, but nature itself has defined them in unwritten laws and in the customs of mankind. Aeschines has so surpassed all men in malicious savagery that he blames me for what he himself has called the results of bad luck.

(276) Besides this, as if all his words were straightforward and patriotic, he told you to watch me and be careful that I didn't confuse or deceive you, calling me eloquent, a magician with words, a sophist, and similar epithets, assuming that the fact that he attributes his own qualities to me first will make it so and that his audience will not further consider who is making these statements. I am sure that all of you know him well and believe that these qualities belong much more to him than to me. (277) And I am aware

of my skill as a speaker, so far as I have it. Yet I see that the audience has the most control over the impression speakers make. For the way that you listen and the amount of good will you have toward each speaker determines your opinion of his wisdom. If I do have a skill of this sort, you will find that, in public matters, it is ranged always on your side, never against you nor for private profit; conversely, Aeschines' skill is used not only to help our enemies, but also against people who might have caused him some trouble or crossed him in some way. He does not use it for just causes or for the city's advantage. (278) The respectable and honorable citizen should not ask jurors who have come here to judge matters affecting the whole city to confirm his anger or hostility or any similar feeling, nor should he appear before you for this purpose but, best of all, these feelings should not be part of his nature; if he must have them, they should be mild and moderate. In what instances should the political speaker be vehement? When one of the vital interests of the city is at stake, and when the city has to deal with its opponents. These are the concern of the honorable and good citizen. (279) But for a person, who has never demanded that you inflict a penalty on me for any public crime—I will add, nor for a private offense—to satisfy the city or to satisfy himself, to come here concocting accusations against a motion to crown and praise me is the mark of personal enmity, of spite, of a mean spirit, not of a worthwhile citizen. To go further and, dismissing the chance of suits against me, to attack Ctesiphon is the ultimate in worthlessness. (280) With this approach, Aeschines, you seem to me to have chosen to make this a contest of eloquence and of declamation, not to demand punishment for any crime. The language of the speaker, Aeschines, is not a valuable thing, nor the pitch of his voice; it is to choose the same policy as the people, to hate and admire the same persons his country does. (281) One with such a spirit will say everything he says with patriotism his guide; he who courts those from whom the city sees some danger to itself does not ride at the same anchor with the people and cannot have the same expectation of safety. But, don't you see, I can. I chose to act in the interests of these citizens and had no separate or personal interest. (282) Can the same be said of you? How could it be? Immediately after the battle, you went as envoy to Philip, who was responsible for the disasters that those days brought upon your country, although, as everybody knows, you persistently denied any connection with him before that. Yet, who is the one who deceives his city? Is it not he who does not say what is in his mind? Is it not he upon whom the herald lays a solemn and just curse? Is it not a man like Aeschines?

What greater crime can be imputed to a political speaker than that what he says and what he feels are two different things? This was found to be true of you. (283) Can you still speak, do you still dare to look these jurors in the face? Do you think they don't know who you are? Or do you think they are so sleepy and so forgetful that they do not remember the speeches you made in the Assembly in the course of the war, solemnly avowing and swearing on oath that there was nothing between you and Philip, but that I was charging you with this because of my own hostility toward you and knew that the charge was untrue. (284) As soon as the result of the battle was reported, you owned up to it immediately, unconcerned with what you said before, and claimed that you were his friend and his guest, substituting "friend" for "hireling." What claim of equality could justify any relationship which makes Aeschines, the son of Eyegleam, the drum-beater, the guest or friend or even acquaintance of Philip? I see none, but the fact is that you sold yourself to pervert the interests of these citizens. In spite of this, Aeschines, although you are caught by the evidence which shows you to be a traitor and have so testified against yourself after the events, you insult and abuse me for results for which you will find everyone else more responsible than me.

(285) Our city, through the policies advocated by me, Aeschines, has had many great and glorious successes, which it has not forgotten. For when the Athenian people were electing a speaker to deliver the eulogy over the dead at the very time of these events, they did not elect you when you were nominated, although you had a fine voice, nor Demades, who had just negotiated the peace, nor Hegemon, nor any other of your friends; they elected me. And when you and Pythokles came forward like savage and ruthless animals, by Zeus and the gods, and made the same abusive accusations which you are making now, the people voted for me all the more eagerly. (286) You are not unaware of the reason, but I will tell you anyway. For the people knew our two qualities, the patriotic zeal which directed my actions, and your injustice. For you and your accomplices admitted, when the city was defeated, what you had denied on oath, when its fortunes were flourishing. The people realized that those who spoke their minds with an impunity gained from the disaster we suffered had been their enemies long before, but then were clearly proved so. (287) They thought it proper that the eulogist who was to adorn the courage of their dead not be under the same roof with nor share the same sacrificial ritual with those who had fought against our dead; that he should not revel in Philip's camp, singing

songs of victory at the disaster to Greece in the company of the murderers and then come here to receive distinction; that he should not lament their fate like an actor with tears in his voice, but share our grief in his heart. They saw these qualities in themselves and in me, not in you. (288) This is the reason they elected me and not you. Nor was it the case that the fathers and brothers of the dead, who were chosen by the people to arrange the burial, felt any differently, but, when it came time for them to hold the funeral banquet at the home of the person who was closest to the dead, as is the custom at public funerals, they held it at my home. And with reason. For while one individual was closer to another by reason of birth, no one was closer than I to them all together. The man who was most concerned with their safety and success was the one who had the largest share of grief at the lamentable fate of them all.

(289) Read for him the epigram which the city selected to be inscribed at public expense at their graves, so that you may realize, Aeschines, how pitiless, how malign, how disgusting even this epigram shows you to be.

EPIGRAM

(290) Do you hear, Aeschines? "Never to fail, always to succeed, is a privilege of the gods." It is not to the adviser, but to the gods, that the poet attributes the power to guarantee the success of soldiers in combat. Why then, accursed man, do you abuse *me* with this charge and make remarks which I pray the gods to turn upon the heads of you and your accomplices.

(291) Aeschines has made many other false accusations, men of Athens, but I was especially surprised that, when he was mentioning the catastrophes to our city, his attitude was not that of a patriotic and just citizen, he shed no tear, he felt no such emotion in his heart; but he shouted and roared and strained his voice, quite clearly thinking that he was accusing me but in fact producing evidence to his own discredit and proving that he did not share the feelings of the rest of us at these distressing events. (292) Yet one who claims, as he does, to be concerned for our laws and our constitution, must have this quality at least, if no other, that he shares the same grief and the same joy as the majority of his fellow citizens, and must not, in matters of public policy, be lined up on the side of their opponents. The purpose of what you have now been doing is obvious: you claim that I am to blame for everything and that the city met with its troubles because of me, since it was not from my policy that you citizens began to send assistance to other Greeks. (293) For if you concede that it was through my influence that you

opposed Philip's rising dominion over Greece, you would be granting me a gift greater than all the gifts you have ever bestowed on others. But I would not say this (for I would be doing you an injustice) nor, I know, would you concede it. If Aeschines were acting fairly, he would never damage and disparage the greatest of your glories, because of his hostility toward me.

(294) But why do I object to this behavior, when he has attacked me with far more shocking lies? If he accuses me, for heaven's sake, of Philippizing, what would he shrink from saying? Yet, by Herakles and all the gods, if you should look at the truth of it, discarding his lies and any statements motivated by his hostility, and ask who really were the men to whom all would reasonably and fairly attach the blame for what has happened, you would find that they were the men in each city like Aeschines, not like me. (295) When Philip's power was small and quite insignificant and we were constantly warning and urging and advising excellent policies, it was these who, with their shameful desire for personal profit, sacrificed the common interest, each deceiving and corrupting his fellow citizens until he enslaved them: in Thessaly, Daokhos, Kineas, Thrasydaos; in Arkadia, Kerkidas, Hieronymos, Eukampidas; in Argos, Myrtis, Teledamos, Mnaseas; in Elis, Euxitheos, Kleotimos, Aristaikhmos; in Messene, Neon and Thrasylokhos, the sons of that damned Philiades; in Sikyon, Aristratos, Epikhares; in Corinth, Deinarkhos, Demaretos; in Megara, Ptoiodoros, Helixos, Peril-los; in Thebes, Timolaos, Theogeiton, Anemoitas; in Euboea, Hipparkhos, Kleitarkhos, Sosistratos. (296) The day will not be long enough for me to list the names of the traitors. All of these, men of Athens, had the same pur-poses in their own countries as Aeschines and his associates here, fawning flatterers of Philip and polluted with a guilt that cries for vengeance; each of them crippled his own country, sacrificed its freedom, first to Philip, now to Alexander, measured happiness by his belly and his ugly desires, and subverted the standards of freedom and rejection of tyranny, which to Greeks before were the prime criteria for success.

(297) As a result of my policies, our city is guiltless in the eyes of all mankind and I am guiltless in your eyes of this shameful and notorious conspiracy of evil—or rather, to speak precisely, of betrayal of the freedom of Greece. Do you then ask me, Aeschines, for what special excellence I claim to deserve honor? I say to you that, when all the political leaders in Greece, beginning with you, had been corrupted, (298) no opportunity, no courteous language, no large promises, no hope, no fear, nothing inspired or induced me to betray any of the interests, which, in my judgment, were

proper and good for Athens. Unlike your group, none of the advice I gave these citizens was weighed, as on a scale, to my own profit, but was given with correct, just, and uncorrupted motives. More than any of my contemporaries I took charge of important affairs and handled them fairly and beneficially. For this I claim to deserve honor. (299) The fortification of the walls, my part in which you ridiculed, and the trenchworks deserve, in my judgment, gratitude and praise. Why shouldn't they? But I put them near the bottom of the list of my political achievements. It was not with stone or brick alone that I fortified this city, nor did I think this the greatest of my acts. But if you wish to examine the protective measures I took fairly, Aeschines, you will find weapons and cities and places and harbors and ships and horses and men for their defense. (300) This was the shield I put in front of Attica, as much as was possible by human calculation, and this is how I fortified our land, not with a wall around the Peiraios or around the city. I was not defeated by the calculations of Philip, far from it, nor by his preparations; but the generals of our allies and their forces were defeated by fate. What are the proofs of this? They are clear and obvious. Consider them.

(301) What was the duty of the patriotic citizen, what the duty of the man whose action for his country was based on forethought, zeal, and justice? Was it not to gain Euboea for Attica as a shield against attack from the sea, to gain Boeotia against attack from the plains, to gain the states on our southwestern borders against attack from places in the Peloponnese? Was it not to ensure that provisions of grain would be shipped along friendly coasts until they reached Peiraios? (302) Was it not to secure some of these areas, Prokonnesos, the Chersonese, Tenedos, by sending troops to help them and by advising and proposing such measures; to make other areas, Byzantium, Abydos, Euboea, dependable friends and allies? Was it not to cut off the principal resources of the enemy and to supply resources which Athens lacked? All of these measures were brought to fulfillment by my decrees and my policies; (303) if one wishes to examine them without spite, men of Athens, he will find that they were planned with precision and properly executed and that I did not neglect or ignore or let slip the opportunity to act on each of them; so far as was within the power and the calculation of one man, I left nothing undone. If some divine force, or fate, or the weakness of the generals, or the evil of you who betrayed the cities, or all of these together damaged our whole effort, until it finally was ruined, for what wrong can Demosthenes be blamed? (304) If there had been one man in each of the Greek states who took the same position in

the struggle as I did in Athens, or, rather, if Thessaly had provided only one man, if Arkadia had provided one man who had the same sentiments as I, none of the Greeks on this side of Thermopylae or beyond Thermopylae would be in their present trouble (305) but all of them would now be living happily in their own countries, in freedom and autonomy, with complete security and safety, with gratitude for their many blessings to you and to the rest of the Athenian people, because of my efforts. To show you that my words do not adequately describe the results I achieved, since I wish to avoid causing envy, read, please, the list of military expeditions we sent according to my decrees.

LIST OF MILITARY EXPEDITIONS

(306) These and similar actions were the duty of the honorable citizen, Aeschines; if their results had been successful, we would have been without doubt—and, I may add, with justice—preeminently great, and, although their results have been different, we have at least a good reputation and the consolation that nobody censures our city or its policy but all blame the fate which determined events to that result. (307) It was, by Zeus, no one's duty to abandon the interests of the city and sell himself to its opponents, to attend to opportunities favorable to the enemy rather than to his own country, to abuse the man who took it upon himself to advise and propose measures worthy of our city and to persevere in them, to watch and remember any harm done to him personally, and to withdraw from public life, as you frequently do, only to remain in the background like a festering sore. (308) There is indeed a kind of political inactivity, which is proper and helpful to the state and which most of you citizens enjoy honestly. That is not his inactivity, far from it. He withdraws when it pleases him (and it pleases him often) but watches for an occasion when you have had your fill of your constant adviser or fate causes some reverse or something else unpleasant happens (there are many such occasions in human affairs): that is the time for him to appear on the political scene like a sudden wind, with well-trained voice and a repertoire of words and phrases which he cleverly strings together without catching his breath; but these don't provide any help or any good result, they bring only disaster to each of the citizens and disgrace to all. (309) Yet if this training and practice in speaking were based on the proper motives and had the good of the country as its purpose, it should have produced fruits which were good and honorable and helpful to all the citizens, alliances with other cities, sources of revenue,

commercial rights, helpful legislation, obstacles to our declared enemies. (310) Athens searched for all of these in the past, and time provided many such opportunities to the honorable man, but you won't appear on the list of honorable men, not first, not second, not third, not fourth, not fifth, not sixth, nowhere, for services which strengthened our country. (311) What alliance did you negotiate for Athens? What help did Athens receive, what good will or glory did it gain? What embassy, what service of yours brought the city greater honor? What success in internal policy or in Greek policy or in foreign policy was achieved under your leadership? What warships did you provide? What weapons? What dockyards? What fortifications? What cavalry? Of what use were you in anything? What public financial aid did you provide for rich or poor? None. (312) But, my friend, if none of these, at least you offered patriotic zeal. Where? When? You are the worst of all citizens; not even when all the speakers who had ever used the platform contributed for the city's security and, finally, Aristonikos contributed the money his friends had collected to restore his civic rights, not even then did you come forward and contribute a thing. It was not because you were poor. How could it be? You inherited more than five talents from the estate of Philon, your brother-in-law, and the leaders of the symmories made you a gift of two talents to wreck the trierarchic law. (313) But I won't mention that story, to avoid diverting myself from the topic before us by speaking of one thing after another. It is obvious that your failure to contribute was not caused by poverty; you guarded against any act of opposition to those who were the beneficiaries of all your political acts. What were the occasions on which you showed your vigor and your brilliance? When it was necessary to speak to the detriment of the people, then you were most brilliant of voice, and had memorized your part well, an excellent actor, a tragic Theokrines.

(314) You do well to remind us of the men who proved to be great in the past. However, men of Athens, it is not right for him to take advantage of the good will you have toward the dead and in comparison to them to examine me, who am still living among you. (315) Who does not know that all living men are more or less exposed to envy, but that no one, not even an enemy, continues to hate the dead? Since this is a fact of human nature, am I now to be judged or compared with those before me? No. It is neither fair nor equitable; it is fair, Aeschines, to compare me with you or with any other living person who shared your policies. (316) Consider this point, also. Is it better or more honorable for Athens to expose to ingratitude and abuse services to the present generation because of the existence of the immeasurably great

services of the men of the past, or should all who act with patriotism share the honor and affection of these citizens? (317) And if it is I who must say it, my political policy, if examined, will prove to resemble and to have the same purposes as the policies of men who were praised in the past, while your policy, Aeschines, is like that of the people who maliciously attacked such men. For it is clear that there were people then who ridiculed contemporary statesmen while praising their predecessors, doing the same spiteful thing as you. (318) Do you now say that I am not at all like the men of the past? Are you, Aeschines? Is your brother? Is any other politician of the present day? I say there is no one. Compare a living man with the living, my good fellow (to use no other name for you) and with his competitors, as we do in all other cases, poets with poets, choruses with choruses, athletes with athletes. (319) Philammon did not leave Olympia without a crown because he was inferior to Glaukos of Karystos and other athletes before his own time, but he was crowned and proclaimed victor because he fought best of those who competed against him. And compare me with speakers of our own day, with yourself, with anyone you wish. I do not shrink from being compared with anyone. (320) When our city was free to choose the best policy and a prize for patriotism was open to all, I advised the strongest measures and all our affairs were conducted by my decrees and laws and embassies; no one of your group was anywhere to be seen except when you felt a need to discredit my proposals. But when that unfortunate defeat was suffered, and there was a call no longer for advisers but for men who would submit to orders, who were ready to harm their country for pay, who were willing to court another, then you and each of your comrades were at your post, fine, important people with handsome stallions. I was powerless, I admit it, but I was more patriotic than you.

(321) The well-meaning citizen (to speak about myself in this way cannot cause envy) must have two qualities, men of Athens: when he is in authority, he should persist in the policy which aims at the city's preeminence and honor, but at every time and in every action, he should be patriotic. For his nature controls this quality, other factors control his power and his strength. You will find that I have been constant in my patriotism. (322) Look at the facts. When Alexander demanded me, when they indicted me before the Amphictyonic Council, when they threatened me, when they made promises, when they set this whole damned group on me like wild animals, at no time did I betray my patriotism. From the very beginning of my political career, I chose the path of honesty and justice; I chose to foster,

to increase, to associate myself with the honors, power, and reputation of our country. (323) I do not walk around the market place, with a smile on my face, exulting in the successes of our enemies, offering my hand and telling the good news to those I thought would report to Macedonia. I do not shudder and moan and hang my head when I hear of some good fortune of our city, like these impious men, who disparage our city, as if, by doing so, they are not disparaging themselves at the same time, who look abroad, who approve the success of another—a success gained at the expense of Greece—and say that we should ensure that his success last forever.

(324) I pray to all the gods that they refuse assent to this desire but rather implant in these men a better mind and a better spirit; if they are beyond cure, may they, and they alone, be quickly and utterly destroyed, wherever they might be, and may the rest of us be granted swift release and safe security from the terrors which hang over us.

PART TWO

Rhetorical Evaluations

4. A STRUCTURAL ANALYSIS OF THE SPEECH ON THE CROWN

Francis P. Donnelly, SJ

DEMOSTHENES' SPEECH ON THE CROWN

Exordium

GOOD WILL FOR D. (1–8)

By request 1–2	D. has shown it constantly
	Judges should show it fully
Through pity 3–4	D. may lose it; A. nothing to lose
	D. has odium of self-praise; A. pleasure of abuse
By right 5–7	The law demands it
	The defendant (second speaker) needs it. Request
	repeated. 8

Reprinted by permission of the publisher from *The Oration of Demosthenes on the Crown*, translated by Francis P. Simpson; rhetorical commentary by Francis P. Donnelly, SJ (New York: Fordham University Press, 1941), pp. 340–45.

Editor's note.—The complex relationships between the various parts of Demosthenes' speech may be seen quickly in the detailed outline provided here. The numbers used refer to sections of the speech, marked by marginal numbers in the translation.

Proposition and Division (suggested) 9

Confirmation

OUTSIDE THE INDICTMENT (10–52)

Private Life.—D. leaves it to judges (10); A.'s cunning foiled (11)

PUBLIC LIFE (12–52)

A.'s malicious method (coming years after; attacking D. through Ctes.) (12–16).

Status Translationis.

For this status, *transferring* the trial to another person, time, etc., cp. Cic. *De Inv.*, 1.16; *Ad Her.*, 1.22. The scholiasts say that, according to old commentators, D. uses this argument seventy-two times in the speech (22, 34, 83, 117, 121 sq, 139, 188, etc.).

PEACE 17–24

D. not the cause 18–20	Circumstances, the cause 18–20	Strife in Greece / Scheming of P.
	A.'s friends, the cause 21	Promoters / Abettors
D. did not prevent alliance 22–24	None proposed 22–23	No statement from A. / No embassy to Grecians
	None could be 24	It would be deceitful / It would be absurd

EMBASSY 25–52

Treachery 25–41	Ambassadors slow 25–30	D.'s law framed 25–27	To help others / To check P. in Thrace
		D.'s law ignored 28–30	A. cites a petty decree / Ambassadors loiter
	A. bribed 31–41	His deception 31–35	Furthering P.'s designs / Speaking lies
		The results 36–41	Phocis destroyed / Thebes, etc., alienated / A. shedding feigned tears

EMBASSY 25–52 (*continued*)

Consequences 42–52	Ruin of Greece 43–45	Thebes. etc., bewitched by P. Other Greeks warred on by P. D. warned by a diseased country
	Ruin of traitors 46–49	General (46–47) Particular (48–49)
	Guilt of A. 50–52	Accusing D. of A.'s crimes Hiring himself to P. and Alex.

INSIDE THE INDICTMENT (53–296)

Proposition (53); Division (56–58); Status (59).

JUSTIFICATION OF CTESIPHON'S DECREE (60–109) A.

D.'s Actions for Best Interests of Athens

OPPOSING P. IN GENERAL 60–78

Expedient 60–65	From P.'s advantages 61–62	Greece was full of traitors Greece was divided
	From D.'s policy 63–65	Alternatives were alliance or neutrality Athens fared better than allies or neutrals
Honorable 66–68	From policy 66–67	Of Athens Of P.
	From antecedents 68	Of P. Of Athens

OPPOSING P. IN GENERAL 60–78 (*continued*)

Just 69–78

From aggressions of P. 69–72
- Remote
- Recent

From documentary proofs 73–78
- Decrees acquit D. of starting war
- Letter of P. absolves D.

OPPOSING P. IN PARTICULAR 79–109

Abroad 79–101

Expeditions 79–94
- Summary described (79); proved best (80)
- Euboea described (81–82); proved best (83–86)
- Byzantium described (87–88); proved best (89–94)

Disinterested policy 95–101
- Against Sparta for Thebes and Corinth
- Against Thebes for Sparta
- Against Thebes for Euboea
- In many precedents for D.'s actions

At home 102–109

Enactment of naval law 102–106
- Against injustices
- Despite prosecutions
- Despite attempted bribery

Excellence of naval law 107–109
- Successful in war
- Best for interests of city
- Identical in spirit with D.'s policy abroad

Conclusion and transition, 110.

A Structural Analysis of *On the Crown*

LEGALITY OF CTESIPHON'S DECREE (111–125)

A.'S CHARGES 111–121	
Accountability 111–119	Law demands account for office only (111–112) Ctes. praised D. for gifts (113) Precedents justify Ctes.' act (114–117) A. indicts thanks for gifts; not fact of gifts (118–119)
Proclamation 120–121	Proclamation often had Proclamation for good of people Proclamation prescribed at times by law
A.'S SPIRIT 121–125	
Spiteful 121–122	Garbling laws Arbitrarily defining a statesman
Perverse 123	Accusation deals with laws; abuse with calumny Courts are for convictions; not for contumely
Hostile to city 124–125	Avoiding a possible conviction Urging an impossible conviction

JUSTIFICATION OF CTESIPHON'S DECREE (126–296) B.

INDIRECT DEFENSE (126–159)

D's Opposition to A., Philip's Friend

PRIVATE LIFE OF A. 126–131

Character 126–128 ⎰ Worthless
Hypocritical

Parents 129–131 ⎰ Disgraceful in their beginning
Absurd in their pretensions
Unfortunate in their son

PUBLIC LIFE OF A. 132–159

Before war, P.'s ally 132–138 ⎰ Antiphon
Python
Anaxmus

Afterwards, P.'s tool in Amphissian War 139–159

A.'s guilt 139–140 ⎰ Enacts no laws to check P.
Strives volubly to escape
Amphissian charge

D.'s opposition 141–144 ⎰ Solemnly protests truth now
Vainly protested formerly

Plans of P. 145–148 ⎰ Without Thebes, etc., P. could not reach Athens
Without Amph. Council, P. could not persuade Thebes
Without an Athenian, P. could not deceive Amph. Council

Cooperation of A. 149–151 ⎰ A. elected delegate
A. proposes an attack on Amphissia
Amphictyonic Council calls in P.

Results 152–159 ⎰ P. captures Elatea
D. checks P. by Theban Alliance
A. is cause of Greeks' downfall

DIRECT DEFENSE—POSITIVELY		
D.'s Actions for Best Interests of Athens (160–251)		
THEBAN ALLIANCE 160–226		
Beginning 160–210	Enmity of Thebes 160–168	Opposed by D.
		Opposed by Arist. And Eubu.
		Fostered by A. and P.
	News of Elatea 169–188	Tumult
		D.'s measures (174–188)
	Value of D.'s measures 188–210	Only possible course then or now 188–191
		Only prudent course; best for Athens; better than A.'s course 192–198
		Only honorable course; following precedent, without mistake 199–210
Completion 211–226	The acts 211–226	Persuasion of Thebes 211–214
		Campaign 215–216
	Their appraisal 217–226	By Aeschines (217)
		By Philip (218)
		By Demosthenes (219–221)
		By decree (222–226)
ALL D.'S ACTS 227–251		
Before Chaeronea 227–243	A.'s reckoning 227–231	Condemns himself (228)
		Omits opposite evils (229–230)
		Omits positive benefit (231)
	D.'s reckoning 232–243	Situation of Athens, P., D. 234–236
		Measures of D. 237–243
Chaeronea 244–247	Not due to D. as ambassador 244	D. victorious
		P. uses force
	Not due to D. as statesman 245–246	Not master of life and fortune
		Successful in statesman's work
	Due to arms and bribery 247	D. not leader of army
		D. not bribed by P.
After Chaeronea 248–251	D. elected 248	To safeguard city
		To be food commissioner
	D. acquitted 249–251	In various trials
		Never indicted by A.

DIRECT DEFENSE—Negatively (*Refutation*)

D. Not to Blame for Athens's Woes (252–296)

FORTUNE 252–275

Of Athens 252–255	Good Better than that of other cities Not controlled by D.'s fortune	
Of opponents 256–269	Demosthenes— 256–257	Private Public
	Aeschines— 258–264	Private Public
	Both— 265–269	Comparison Proof
Of Athens 270–275	Not due to D.	All people have suffered D. not the only statesman
	D. unjustly accused by A.	A. did not come forward before A. blames even the accidental

ELOQUENCE 276–296

Eloquence of A. hostile 276–284	To individuals 276–281	Attacking from spite Attacking to show off eloquence
	To state 281–284	Fraternizing with P. Pretending to be P.'s friend
Eloquence of D. patriotic 285–290	D. gave funeral oration 285–287	A. and party were enemies Exulted with P. over Chaeronea
	D. had funeral meal at house 288–290	Nearest to all bereaved Justified by public inscription
Eloquence of A. traitorous 291–296	Exulting over Chaeronea 291–293	Not sad over Athens's defeat Attacked Athenian principles
	Responsible for ruin of Athens 293–296	Same acts as other traitors Same principles as other traitors

PERORATION (297–324)		
D. is worthy 297–306	No traitor 297–298	Resisted all temptations / True as beam of balance
	True patriot 299–302	Building material wall / Building national wall
	Successful statesman 303–306	Left nothing undone / All would be free, if D. had assistants
A. is unworthy 307–313	Traitor 307–308	Assisting enemy / Keeping treacherous silence
	Unsuccessful statesman 309–313	Measures (309–311) / Money contributions (312–313)
D. and the ancients 314–324	Comparison with ancients unfair 314–317	They are respected; living are envied / Their great benefits do not destroy our smaller ones / They are akin to D. not to A.
	Comparison with contemporaries fair 318–324	As in all contests / With A.'s party traitors, before and now

PROPOSITION (*entire speech*): Ctesiphon's decree is lawful.

PROPOSITION (*omitting 111–121 and digressions, e.g., private life*): D. acted for the best interests of Athens.

STATUS: Because D. opposed P. (A. is shown to be P.'s friend and was opposed by D.)

SYLLOGISM: He who opposed P. acted for the best interests of Athens. But D. opposed P. The general question of opposing P. and safeguarding Athenian liberty is discussed principally in 60–72, 95–102, 188–210, by an appeal to precedents. The particular measures of D. are proved in each case advantageous by a presentation of the facts, corroborated by documents.

POINTS IN DISPUTE: I The grounds or justification of Ctesiphon's decree; II The omitted proviso, "When he has handed in his accounts." (Accountability): III The proclamation in the theater.

ORDER: In Ctesiphon's decree and A.'s indictment. I, II, III: in A.'s speech, II, III, I; in D.'s speech I (outside indictment, 10–52; inside indictment, A, 53–110), II, III, I (inside indictment, B; indirect defense, 126–159; direct defense, 160–296).

5. ĒTHOS IN ON THE CROWN

David C. Mirhady

Near the beginning of his speech Demosthenes uses a very common form of argumentation in forensic oratory, the challenge (*proklesis*), whereby the speaker offers to allow the entire dispute to rest on a single issue, often to be decided even by a specific procedure, such as the torture of a slave or someone swearing an oath. Here Demosthenes argues that the case should rest entirely on the type of person he is versus the type of person Aeschines is.[1] That is, he wants the case to rest on the question of character. From a legal point of view the offer is meaningless—there was no established legal procedure for deciding one character versus another—but in terms of rhetoric it is actually an accurate harbinger of where emphasis will be put in Demosthenes' speech. Demosthenes wants to show that he should win his case because he is a "better man," as some people say in modern political contexts. The rhetorical theory of his time, as exemplified in Aristotle's *Rhetoric*, had interesting things to say about assessing character and its role in oratory, but as we shall see, Demosthenes was in no way limited by theory.

In his various theoretical writings, Aristotle deals with character (*ēthos*) in several different ways.[2] Of course, in his *Ethics* we have three lengthy philosophical treatises on the subject: *Nicomachean Ethics, Eudemian Ethics*, and *Magna Moralia*.[3] In *Poetics* 6, he also includes character, along with plot, style (or language), thought, melody, and spectacle, as key elements of tragedy.

But Aristotle's signal achievement in rhetorical theory was in advancing the view, albeit very briefly,[4] that the character of the speaker (along with the logical elements of a speech (*logos*) and the emotional reaction (*pathos*) of the audience) was one of the three key means or vehicles of persuasion (*pisteis*). One of the great questions about Aristotle's conception of character as a rhetorical *pistis* (basis for belief), however, is the extent to which it involves explicit arguments or statements about the character of the speaker. Or is it implicit in everything the speaker says and does? It certainly appears that each of the *atechnoi pisteis* (the proofs that do not come from the compositional art of the speech writer) involve such explicit statements, such as the text of a law, the wording of witness testimony, a contract, or an oath.[5] Even the "torture of a slave" (*basanos*) actually seems to refer to a statement that might be elicited from the torture, or to the challenge to have the torture done, rather than the act of torture itself. But it seems as if the character of the speaker is immanent whenever he is speaking, just as the emotional state of the audience is always being affected. So, for instance, if a speaker asks a rhetorical question in a sarcastic way, we learn about his character even if the question has nothing to do with his character.[6]

Aristotle's actual teachings on the role of character in rhetoric are quite straightforward, but it is important to keep them straight since there are many possibilities for misunderstanding. Aristotle argues that speakers' characters are credible if the speakers can be shown to have moral goodness (*arete*), practical intelligence (*phronesis*), and goodwill (*eunoia*) toward the audience.[7] Aristotle argues that the audience has to be convinced of all three in order to find a speaker credible. They have to think that the speaker knows what he is talking about, that he is morally good, and that he has their best interests at heart. This concept is compelling, but Aristotle does not actually develop it at length.

Another area of Aristotle's *Rhetoric* that touches on character is his teaching that the epideictic speeches are devoted to praise (*epainos*) and criticism (*psogos*) of the honorable (*to kalon*) and the disgraceful (*to aischron*).[8] The object of that praise and criticism tends to be human character, and Aristotle recognizes that his teachings in this area overlap with those on character as a rhetorical *pistis*.[9] Here he lists the aspects of moral goodness (*arete*) that are the object of praise: a sense of justice, courage, self-control, magnificence, magnanimity, liberality, gentleness, and practical and speculative wisdom.

Aristotle also includes several chapters in which he conveys general observations about character with regard to age, heredity, wealth, and power,[10] but he does not connect those chapters with his central teachings about character, that is, with regard to moral goodness, intelligence, and goodwill. He likely took over this material from other rhetorical handbooks with little intellectual commitment.

Likewise, he also takes over a chapter on slander (*diabole*),[11] which was originally developed within the handbook tradition on the arrangement of the parts of a speech. The idea was that a speaker should begin a speech either by blackening the character of the opponent or by polishing his own character, which had been blackened by the opponent, before going on to the rest of the speech. This approach to character is actually closer to Aristotle's own interests in character as a rhetorical *pistis* than the chapters on age, breeding, and so on, inasmuch as it pertains to the persuasiveness of the speaker himself, but Aristotle again does not connect it back to his original teachings on character with regard to moral goodness, practical intelligence, and goodwill. When character becomes not just a means of persuasion, but, as in Demosthenes' speech, a central subject of the speech itself, it moves beyond the focus of Aristotle's teachings on the character of the speaker *per se*. Aristotle also wants to make a distinction between law court speeches—which Demosthenes' speech *On the Crown* ostensibly is—and epideictic speeches, whose subject matter is so often praise or criticism of the character of some individual or group, but Demosthenes blurs the lines by including so much criticism of Aeschines and praise of himself. So we need to look beyond Aristotle's teachings for the sources of Demosthenes' argumentation on character.

Students who come to *On the Crown* for the first time from a twenty-first-century perspective will find something about it that is very familiar, and not particularly attractive. Contemporary political discourse has sadly become largely negative—politicians and media pundits are continually attacking their rivals' characters as much as their policies—and that is abundant in Demosthenes' speech as well.[12] The reasons for this situation today are, I am glad to say, *exo tou pragmatos* (outside the subject of this chapter). But the reasons for the negativity of Demosthenes (and of his rival Aeschines) are not so hard to discover. Under Demosthenes' leadership, Athens lost a great deal of its power and prestige, particularly as a result of the defeat at Chaeronea in 338, where the forces of Philip of Macedon defeated an army of allies that Demosthenes had worked hard to assemble. Athens was set to become a second- or third-rate power in the years ahead.

Yet, through his friend Ctesiphon, Demosthenes was demanding a crown in recognition of his superior leadership. To Aeschines it seemed a vain attempt to suggest that Demosthenes' leadership had been good even though the results were disastrous. Athens's other great leaders had been renowned for victories. In the fifth century, Themistocles, Aristides, and Cimon had all led Athens to victories over the Persians, and Pericles later kept the Spartans at bay while lavishing Athens with unprecedented wealth. Even those statesmen experienced severe personal and political setbacks, but they had all led Athens to triumphs.[13]

Athens's democracy was demanding. In defeat, Demosthenes had to defend not only his decision to lead the resistance against Philip, but his entire career. His most important weapon? Blaming the other guy. Aeschines has historically been somewhat vilified as a result. More of the mud that was flung between the two stuck to him than to Demosthenes. Other notable Athenians of the time had also followed a different policy from Demosthenes. While Aeschines' opposition to the Macedonians may have been more mitigated than Demosthenes', the essayist Isocrates had actually embraced Philip as a Panhellenic champion even before Chaeronea. So Demosthenes' path was not inevitable. It followed choices he made based on his political and strategic calculations. The hegemony of Athens was more important to him than Greek unity.

But it was not just defeat that led to invective (mudslinging) playing such a dominant role.[14] Character assassination is on display in speeches composed before Chaeronea in 338, for instance in Aeschines' *Against Timarchus* and the speeches of Demosthenes and Aeschines *On the (False) Embassy*, all from the 440s. Clearly, an intense political and personal rivalry raged in mid-fourth-century Athens between these men.

Early in Athens's democracy the institution of ostracism was used to remove political rivals. As a result of Cleisthenes' democratic reforms in 509 BCE, the Athenians began to hold a yearly vote about whether to ostracize someone, and many of the leading men of Athens were subjected to a ten-year enforced absence, including the great Aristides, Themistocles, and Cimon who had led Athens to victories. Ostracism left the rivals of the ostracized politicians relatively free to guide Athenian policy. But that ended in 415 BCE, when the ostracism not of a leading man but of the minor demagogue Hyperbolus revealed that the system was open to abuse. Although it stayed on the books, ostracism as an institution fell into disuse. As Athens had no elections in the modern sense, in which a governing party received a mandate to control the political agenda, every day brought a new opportunity for rivals to contest the issues and each other. Ostracism had offered a means of removing rivals from the scene, under the pretext that the greatness of certain leaders was a danger to the egalitarian political order.

In the absence of ostracism, fourth-century Athenians promoted their own agendas by sidelining their opponents. Sidelining might include impeachment (*eisangelia*), scrutiny of orators (*dokimasia rhetoron*), and indictment for illegal proposals (*graphe paranomon*), such as the one that Aeschines brought against Ctesiphon, which provoked the speech *On the Crown*.[15] Since ostracism required no trial for political wrongdoing, little political rhetoric developed from it. But we find language from each of these later procedures finding its way into discussions of character in political speeches in the fourth century. So here is a source of rhetorical topics for character criticism that we do not find in the handbooks, such as Aristotle's. For instance, in an impeachment an orator could be charged with "not giving his best advice while accepting bribes." Demosthenes makes implicit reference to this law several times in the speech when he speaks of his role as "adviser" (e.g., §§ 50, 57, 184, 295, and 320); he may also be doing so indirectly whenever he mentions his opponent's venality (*mistharnia*). He attacks Aeschines' character, but he no longer makes a charge against him, as he had in the earlier embassy case, of a specific wrong act. Otherwise why wouldn't he have brought a charge?[16] The law on the scrutiny of orators seems to have mentioned four criteria that would lead an orator to fail his scrutiny: mistreatment of parents, shirking military service, prostitution of himself, and squandering his estate. Aeschines had used all of these criteria against Demosthenes' colleague Timarchus and won,[17] but neither Demosthenes nor Aeschines seems to be open to such accusations. Nevertheless there are references in *On the Crown* to parents, to military service, to selling of oneself, and to personal finances.

Constitutional changes, such as the disuse of ostracism, and legal procedures influence some of the rhetoric of character in the speech, but there were other factors. In an important article Galen Rowe remarks that it was not Demosthenes' intention "to represent the real Aeschines but to create an idealized, and therefore fictional, type who would play a well defined role among the other *dramatis personae* of his oration."[18] Rowe argues that Demosthenes' terms of abuse are "highly suggestive" of comedy. A great number of his derogatory epithets (39 of 47) are also found in the comedies of Aristophanes, which were performed between the 420s and 380s. Of course, as

Rowe acknowledges, many of these are also found elsewhere, but he argues that Demosthenes' apparent quest for bizarre effects that result from neologisms and strange compounds is thoroughly comic. He notes *diakukon* ("thoroughly jumbling" § 111), *spermologos* ("seed picker" § 127; "idle babbler" Keaney), *iambeiophagos* ("insult gobbler" § 139[19]), *grammatokuphon* ("letter-plower" § 209[20]), and *autotragikos* ("thoroughly tragic" § 242). To these might be added "faultfinder" (*philaitios* § 242). Demosthenes also uses derogatory diminutives such as *anthropion* ("manikin" § 242; "paltry man" Keaney) and *archidiois* ("magistratelets"; "minor officials" Keaney), and his use of animal terms is also comic: *kinados* ("fox" §§ 162, 242; "sly beast" and "animal" Keaney), *pithekos* ("monkey" § 242), and *lago* ("rabbit" § 263). Rowe argues in particular that Demosthenes illustrates Aeschines' venality, corruption, and hypocrisy through recurrent images of him as the political hireling, quack doctor, and third-rate actor.[21] These all contribute to his portrayal as a comic *alazon*, a "pretender" or "braggart." Demosthenes' goal is "to expose Aeschines as something less than he pretends to be."[22]

Rowe probably overstates Demosthenes' reliance on comedy, a point made by Andrew Dyck.[23] Dyck himself emphasizes the black and white shades of Demosthenes' portraits of Aeschines and himself. He notes Plutarch's praise of Demosthenes for achieving inoffensive self-praise[24] and argues that "the portrayal of Aeschines is intimately bound up with the rhetorical strategy of the speech as a whole."[25] This portrayal of Aeschines is especially concentrated in two sections (126–59 and 252–96). The first is "unrivalled in scurrility in the extant work of an Attic orator" and is "at best a caricature of the real man."[26] Dyck argues that Demosthenes uses this strategy in part to distract attention from his own weakest arguments.[27] Moreover, with the changed time and circumstances, between Aeschines' launching of his suit in 336 and the speeches in 330, Demosthenes was freer to indulge his fancy for invective than he had been when prosecuting Aeschines a dozen years before in the case of the embassy in 342. Since Aeschines is not now on trial, as he had been before, there is no expectation that any of Demosthenes' criticisms of his character relate to a particular charge that he had brought against him. Moreover, Aeschines' father, who might have challenged Demosthenes' account of Aeschines' birth and childhood, has died in the meantime.[28]

To take Plutarch's point in another way, Demosthenes' strategy seems largely dictated by his own claim that "it is a natural characteristic of all men to enjoy listening to insults (*loidoriai*) and accusations, but to be offended when they hear men praising themselves" (§ 3; cf. § 138). At that point in the speech Demosthenes argues that Aeschines has an advantage because he is the accuser (and so more likely to insult). Demosthenes ignores the fact that he himself is not on trial while Aeschines is taking the risk of being fined for receiving less than 20 percent of the votes.[29] Demosthenes claims that he is himself at a disadvantage, but he turns the tables and devotes much of his speech to attacking Aeschines' character, which, as he says, he knows the judges will enjoy (§ 3).

Demosthenes uses several different words to describe invective: *diabole* (§§ 7, 11, 14, 20, 24, 28, 111, 225, 293); *loidoria* (§§ 3, 10, 11, 12, 15, 20, 123, 138, 256, 274, 284, 285, 290); *pompeia* (§ 124); *blasphemia* (§§ 34, 95, 123, 126, 256, 272); and *diasurein* (§§ 27, 126, 180, 218, 299, 317, 323, literally, "tearing to pieces," i.e. "ridicule").[30] It would be extremely difficult to translate these terms distinctly and consistently. But Demosthenes attempts some distinctions: "I believe the difference between insult (*loidoria*) and accusation[31] lies in this, that accusation is directed at crimes for which there are penalties in the laws, while insult involves slander (*blasphemia*), which naturally involves only the statements that personal enemies make about each other" (§ 123). From *loidoria*, "insult," however, Demosthenes also goes on to suggest that Aeschines has been hurling "libelous statements" (*aporrhemata*) at him. These are not just libelous in the sense of being defamatory, i.e. diminishing someone's reputation; they are specific claims that are especially forbidden by law (unless they can be demonstrated to be true), such as that someone "beats his father" or "throws away his shield (and runs away in battle)." If a person did any of these things, he ought to be prosecuted. In each case Demosthenes is accusing Aeschines of engaging in these various forms of invective. He is silent on whether he is doing it himself, but he clearly is.

Following Aristotle, we might be tempted to concentrate on how Demosthenes shapes the *ēthos* or *persona* of himself *as the speaker*. But Demosthenes clearly fashions this *persona* dialectically, in contrast with and in response to his opponent Aeschines, so we must look at how he shapes that contrasting view as well. If we take nothing else from this discussion, we should appreciate the extent to which the idea of "negative campaigning" was well understood long before modern mudslinging. Aristotle would have us understand the character of the speaker as a distinct element of persuasion (or *pistis*). In the case of this speech, however, that character is unavoidably confused with the character of the man whose career is being debated; they are the same man.

In his prosecution speech Demosthenes' opponent Aeschines recounts a more elaborate list of characteristics than Aristotle's moral goodness (*aretê*), practical intelligence (*phronêsis*), and goodwill (*eunoia*) toward the audience.

> I think you would all acknowledge that the following qualities ought to be found in the "friend of the people": in the first place, he should be freeborn, on both his father's and his mother's side, so that he is not, because of misfortune of birth, disloyal to the laws that preserve the democracy. In the second place, he should have as a legacy from his ancestors some service that they have done to the democracy, or at the very least there must be no inherited hostility against it, so that in the attempt to avenge the misfortunes of his family he does not undertake to injure the city. [170] Thirdly, he ought to be temperate and self-restrained in his daily life, so that he does not take bribes to support his wanton extravagance against the people. Fourthly, he ought to be a man of good judgment and an able speaker; for it is well that his discernment choose the wisest course, and his training in rhetoric and his eloquence persuade the hearers; but if he cannot have both, good judgment is always to be preferred to eloquence of speech. Fifthly, he ought to be a man of brave heart, that in danger and peril he may not desert the people. (Aeschines 3.169–70, Loeb translation by Charles Darwin Adams)

Aeschines' first two criteria, free birth and family service, correspond to a commonplace of speeches of praise, namely, the genealogy of the person to be praised.[32] But Aeschines actually interprets such "genealogy" as a genetic loyalty to democracy, in a way that corresponds to Aristotle's goodwill to the audience. The third criterion, temperance and self-restraint (or moderation) in private life, corresponds to Aristotle's moral goodness (*aretê*), since in the Greek moral vocabulary temperance is a kind of moral goodness (as are a sense of justice and bravery). The fourth criterion, good judgment, is essentially the same as Aristotle's practical wisdom. The fifth criterion, bravery, is another form of virtue, this one not private but public. Aeschines' subsequent discussion, in which he discusses at length the relationship between good judgment and speaking ability, seems to reveal an ongoing discussion about these issues not only in law court and political contexts, but also in the philosophical circles and rhetorical classrooms of the fourth century.

Demosthenes himself also advances a triad of characteristics that he thinks are required of the loyal citizen: forethought (*pronoia*), zeal (*prothymia*), and a sense of justice (*dikaiosyne*) (§ 301). These can easily be associated with Aristotle's triad, forethought with practical wisdom, zeal with goodwill (loyalty), and justice with virtue or moral goodness. Note the prefix *pro-* ("fore") in each of the first two words. In this context Demosthenes wants to emphasize that he was, as the modern saying goes, "proactive."[33] He anticipated events rather than just reacting to them, perhaps the most important trait in a politician or military leader. Elsewhere Demosthenes formulates the triad somewhat differently, as goodwill, intelligence derived from following events closely, and wealth (§§ 171–72). He contrasts his own zeal with Aeschines' injustice (§ 286), and in still another passage he identifies zeal with loyalty and describes how Aeschines has betrayed it by taking a big bribe (§ 312). Loyalty, he says, means having the same friends and enemies as the people, and thus the same policies (§§ 280–81).

Demosthenes even extends a very similar triad to the Athenians as a whole: "you [Athenians] not only had their [the Thebans'] best interests at heart [*eunous*],[34] but you were also prudent men [*phronimoi*] and even prophetic [*manteis*]" (§ 80). Two of these three terms correspond exactly to Aristotle's. The other, "prophetic," imbues the Athenians with a divine characteristic rather than a moral one—religious matters seem to have been a blind spot for Aristotle—but its ability to foresee events put it in the realm of practical intelligence. Demosthenes dwells specifically on the point of character, saying that he had the same character (*ēthos*)[35] in internal politics and in Greek affairs (§ 109), and he specifically claims two parts of his triad (from § 301) when summing up the narrative of his early accomplishments (§ 110). He also tries his hand at describing the values that inform Athenian character: "a free gift deserves gratitude and praise.... [§ 114] I will easily show with many examples that this procedure is defined in your characters[36] as well as in your laws."

Demosthenes echoes another aspect of Aristotle's thought when he argues that the choice to oppose Philip, though unsuccessful, revealed something distinct in the Athenians' character (206). In his *Poetics*, Aristotle points out: "Character is that which reveals choice, shows what sort of thing a man chooses or avoids in circumstances where the choice is not obvious, so those speeches convey no character in which there is nothing whatever which the speaker chooses or avoids" (*Poetics* 6 1450b [Loeb translation by W. H. Fyfe]).[37] According to Demosthenes, the choice to take risks for the sake of freedom was also demonstrated by the Athenians at Marathon, Artemisium, Salamis, and Plataea (§ 208). The place names alone, all concerning events in 490–479 BCE, evoke Athenian patriotism. The defense of freedom, even if unsuccessful, has preserved the Athenians' good reputation (*eudokimein* § 306). Aeschines, on the other hand, chose a public policy that aligned him with the enemy (§ 292).

Later (§ 321), Demosthenes narrows the qualities of character (or nature) in the "well-meaning" (*metrios*) citizen to two: loyalty and choosing the city's preeminent nobility. Again, these might be identified with two of Aristotle's three qualities, goodwill and morality (cf. § 291). The third quality, practical intelligence, Demosthenes does not emphasize as much. Intelligence would suggest success, and while Demosthenes can claim to have anticipated events and to have been successful at putting together what might have been thought an unlikely and large alliance, that alliance was defeated. So he was unsuccessful in a very important sense. Nevertheless, he does point out that Aeschines had no more success than he himself did (§§ 309–11).

Returning to religion, we might, for instance, point out Demosthenes' piety in beginning his speech with a prayer—piety lends credibility, after all—but when that prayer entails a wish that the judges have as much concern for him as he has had concern for them and for Athens, which might be understood as a comment on his own character as speaker, he immediately engages the question that is *sub iudice*, since the trial depends largely on whether the judges think that he provided good leadership. Demosthenes further signals the dialectical nature of his characterization by referring to Aeschines' demand that he rebut Aeschines' claims in the order Aeschines made them as "appalling" or (in Keaney's translation) "harsh" (*skhetlios*). The word is striking, and clearly meant to refer not only to Aeschines' demand but also, by metonymy, to the character of Aeschines himself.

So begins a series of competing adjectives in which Demosthenes describes himself and the judges and their actions as goodwilled, advantageous (§ 101), fair (§§ 56, 58), straightforward (§ 58), most glorious (§ 65, cf. 95), noble (§§ 89, 100), humane and generous (§§ 112, 268), and so on, including those characteristics cited in § 301.[38] Aeschines, on the other hand, is described as malicious (§§ 119, 212), base (§§ 47, 50, 131, 242, 303), most petty[39] (§ 197), traitorous (§§ 49, 61, 134, 136, 284), imperceptive and stupid (§§ 120, 128), wretched (§ 121), hostile to his country (§§ 137, 197), polluted (§§ 134, 141), rotten (§ 227), scummy (§ 128), ungracious (§ 131), derisive (§ 180), insulting (§ 180), unjust (§§ 31, 314, 315), histrionic (§ 313), criminal (*kakourgema* § 31), shameless (§§ 22, 285), crude (§§ 275, 285), contemptible[40] (§§ 33, 196), corrupt (§ 61), spiteful and mean-spirited (§ 279), venal (§ 50), mendacious (§ 282), hating or hated by the gods (*theois ex-throi* §§ 46, 119, 61, 119), and impious (§ 240).[41] To Athens's enemy Philip, Aeschines was a hireling (§§ 38, 49, 52, 149, 236, 284, 307), an assistant and comrade (§§ 41, 61), a friend or a guest (§§ 46, 51), a flunky[42] (§ 46), and a spy (§ 137).[43] Translators risk wearing out their thesauruses searching for precise translations of the many words for immorality and bad character that Demosthenes uses of his opponent. It seems unlikely that there is any great system to Demosthenes' terminology, though an enterprising student may find one.

Aside from his fusillade of adjectives, Demosthenes also resorts to a series of derisive rhetorical questions to Aeschines that also illustrate his own character (and to some extent Aeschines' as well): "What do you and yours have to do with 'virtue,' you scum? How can you distinguish the noble from the ignoble? Where did you get this knowledge? How can you claim it?" (§ 128) It is pretty strong stuff, comparable to the worst mudslinging we see among contemporary politicians. Between Athens and Philip Demosthenes describes a contest over honor and glory (*time* and *doxa*); for Athens it is achieved through love of honor (*philotimia*) and benefits for all (cf. § 80), for Philip (and by extension through Aeschines) it is achieved through rule and domination (§§ 66–67).

Demosthenes won the case with over 80 percent of the votes, forcing Aeschines to pay a fine and go into retirement on the island of Rhodes, ironically as a teacher of rhetoric. We have no way of knowing what factors actually influenced the large democratic jury to vote the way it did. Was it a vain attempt to support independent Athenian policy? Was it thought trivial to deny Demosthenes a crown after crowns had been liberally awarded earlier to others, as well as to Demosthenes himself? Or did they simply embrace Demosthenes' negative campaigning?

One of the most interesting issues related to character that Demosthenes takes up is the role that he and Aeschines were to play. Here he adopts the term "adviser" (*symboulos*)[44] rather than "speaker" (*rhetor*), even though it was actually as a *rhetor*[45] that he spoke and wrote decrees for proposal when he took to the platform (*bema* § 66; cf. §§ 69, 209, 272–73). Sometimes, however, he embraces both roles, claiming responsibility for what is accomplished through speech (as speaker) and through deliberation (as adviser) (§ 212). Elsewhere, he contrasts the role of the adviser with that of Aeschines as sycophant, or malicious prosecutor (§ 189): "the one reveals his opinion before the events and makes himself responsible to those he has persuaded, to fortune, to opportunities, to anyone who wishes (to prosecute him); the other, who was silent when he should have spoken, cavils if anything unpleasant results" (cf. §§ 232, 237, 242, 266, 275, 289, 308–9). His discussion of the role of the adviser is extended (§§ 192–94). He likens it to that of a shipper[46] whose ship may be wrecked as a result of bad luck in a storm (§ 194). Like a shipper, Demosthenes had organized the alliance for the battle, but he was not the general who directed the Athenian strategy and tactics. In fact, he participated in the battle of Chaeronea in 338 as a regular solider, a hoplite. So he was not like the captain or steersman of the boat.

Demosthenes also, however, elsewhere embraces the company of several other speakers (*rhetores*), such as Callistratus, Aristophon, Cephalus, and Thrasybulus (§ 219), though he does not quite put himself in the company of the legendary Themistocles (§ 204; cf. §§ 238, 314–19).[47] This may be because, as a fifth-century leader, Themistocles had a legend that had been allowed to grow, while the others were all fourth-century leaders. It may also be, however, because the term *rhetor* did not come into common use until the fourth century. Late in the speech (§§ 314–18), Demosthenes explicitly takes on Aeschines' arguments that he does not compare well to the great fifth-century leaders.[48] He argues that he should not be compared to them but to the other leaders of his own time, including, of course, Aeschines.

One of Demosthenes' extended attacks on Aeschines' character begins by citing his "insensitivity [*agnomosune*] and his spitefulness [*baskania*]" (§ 252). As he goes on, it becomes clear that Demosthenes is referring to Aeschines' attack on Demosthenes that is based on the "bad luck" of the loss at Chaeronea. Demosthenes responds with two words of his own: his account is "more truthful and more humane." This matrix of terms goes deeply into the Greek vocabulary of morality and jurisprudence. "Insensitivity" (*agnomosune*) is clearly the opposite of *syngnome*, the propensity to forgive mistakes and feel pity, what Aristotle calls *epieikeia*;[49] "spitefulness" (*baskania*) connotes a sense of sorcery, of malice specifically associated with bad luck. If we were to see these terms as corresponding opposites to Aristotle's three aspects of character, insensitivity would be the opposite of morality and spitefulness the opposite of goodwill.

Aristotle might ask what moral or ethical lessons such works as Demosthenes' *On the Crown* offer? Certainly it has moments of elegy for a democratic sense of statehood and independentist foreign policy that are worth considering. These things are revered even when the political winds are against them. But more importantly, the speech may illustrate a kind of verbal violence done in order to eliminate other violence, similar to a police intervention. It was Aeschines, after all, who had begun this round of negative campaigning by initiating his suit against Ctesiphon instead of acquiescing in Demosthenes' vainglorious desire for a crown. Other Athenian political figures of the time, such as the rhetorician and essayist Isocrates, had embraced the advent of Macedonian hegemony without stooping to personal attacks on rivals. But once the door is opened to negativity, it is hard to close it again.

As Demosthenes admits, audiences prefer to hear invective directed against character rather than praise. That fact brought some scorn on democratic rhetoric from philosophers such as Plato and Aristotle, and even from the comic playwright Aristophanes, who reveled in political invective himself. For all the artistry of Demosthenes' language and his devotion to Athens and its democracy, his descent into such sustained invective should give readers today some uneasiness about the tendency of democracies to fall under the sway of negative discourse.

NOTES

1. Demosthenes, *On the Crown* 18.10.

2. Aristotle certainly knew of Demosthenes when he was composing at least parts of his *Rhetoric,* but his only comment on him is to illustrate the fallacy of a *post hoc propter hoc* argument by Demosthenes' rival Demades, namely, "that the policy of Demosthenes was the cause of all the evils that happened, since it was followed by the war" (Aristotle, *Rhetoric* 2.24.8).

3. The Latin equivalent for the Greek *ēthos* ("character"), which gives us "ethics," is *mores,* which gives us "morality." Moreover, the spelling of *ēthos* differs from *ethos* ("custom") in that its first letter is the long *eta,* whereas *ethos* begins with *epsilon,* its short version. It is important not to confuse the two words although they are clearly related. The Latin *mos* ("custom") is the singular form of *mores* ("customs/character").

4. See Aristotle, *Rhetoric* 1.2.3–4 and 2.1.1–7.

5. Aristotle deals with the *atechnoi pisteis* systematically in *Rhetoric* 1.15.

6. It is not the task of this essay to resolve such questions. See William W. Fortenbaugh, "Aristotle on Persuasion through Character," *Rhetorica: A Journal of the History of Rhetoric* 10 (1992): 207–44.

7. Aristotle, *Rhetoric* 2.1. Aristotle was not the first to conceive of this sort of triad. Homer's depiction of Nestor in *Iliad* 1 and 9 seems to follow it. Thucydides the historian has the Athenian leader Pericles appeal to it (Thucydides 2.60.5–6), and Plato has Socrates cite something very much like it as a set of qualities

he would like to see in a partner in a philosophical investigation (Plato, *Gorgias* 487a). Even Aristotle himself notes something like it as a set of qualifications for a politician in his *Politics* (*Politics* 5.9 1309a33–37).

8. Aristotle, *Rhetoric* 1.3, 1.9.

9. Ibid., 1.9.1.

10. Ibid., 2.12–17.

11. Ibid., 3.15.

12. Brad Cook has recently described a part of this phenomenon as "swift-boating" and connected it to techniques in the crown dispute.

13. Demosthenes has his own response to this criticism (18.314–319).

14. In English we have many names for this activity: slander, invective, character assassination, incitement of prejudice, mudslinging, etc. The Greek rhetoricians, including Aristotle, called it *diabolē*, which may actually be closest metaphorically to "mudslinging," since it refers to throwing (*bolē*) across (*dia*).

15. On impeachment, see Hyperides, *Against Athenogenes*, 3.7–8. On the scrutiny of the orators, see Aeschines, *Against Timarchus*, 1.28–32.

16. Demosthenes repeatedly brings this criticism against Aeschines, who could have brought charges of malfeasance but never did.

17. See Aeschines, *Against Timarchus*, 1.

18. Galen O. Rowe, "The Portrait of Aeschines in the Oration *On the Crown*," *Transactions of the American Philological Association* 97 (1966): 397–406.

19. In his translation, Keaney opts for an alternative reading in the manuscripts, *iambeiographos* ("writer of lampoons"). As well as these fantastic terms, Demosthenes also employs two-word expressions that seem pretty novel: "court hack" (perhaps better as "market tramp" [*peritrimma agoras*]).

20. When he translates the three words *katarate kai grammatokuphon*, Keaney ignores the *kai* ("and") and gives us "abominable clerk." A literal translation, "(you) damned (man) and letter-plower," is admittedly very awkward. Keaney sees the common Greek stylistic figure *hendiadys*, by which one says one thing (*hen*) through (*dia*) two (*dys*) words.

21. Rowe, "Portrait of Aeschines," 399–402. For greed see §§ 296, 260, 261, 262, 298; corruption §§ 38, 41, 47, 49, 50, 138; actor *tritagonistes* §§ 129, 262, 265, 267; cf. tragic Theocrines § 313, rustic Oenomaus § 242 (cf. § 180). In contrast, Demosthenes has fun with his own reputation for lisping, adopting the name Lisper ("Battalos," perhaps to be lisped as Bathaloth) as that of a mythological hero (§ 180).

22. Rowe, "Portrait of Aeschines," 399.

23. Andrew R. Dyck, "The Function and Persuasive Power of Demosthenes' Portrait of Aeschines in the Speech *On the Crown*," *Greece & Rome* 32 (1985), 42–48. Cf. *Nicomachean Ethics* (4.7 1127a21f.) in which Aristotle says, "the boaster

is a man who pretends to creditable qualities that he does not possess, or possesses in a lesser degree than he makes out." Demosthenes' goal is not comedy but invective, but it does not seem as if the shading would have to change a great deal for Demosthenes' portrayal to take on a comic light. He himself comments on the enjoyment people have in hearing invective; it is somewhat like that with comedy.

24. Plutarch, "On Praising Oneself Inoffensively," 542b and 543b.

25. Dyck, "Function and Persuasive Power," 42.

26. Ibid., 43.

27. Dyck, "Function and Persuasive Power," 44. Specialists in Greek law have tended recently to argue that Demosthenes' legal case was not as weak as was once thought. See Michael Gagarin, "Law, Politics, and the Question of Relevance in the Case *On the Crown*," *Classical Antiquity* 31 (2012): 293–314, and Edward M. Harris, "Law and Oratory," in *Persuasion: Greek Rhetoric in Action*, ed. Ian Worthington (London: Routledge, 1993), 141–48.

28. Demosthenes attacks Aeschines' father as a slave, which he clearly was not, and his mother as a prostitute, an equally dubious claim (§§ 129–30).

29. He alludes to the fact later (§ 82).

30. Thomas M. Conley, "Topics of Vituperation: Some Commonplaces of 4th-Century Oratory," in *Influences on Peripatetic Rhetoric: Essays in Honor of William W. Fortenbaugh*, ed. D. C. Mirhady (Leiden: Brill, 2007), 231–38. Conley gives a short but systematic and accessible account of invective at the time of Demosthenes. He argues (p. 232) that vituperation is generally aimed at two classes of individuals, "hot shots" (*hybristeis*) and "lowlifes" (*poneroi*).

31. A more precise translation of *kategoria* would be "prosecution speech" in court, the sort of speech Aeschines has delivered. An "accusation" in the sense of the formal charge of the prosecutor is an *aitia*.

32. Cf. Demosthenes 18.98. Aristotle does not actually include genealogy in his account of epideictic speeches, but it does appear in the contemporary work known as the *Rhetoric to Alexander* (§ 37.5–10). Demosthenes admits to having been born into fortunate circumstances, which allowed him to do many of the things associated with the wealthy (§ 257). To us this might seem just a matter of luck, not a matter worthy of praise. To a Greek it was also a proper reflection of character. One of the principal terms for bad character is *poneria*, literally a condition characterized by having to do labor (*ponos*). So almost by definition laboring people had bad character.

33. See § 27, "I foresaw the result," and § 45, "I warned and protested." Cf. §§ 63, 72, 199. Of Aeschines, in contrast, he says, he was "a doctor who diagnoses illness only after death" (§ 243).

34. He uses the opposite word, *kakonous*, of Aeschines (§ 135).

35. Keaney translates it here as "quality."

36. Keaney translates êthesin as "customs," as if it were *ethesin*, which indeed was read by some ancient commentators, but does not appear in the manuscripts.

37. Cf. Aristotle, *Nicomachean Ethics* 3.2 1111b and 6.2 1139a-b.

38. While Demosthenes claims many fine adjectives for himself and the Athenians, he also denies their opposites: "No policy of mine was ever vindictive, malicious or malign, nor paltry, nor unworthy of Athens" (§ 108).

39. Keaney translates *phaulotatos* as "worst type." The word generally has a connotation of insignificance.

40. The Greek word *kataptupistos* literally means "to be spat down on." Demosthenes also faults Aeschines for being *diaptuon* ("contemptuous"), literally "someone who spits on others." (Note the onomatopoeia.)

41. Athens actually had ritual contexts for invective, for instance in comedy and in the rites of Demeter, in which abuse was hurled by and at initiates who were being pulled on a wagon in a procession. Demosthenes also refers to this ritual (§ 122). Demosthenes begins his speech with a prayer that is, as Harvey Yunis, *Demosthenes: On the Crown*, (Cambridge: Cambridge University Press 2001) 20 points out, "pious, moving, and utterly artificial."

42. Keaney's translation. The Greek word *kolax* is normally translated "flatterer."

43. Demosthenes also uses complimentary language ironically: "worthy gentlemen" (§ 89), "mouther of noble phrases" (*semnologos* § 133), "most brilliant of voice, best memorizer, best actor" (§ 313), as well as ambiguous language ("he becomes subtle" § 227 and "haughty" *semnos* § 258). And he throws back at him Aeschines' claim that Demosthenes is "clever, a wizard, and a sophist" (§ 276).

44. Keaney translates as "statesman." Cf. § 192.

45. In the Athenian law on impeachment, the *rhetor* and general are linked side by side (cf. § 205), seemingly as the individuals who provide political and military leadership.

46. Keaney translates *naukleros* as "(ship) owner," but owners were often not on the ships. This figure is also not the steersman or captain (cf. § 194), but the one who is on the ship and responsible for the overall shipping operation although he is not actually steering the boat.

47. One might argue that by even mentioning Themistocles' name Demosthenes is drawing connections between Themistocles and himself.

48. Aeschines 3.178–88.

49. See Aristotle, *Nicomachean Ethics* 5.10 and *Rhetoric* 1.13.

6. CRAFTING NOSTALGIA: *PATHOS* IN *ON THE CROWN*

Richard A. Katula

A good lawyer knows the law; a great lawyer knows the judge.

—Anonymous

Demosthenes' performance in *On the Crown* is, perhaps, the quintessential testament to the words of Quintilian, "The orator must be at his greatest when the proofs are against him; his finest achievement is a tear in the eye of the judge. In awakening it, he performs his most characteristic function."[1] From a strictly legal point of view the proofs were against Demosthenes. Aeschines had the better case, and for three reasons.[2] The decree to award Demosthenes a crown was challenged by Aeschines through a *graphe paranomon* (prosecution for illegalities) against Ctesiphon in 336 BCE. By a strict reading of the law Aeschines was correct in doing so, and his nostalgic appeals to the Solonian democracy coupled with his comments about the current state of affairs in Athens might have carried the day. But Demosthenes' oration engulfed the event with his delivery, his blended style of oratory, and with his own nostalgic appeals to the past.[3] As Charles Rann Kennedy says, "His eloquence would have been of no avail [since Ctesiphon was guilty], had it not touched the true chord of Athenian feeling."[4] He alluded to the golden age of Pericles, to the past honor and dignity of Athens, to Athenian culture and common experience, to the memory of the men buried in the *Kerameikos*, to the hopes and dreams of the generation of patriots he had helped raise by his oratory.[5] And he spoke of democracy, that system of government the jurors had come to cherish. By doing so Demosthenes won the day.

This essay employs Aristotle's canons of rhetoric and his theory of *pathe* (emotional proof) to explore the ways that Demosthenes brings to the surface, throughout the speech, emotions lying deep within the audience: through his use of delivery and memory, his archaizing style of oratory, the arrangement of the speech, and his artful, nostalgic crafting of public memory in the service of his personal reputation and his public record. The essay also looks at the oration of Aeschines with its focus on the legalities of the case and the underlying emotional appeal (pathos) made by him in contrast to Demosthenes, since it is in this contrast that we see most clearly the difference between the two speeches. The argument in this essay is that while both orators made use of nostalgia as the emotional element in their orations, Demosthenes reminds the audience of their traditions of courage, honor, bravery, and leadership, while Aeschines appeals to their past glory and honor as opposed to their shamefulness (aiskyne) in their present political status and in the corruption caused by their degradation of Solon's constitution. When it was a decision between the two emotional strategies—qualities of character versus corruption of the law —Demosthenes won.

EMOTIONS AND EMOTIONAL CONTAGION

What is an emotion? Emotions are feelings. They are "packages" of stimuli, both positive and negative, and they predispose the individual to bivalent behavior. An emotion is "a complex functional whole including appraisals or appreciations, patterned psychological processes, action tendencies, subjective feelings, expressions, and instrumental behaviors.... Emotions fit into families, within which all members share a family resemblance but no universal set of features."[6] Aristotle, in his *Rhetoric*, calls these feelings "states of mind," and he says that the state of mind that accompanies distress is also the state of mind in which people take pleasure in the opposite emotions. Indeed, circumstances like the trial of Ctesiphon bring with them the potential for bivalent states of mind,[7] and the orators craft a speech that favors their position on the issue.

Furthermore, "emotional contagion," is one of the most observable features of emotion, and the feature that speakers use most effectively for persuasion. It is defined as a "multiply determined family of psychophysiological, behavioral, and social phenomena."[8] In their delivery, style, and in their narratives, orators use the mimicry and synchrony that people of a particular family or culture share to "infect" the crowd. As Pickard notes about the typical Athenian juror,

> Men who are assembled in a crowd do not think, unless they are forced to do so by something extraordinary; it is generally the shallowest minds which are the most quickly made up, and which affect the rest of the crowd by a kind of contagion; and so the art of rhetoric is different from reasoning. In 4th century Athens, orators had often to use rhetorical techniques which no logic can defend, and to employ methods of persuasion upon a crowd which he would be ashamed to use if he were dealing with a personal friend.[9]

In rhetorical theory, emotional proof (*pathos*) is an ambiguous term, sometimes mixed in with logical proof, as in Aristotle's discussion of emotional proof as cognitive,[10] and sometimes conflated with ethical proof, as in Quintilian's and Cicero's theories of rhetoric.[11] But for the practicing orator, there is no confusion. The orator knows that the whole address is an emotional experience for the audience, and he/she knows what that means. Oratory, he/she knows, is the psychagogic art, the art of putting together all the modes of proof in one's demonstration so as to win the case. Quintilian puts it this way:

> There are, and always have been, a considerable number of pleaders capable of discovering arguments adequate to prove their point. . . . But few indeed are those orators who can sweep the judge with them, lead him to adopt that attitude of mind which they desire, and compel him to weep with them or share their anger. And yet it is emotional power which dominates the court, it is this form of eloquence that is the queen of all. . . . The peculiar task of the orator arises when the minds of the judges require force to move them, and their thoughts have actually to be led away from the contemplation of the truth. No instruction from the litigant can secure this, nor can such power be acquired merely by the study of a brief. Proofs it is true, may induce the judges to regard our case as superior to that of our opponent, but the appeal to emotions will do more, for it will make them wish our case to be the better. And what they wish they also believe. For as soon as they begin to be angry, to feel favorably disposed, to hate or pity, they begin to take a personal interest in the case, and just as lovers are incapable of forming a reasoned judgment on the beauty of the object of

their affection, because passion forestalls the sense of sight, so the judge, when overcome by his emotions, abandons all attempt to enquire into the truth of the arguments, is swept along by the tide of passion, and yields himself unquestioning to the torrent. . . . For it is in the power over the emotions that the life and soul of oratory is to be found.[12]

Two of the canons of rhetoric that Demosthenes employs to bring the audience into the state of mind of which Quintilian speaks are delivery and its related canon, memory.

DELIVERY, MEMORY, AND EMOTIONAL PROOF

So aware were orators of the day of the typical Athenian juror, an old man unacquainted with the law,[13] that they saw courtroom oratory as perfor-mance art, in delivery as well as in strategy. Demosthenes was foremost among equals in this art.

We know a good deal about Demosthenes' delivery. The influence of Isocrates' handbook, the oratory of Callistratus, and the criticism of the actor Satyrus all played a part in Demosthenes' development as a speaker.[14] While some of what we know may be hyperbole or legend, we have it on pretty good evidence that Demosthenes began his career in the courts and the assembly as a notoriously poor performer. His problems were difficult to overcome: a weak voice, a lisp, poor breathing, and trouble making the letter R, and when he first addressed the people, Plutarch (as well as others[15]) tells us, "he was derided for his strange and uncouth style."[16] Pickard adds that more than once his periods fell into confusion and were met with laughter. But he practiced assiduously to eliminate flaws in his speaking, going so far, legend tells us, as to practice with pebbles in his mouth, repeating difficult phrases many times, and trying to speak above the breakers on the shore at Phalerum, reciting while running uphill, and speaking before a mirror to perfect his gestures.[17] Demosthenes began to regard oral delivery, or action, as the essential element of his oratory.

And Demosthenes understood the importance of tone of voice. Plu-tarch recounts how a man came to ask for Demosthenes' assistance as a pleader, relating that he had been assaulted and beaten. "Certainly," said Demosthenes, "nothing of this kind could have happened to you." Upon which the man, raising his voice, exclaimed loudly, "What, Demosthenes, nothing has been done to me." "Ah," replied Demosthenes, "now I hear the voice of one that has been injured and beaten." Apocryphal perhaps, but the story reminds us that Demosthenes placed great value on tone of voice. This aspect of his oratory is why MacDowell notes, "Only by reading aloud sections of *On the Crown* in Greek can one truly appreciate the power and authority of his prose."[18]

Furthermore, we know that his speeches gained a certain passion drawn from a tone of bitterness when he was strongly moved.[19] This tone, which may be heard sometimes as sarcasm, sometimes as irony, or at times "moroseness," as some scholars have termed it, may have developed when he was prosecuting his guardians who had stolen or squandered the fortune left to him by his father, or, it may have been intrinsic to his personality. Personal attacks on one's opponent were customary in the courts of the time, and Demosthenes, in his work as a speechwriter (logographer), did not hesitate to use it.[20] The tone is most evident in his ad hominem attacks on Aeschines. We may hear some of this sarcasm if we read aloud (even in English) some of the remarks Demosthenes makes about Aeschines' lineage and his mother's line of work: "(§129) I have no difficulty in finding things to say about you and your family; my difficulty is where to begin. Should I say that your father, Trembler, was a slave in the elementary school of Elpias, near the Thesium, wearing leg irons and a collar? Or that your mother plied her trade in the daylight marriages in the little shack near the statue of Kalamites, she who raised you, her pretty little doll, to be the paragon of third-rate actors?"

Sources such as Plutarch say that by perfecting his delivery Demosthenes "came to have the pre-eminence of all the competitors in the assembly."[21] And Dionysius, writing four hundred years later, remarks,

> How must the Greeks have been excited at the time by the orator addressing them on live and personal issues, using all his prestige to display his own feelings and to bare his soul, and adding beauty and colour to every word with the appropriate delivery, of which art he was, as everyone agrees, the most brilliant exponent.... If then, the spirit with which Demosthenes' pages are still imbued after so many years possesses so much power, and moves his readers in this way, surely to hear him delivering his speeches at the time must have been an extraordinary and overwhelming experience.[22]

Indeed, people admired him as much for his performance of the speech as for his arguments. After all, as MacDowell tells us, the courtroom in the fourth century was the cultural heir of the theatre in the fifth century, and drama was considered an essential part of it.[23] Since so much was at stake, we can assume that Demosthenes was at his emotional best in *On the Crown*.

In fact, Demosthenes comments on his speaking prowess in §§ 277–78, noting that his eloquence is put to the service of the "vital interests of the city." These comments are intended to respond to Aeschines' charge in § 40 that Demosthenes' eloquence is a way of blinding the audience to the truth of the charges made against him: "His speeches have been plausible; his actions traitorous." Even Aeschines was aware of the power of Demosthenes' delivery to sway the emotions of the audience.

Delivery establishes emotional tone, while style and narrative establish mood. Something like the music that accompanies the lyrics. Demosthenes had the range necessary to establish tone at both ends of the register: the white-hot, passionate tone that he uses to insult Aeschines; and the sentimental tone that he uses to discuss the past. Thus, delivery suggests emotion.

Demosthenes was at his best when he had a prepared speech. His attempts at extempore speaking were frustrating early in his career, and he often failed to get his most important arguments in front of the jury. Thus, he mastered the art of "writing to be spoken." Demosthenes reserved his extempore remarks for the insertion of decrees (which was unusual but allowed him to insert evidence when it seemed most timely) and for jests and mockery as he does in *On the Crown* when he issues rejoinders to the insults hurled at him by Aeschines (§§ 122–30). Thus, he worked at his speeches until they were high art and he knew them verbatim. Despite this careful attention to each and every word, Demosthenes avoids the trap of sounding like a sophist (Plutarch tells us that early on Demosthenes was accused by Pytheas, a contemporary, of writing speeches that "smelt of the lamp")[24] or like orators who were known for tricks of the trade and were often rebuked by jurors who spotted them.

STYLE, ARRANGEMENT, AND EMOTIONAL PROOF

Demosthenes paid particular attention to varying the mood, which he did by the phrasing of words and the construction of his sentences. Dionysius of Halicarnassus, in *On the Ancient Orators*, says that Demosthenes perfected the art of mixing styles, whose speeches were "well-blended." He is set against all the earlier writers and orators as the best "eclectic," because, Dionysius says, "he adds vigor to the Lysianic style, lucidity to the Thucydidean, and within the middle or best style he is superior to Isocrates and Plato."[25]

But it is not only in his mixing of these styles that Dionysius notices Demosthenes' genius. It is in his mixing of the *austere* and *refined* modes of speaking that Dionysius finds Demosthenes to be the greatest orator. The *austere* mode of composition is comprised of language that is solemn, noble, and grand and has a certain greatness of spirit and beauty that come from its "patina," a metaphor for the tarnish that develops with age on bronze. The *refined* mode of composition contains language that is pleasurable, melodious, and theatrical and panders to popular taste. Demosthenes became fully cognizant of these modes, and he knew how to exploit them in oratory—the austere because it lent an old-fashioned air to his speeches, and the refined because it appealed to the dramatic, the passionate, and the fourth-century audience's love of spectacle.

Because of this artistic mixing Kim calls Demosthenes not the last classical orator but the first *classicizing* author.[26] His oratory had the "attitude of classicism," seen especially in its references to the politics and culture of the fifth century, the Periclean age—a time when Athenians were at the zenith of their power, when they had jobs, dignity and respect, leisure and money, and when they controlled their own destiny because of the democracy that Pericles supported. This golden age, and all the emotions connected to it, is what Demosthenes conjures up in the audience's minds with his sometimes noble and sometimes fiery rhetoric. By doing so, Demosthenes erases the emotion of shame that many Athenians feel about their present situation, and replaces it with a feeling of pride and honor.[27]

Demosthenes' comments in §§199–205 are a powerful example of the use of the *austere* in *On the Crown*. There is grandeur that derives from its asyndetons, metaphors, and periods. In terms of the *refined* it can be seen in the elevated, theatrical language used to describe Aeschines, his parents' occupations, and Aeschines' life in the theatre (§§ 257–60). This example is typical of the pandering style used throughout his narrative. It is in this mixing of the *austere* and *refined* modes of speaking that Demosthenes wins the crowd over. As Dionysius says,

> It seems to me that he was taught by experience and his own nature that the masses who rush to schools and public festivals do not demand the same sort of things as those who occupy the law courts and the assemblies. The former yearn for artifice and entertainment; the latter for instruction and assistance on the matters which they are investigating. Demosthenes thus thought it was necessary both that a forensic speech not be spoken in a seductive and sweet voice, and that an epideictic speech not be marked by aridity and patina.[28]

And Demosthenes arranges his speech "as he wishes," despite Aeschines protestations to the jury that he respond to the arguments in the order in which Aeschines brings them up. He conditions the audience against Aeschines' attacks on his character and his actions by speaking first of the history of his and Athens's relations with Philip. In § 9, Demosthenes begins his justification of his behavior in the affair with Philip, and in § 22, he introduces what will be one of his key arguments: his attack on Aeschines' shamelessness in remaining silent if, indeed, Demosthenes had sold out Athens to Philip rather than uniting with the rest of Greece against him.

INVENTION AND EMOTIONAL PROOF

Demosthenes continues the emotional unity of his address in the invention of arguments. He will move his audience in two ways: with the passionate arguments about Aeschines' actions and personal characteristics, and with the sentimental arguments about the past glories of Athens. These arguments represent the *refined* and the *austere*. An example of the former has already been shown in §129. These arguments are also at §§10–12, 15, 127–32, 180, 242–45, and 259–65. It seems as though the personal attacks are a theatrical device aimed at pandering to popular taste, but they are an integral part of Demosthenes' strategy, also, in that they show Aeschines to be a shameful person.

The latter line of argument will focus on the nostalgia created by Demosthenes in *On the Crown*. The term "nostalgia" comes from the Greek *nostos*, meaning "to return home," and *algia*, meaning a "painful condition."[29] It has since been defined as "homesickness," exemplified in Homer's *Odyssey* when Odysseus weeps at Ogygia for his beloved home, Ithaca. Nostalgia also has close ties with "public memory" or "collective memory" in the sense that nostalgia is a yearning for yesterday as "yesterday" is painted by historians and orators. Being nostalgic increases the orator's connection to the larger society. Nostalgia makes people feel closer to each other. Routledge found that, "Nostalgia does not have any negative effects on people, but generates a number of psychological benefits."[30] Nostalgia is a "psychological resource that people employ to counter negative emotions and feelings of vulnerability."[31]

The audience (Quintilian's judge) was on an emotional precipice. Plutarch tells us that "never was any public cause more celebrated than this."[32] And Charles Rann Kennedy adds that "the interest excited was intense, not only at Athens, but throughout all of Greece, and an immense concourse of foreigners flocked from all parts to hear the two most celebrated orators of the world. The jury (of not less than 500) was impaneled by the archon, and before a dense and breathless audience the pleadings began."[33] And they were a typical Athenian jury: old, poor, and mostly idle, and subject to the contagion of emotion caused by the dropping of a name or a place, or traditions such as freedom, courage, honor, and dignity.

What was it about the "place" that makes Demosthenes' nostalgic appeals so appropriate and powerful? Miles gives us a hint when she notes that "a number of Greek temples destroyed during the Persian Wars were deliberately preserved by the Greeks to serve as memorials. Archaeological and literary evidence reveals how these memorials sometimes served as rallying points for collective identity."[34] The setting for the speech was near the Agora, the marketplace, which sits below the Acropolis (which had been destroyed during the Persian Wars) and between the Acropolis and the Kerameikos cemetery (which appears just alongside the outer long walls that flank the ancient road from Athens to the Peireas, and which Pericles used to provide jobs for the soldiers when they were not at war), where he delivered the *Funeral Oration* in 430 BCE, and where the soldiers were burned in the funeral pyre following the first year of the Peloponnesian War.[35] What place could be more perfect for an appeal to nostalgia? The crowd was assembled near the Areopagus, and at the top of this hill sat the Parthenon inside of which was the statue of Athena, goddess of power and protection, who could save Athens no longer. As Pieper and Ker tell us, "The extolling of antiquity or nostalgia for a somehow disconnected past, indeed seems ubiquitous in ancient culture."[36]

The comments made about Aeschines' lineage were the kind that would have raised the emotional level of the audience, because Athenians were proud of their heritage. MacDowell tells us that "modern scholars have speculated that Athenian citizens wished to share their privileges with as few others as possible, or that they wished to preserve their racial purity."[37] Athenians were particularly keen to birthright because it signaled for them a person's character, or what Aristotle called "ethics." As Su notes: "With his neologism [the use of Homer's term *ethea* for "ethics," a person's character], Aristotle cemented an idea that had been in circulation at least since Herodotus: namely that an individual's place of birth shapes the way he or she will act; or, to use the more current understanding of the word *ēthos* (the singular form of *ēthea*), place molds an individual's character."[38] Rhetorical appeals to nostalgia are a frequent strategy of the politician and courtroom orator. Parry-Giles and Parry-Giles note that "the rhetorical use of nostalgia invokes an idealized, mythological past to find /construct sources of identity, agency, or community that are felt to be lacking in the present.... For political leaders, and presidents, nostalgia offers an almost irresistible rhetorical tool, given its highly affective and effective rhetorical consequences. Nostalgia becomes a means for the political orator to affiliate his/her image and character with the traditions of the community."[39]

Demosthenes uses this nostalgic rhetoric throughout his narrative to create the mood in *On the Crown*. Parry-Giles and Parry-Giles further assert that "political nostalgia is the limited, distorted narrative of the past-in-memory that argumentatively resurrects and glorifies bygone times and is communicated to achieve an emotional response in the service of a political or electoral goal."[40] Nostalgia is a powerful political/rhetorical strategy because of its emotional resonance with an audience and because of the identification it creates between political leaders and their audiences.

And they were human beings, or, in the case of *On the Crown,* a large group of human beings. Demosthenes senses the emotions that are present. Athens is about to fall, and with it all the traditions of democracy. Both orators will mention these traditions over and over again as a way of reminding Athenians what they are about to lose, but also as a means of guiding their state of mind to either a joyful and pleasurable remembrance of the past or a painful portrait of the future. In opposition to Aeschines' remarks about the consequences of Demosthenes' policies, Demosthenes frames his public memory with the good that the people and his policies have accomplished, thus giving people a choice between opposing valences or states of mind: one that has emotions such as fear and anger and one that would bring calm, confidence, and kindliness.

Demosthenes seizes the moment. In his *prooemium*, he invokes the gods of the community and mentions Solon, the beloved writer of the laws (Aeschines does this also, but for a different reason). He invokes the gods again in §7. Then, in reviewing the events of the past throughout his speech, he references the patriotism of the Athenians, calls Athens a citadel of freedom, talks about the tradition of never letting an ally down, always fighting for freedom instead of a false and temporary security. The nostalgic remembrances come in torrents. In §§ 66–69, Demosthenes invokes Athens's traditions. And again in §§ 72, 80, 85, and 89–93. In §§ 97–98, and especially in § 99, he praises Athens as the city that others turn to, and that now will be lost. Also in §§ 98–102, Demosthenes praises Athenians as the people who fought for and with others despite past grievances when it was in the service of freedom.

Most characteristic of the nostalgia in Demosthenes' speech is the section from 200 to 208. It is here that Demosthenes puts a tear in the eyes of the judges with lines reminiscent of Pericles in the *Funeral Oration*. Statements such as this one appear throughout the text, sometimes more obliquely than others. And they create a mood, much as the décor in a restaurant creates the ambience. Not every line does this, but the overall mood created is one of pride and patriotism, of honor and bravery in the face of crisis, of freedom, which they are about to lose, and of continuity between past and present. It is a nostalgic mood filled with emotional choices that the jurors must make between Aeschines' legal case and Demosthenes' claim that, even if it failed, Athens's defiance of Philip in defense of democracy spoke to their eternal glory. When read aloud, it is the austere mode in word choice, phrasing, and argument that infuses the entire speech.

[§ 200] All that can be said now is, that we have failed and that is the common lot of humanity, if God so wills. But then, if Athens, after claiming the primacy of the nations, had run away from her claims, she would have been held guilty of betraying Greece to Philip. If, without striking a blow, she had abandoned the cause for which our forefathers flinched from no peril, is there a man who would not have spat in your face? In your face, Aeschines: not at Athens, not at me! [§ 201] How could we have returned the gaze of visitors to our city, if the result had been what it is—Philip the chosen lord paramount of all Greece—and if other nations had fought gallantly to avert that calamity without our aid, although never before in the whole course of history had our city preferred inglorious security to the perils of a noble cause? [§ 202] There is no man living, whether Greek or barbarian, who does not know that the Thebans, or the Lacedaemonians, who held supremacy before them,[16] or the king of Persia himself, would cheerfully and gratefully have given Athens liberty to keep what she had and to take what she chose, if only she would do their behest and surrender the primacy of Greece. [§ 203] But to the Athenians of old, I suppose, such temporizing was forbidden by their heredity, by their pride, by their very nature. Since the world began, no man has ever prevailed upon Athens to attach herself in the security of servitude to the oppressors of mankind however formidable: in every generation she has striven without a pause in the perilous contention for primacy, and honor, and renown. [§ 204] Such constancy you deem so exemplary, and so congenial to your character, that you still sing the praises of those of your forefathers by whom it was most signally displayed. And you are right.

Who would not exult in the valor of those famous men who, rather than yield to a conqueror's behests, left city and country and made the war-galleys their home; who chose Themistocles, the man who gave them that counsel, as their commander, and stoned Cyrsilus[17] to death for advising obedient submission? Aye, and his wife also was stoned by your wives. [§ 205] The Athenians of that day did not search for a statesman or a commander who should help them to a servile security: they did not ask to live, unless they could live as free men. Every man of them thought of himself as one born, not to his father and his mother alone, but to his country. What is the difference? The man who deems himself born only to his parents will wait for his natural and destined end; the son of his country is willing to die rather than see her enslaved, and will look upon those outrages and indignities, which a commonwealth in subjection is compelled to endure, as more dreadful than death itself. [§ 206] If I had attempted to claim that you were first inspired with the spirit of your forefathers by me, every one would justly rebuke me. But I do not: I am asserting these principles as your principles; I am showing you that such was the pride of Athens long before my time,—though for myself I do claim some credit for the administration of particular measures. [§ 207] Aeschines, on the other hand, arraigns the whole policy, stirs up your resentment against me as the author of your terrors and your dangers, and, in his eagerness to strip me of the distinction of a moment, would rob you of the enduring praises of posterity. For if you condemn Ctesiphon on the ground of my political delinquency, you yourselves will be adjudged as wrongdoers, not as men who owed the calamities they have suffered to the unkindness of fortune. [§ 208] But no; you cannot, men of Athens, you cannot have done wrongly when you accepted the risks of war for the redemption and the liberties of mankind; I swear it by our forefathers who bore the brunt of warfare at Marathon, who stood in array of battle at Plataeia, who fought in the seafights of Salamis and Artemisium, and by all the brave men who repose in our public sepulchres, buried there by a country that accounted them all to be alike worthy of the same honor—all, I say, Aeschines, not the successful and the victorious alone. So justice bids: for by all the duty of brave men was accomplished: their fortune was such as Heaven severally allotted to them.

In §§170–79, perhaps the most stirring lines of the speech, Demosthenes uses *ethos* as *pathos* in Quintilian's sense; placing himself in the tradition of courageous Athenians, he speaks for defending Athens, when no one else stood to do so, as Philip was approaching.

But the crisis of that day, as it seems, called not only for the patriotic and wealthy citizen, but also for a man who had closely followed the course of events from the beginning and who had correctly reasoned why and with what intentions Philip was acting. For one who did not know this and who had not carefully examined the situation for a long time, not even if he were patriotic, not even if he were wealthy, was any the more likely to know what had to be done or able to advise you. That man, on that day, was I. . . . With these and similar measures, I stepped down. All, together, praised my advice, no one opposed it.

Charles Rann Kennedy says of Demosthenes: "Throughout his whole political career he had been supported by the judgment and convictions of the people. Thus he argued, and the people felt it was impossible for them to find him guilty without passing sentence upon themselves, without condemning the policy which Athens had for a long series of years consistently pursued. The genius of Athens protected her from such disgrace; and by an overwhelming majority, which left the accuser no choice but to retire into exile, a verdict was given for the defendant."[41]

THE SPEECH OF AESCHINES

And what of Aeschines and his speech? Aeschines was also a master of delivery and was noted for his businesslike style. He wrote the depositions and documents that he introduced in his speech. He left nothing to chance, even writing the laws he would cite and leaving out passages of those laws that did not fit his case or that were extraneous to the trial.[42] He was a worthy antagonist of Demosthenes.

Aeschines' speech also employs nostalgia. Through historical allusion he harnesses the power of monuments and places. The laws of Solon are mentioned throughout the speech. Aeschines evokes an idealized past when Solon's code was adhered to as opposed to the present when the awarding of honors such as the crown is abused. He does this as a rhetorical strategy designed to identify his cause with the audience's warm feelings for the past. Hobden synthesizes the case this way:

In *Against Ctesiphon*, Aeschines pursues two principal lines of attack appropriate to a suit concerning illegal decrees and to the precise circumstances of the case: proving the illegality of the decree issued six years earlier by Ctesiphon honoring Demosthenes with a crown, and disproving the terms of the award that Demosthenes "accomplishes the best for the demos in word and deed." Within this framework depictions of the people, city and events of Athens' past enter into the narrative in conjunction with the present day polis at three points; at the beginning and end of the speech, and approximately two-thirds of the way through once the account of Demosthenes' political disservices is complete and a concentrated assault on his democratic character has begun. On each occasion, presentation of the past is accompanied by a discussion of the contemporary city, creating a series of juxtapositions whose individual coherence is signified by a shift in tense and temporal indicators distinguishing past from present.[43]

Aeschines references Solonian democracy in his introduction. Specifically, he refers to the procedure that had the eldest speak first in the assembly as opposed to the present situation when "that most sage and virtuous proclamation is no longer heard, 'who is disposed to speak of those above fifty years old?' and then 'who of the other citizens in their turns?'" This reference to the tradition of the call to the eldest (who made up most of the jurors) to speak first has been ignored, Aeschines argues, and as a result the constitution has been corrupted.

Aeschines appeals next to the jury's sense of shame and disgrace in that, aside from procedural matters that had been neglected, an honor such as a crown of gold had been used rarely throughout Athenian history, and that had made it an esteemed honor. In § 43, he asserts that to bestow it on men such as Demosthenes, a man who, he charges, advocated disastrous policies and who had led a cowardly career of dubious distinction since Chaeronea and Thebes, was to damage the luster of the crown itself, and bring shame to the people. As Pickard notes, "In one striking passage, Aeschines imagines the scene at Dionysia, if, when the orphans of those who had fallen in the service of their country were presented with a suit of armor by the State, Demosthenes, who had made them orphans, was crowned with gold."[44] Truly, Aeschines asserts, this was a shameful event.

And Aeschines' history, as compared with Demosthenes', is crafted as a warning, not a comfort, to the audience. He draws on the past as prologue. Aeschines misses that which is most self-evident: that the Athenians are a proud people, having led the Delian League, institutionalized the rule of law, democratized leadership, and been the most powerful city-state and the leader of the Greek empire. Aeschines' motivation is fear rather than confidence. He is, to put the best term on it, a realist, and the people, he thinks, are realists also, and fearful, indeed, of the day when they must pay the same price as the Spartans. Sections 132–34 demonstrate this emotional appeal.

> What strange and unexpected event has not occurred in our time? The life we have lived is no ordinary one, but we were born to be an object of wonder to posterity. The Persian king, who dug a canal through Mount Athos, who cast a yoke on the Hellespont, who demanded earth and water from the Greeks, who had the arrogance to write in his letters that he was the lord of all men from the rising to the setting sun, surely he is now fighting for his own safety rather than for domination over others?
>
> And do we not see that men who are thought worthy of this glory and of the command against the Persians, are precisely those who freed the sanctuary at Delphi? And Thebes—Thebes the neighboring city—has been erased in one day from the center of Greece. . . . A just punishment, for their misguided policies, and for the blindness and folly that afflicted them, divinely inspired rather than human. And the unfortunate Spartans, who were only involved with these events at the beginning when the temple at Delphi was captured, and who at one time claimed to be the leaders of the Greeks, are now about to be sent to Alexander as hostages to parade their misfortune.
>
> Whatever he decides, they and their country will have to endure, the verdict depending on the moderation of the victor whom they offended. And our own city, the common refuge of the Greeks, which formerly embassies from all over Greece would visit, each city seeking its safety from us, is now no longer fighting for the leadership of Greece, but to defend the land of its fathers. And all this has happened from the moment Demosthenes took over control of affairs.[45]

The eloquence of this passage is typical of orations of the time that were imbued with the prestige of antiquity, but Athenians were not in the mood for the fear it triggers. Theirs, Demosthenes reminds them, is a tradition of courage and freedom. Perhaps there is something in the tradition of freedom that is indispensable to the human psyche. And it is only upon the premise of freedom that a people can be free to develop lofty political responses and take the moral path when it is presented to them. Nostalgia, as a rhetorical strategy, works best when it harkens back to memories of good times, of heroic times, and times when people were happy.

Between Demosthenes' speech and Aeschines' speech lies the potential for bivalence. Both speeches provoke nostalgia—the anger-tinged nostalgia of Aeschines' speech, on the one hand, in which the audience feels that Athenian judicial procedure has been desecrated and with it the glory of Athens itself; and the self-admiring pride and dignity, on the other hand, evoked by Demosthenes' oration, in which the audience feels gratified and triumphant at having done the right thing, at having preserved Athenian honor. The audience is left to choose between the anger and shame of Aeschines or the pride and courage of Demosthenes.

Both men knew the art of emotional appeal, and the power it had for the typical Athenian juror of the time. When Demosthenes' speech and Aeschines' speech are compared, the people have a choice. Demosthenes' speech rings with those mystic chords of memory, while Aeschines' speech falls flat. It comes off as a legalistic and personal attack. Aeschines thought that a legalistic strategy would blunt Demosthenes' strategy of nostalgia, but the mood it creates is overwhelmingly negative. As Routledge says, "Nostalgia is a psychological resource that people employ to counter negative emotions and feelings of vulnerability. Nostalgia allows people to use experiences from the past to help cope with challenges in the present."[46] Demosthenes' speech is thus a triumph of rhetoric, of using all the canons of rhetoric and infusing them with the *pathos* inherent in nostalgia.

NOTES

1. Quintilian, *The Orator's Education,* vol. 2, books 6–8, ed. and trans. D. A. Russell (Cambridge: Harvard University Press, 2001), 6, ii, 7.

2. Douglas M. MacDowell, *The Law in Classical Athens* (Ithaca: Cornell University Press, 1978), 51–52. See also Donovan J. Ochs, "Demosthenes' Use of Argument," in *Demosthenes' On the Crown,* ed. James J. Murphy (Davis, CA: Hermagoras Press, 1983), 160–63.

3. David S. Werman, "Normal and Pathological Nostalgia," *Journal of the American Psychoanalytic Association* 25 (1977): 393.

4. Charles Rann Kennedy, "Demosthenes' Use of History," in Murphy, *Demosthenes' On the Crown* (1983), 156.

5. Ibid., 151.

6. Elaine Hatfield, John T. Cacioppo, and Richard L. Rapson, *Emotional Contagion* (Melbourne: Cambridge University Press, 1994), 3.

7. Aristotle, *Aristotle on Rhetoric: A Theory of Civic Discourse,* ed. and trans. George Kennedy (New York: Oxford University Press, 1991), 160.

8. Hatfield, Cacioppo, and Rapson, *Emotional Contagion*, 4.

9. A. W. Pickard, *Demosthenes and the Last Days of Greek Freedom* (e-book), 107.

10. William W. Fortenbaugh, "Aristotle's Rhetoric on Emotions," *Archiv fur Geschicte der Philosophie* (1970), 52, 40–70. See also Aristotle, *Aristotle on Rhetoric*, 39.

11. Quintilian, *Orator's Education*, 6, ii, 9–12.

12. Quintilian, *Institutes of Oratory*, 6.1.55–2.3.

13. MacDowell, *Law in Classical Athens*, 35.

14. George Kennedy, "The Oratorical Career of Demosthenes," in *Demosthenes' On the Crown*, ed. James J. Murphy (New York: Random House, 1967), 29.

15. George Augustus Simcox and William Henry Simcox, *The Orations of Demosthenes and Aeschines On the Crown* (Oxford: Clarendon Press, 1872), xxxiv–xxxvi.

16. Plutarch, *Plutarch's Lives: The Life of Demosthenes*, trans. John Dryden (Cambridge, MA: Charles River Editors), e-book, 14; Plutarch, *Plutarch's Lives* (Dryden trans.), ed. A. H. Clough (Boston: Little, Brown, 1906), 5:6, under Online Library of Liberty, http://oll.libertyfund.org/titles/1775.

17. Pickard, *Demosthenes and the Last Days*, 30–31.

18. Demosthenes, *Demosthenes, Speeches 27–38*, trans. Douglas MacDowell (Austin: University of Texas, 2004), 7.

19. Pickard, *Demosthenes and the Last Days*, 22.

20. Cf. Demosthenes' speech written for Apollodorus against Phormio.

21. Plutarch, "The Life of Demosthenes," in Murphy, *Demosthenes' On the Crown* (1967), 5.

22. Dionysius, *Dionysius of Halicarnassus: Critical Essays*, trans. Stephen Usher (Cambridge: Harvard University Press, 1974), 324–25.

23. MacDowell, *Demosthenes, Speeches 27–38*.

24. Plutarch, *Plutarch's Lives: The Life of Demosthenes*, 222 (e-book), 18; Plutarch, *Plutarch's Lives* (Dryden trans.), 5:8.

25. George Kennedy, ed., *The Cambridge History of Literary Criticism*, vol. 1, *Classical Criticism* (Cambridge: Cambridge University Press), 269. See also Galen O. Rowe, "Demosthenes' Use of Language," in Murphy, *Demosthenes' On the Crown* (1967), 182.

26. Lawrence Kim, "Archaizing and Classicism in the Literary Historical Thinking of Dionysius of Halicarnassus," in *Valuing the Past in the Greco-Roman World*, ed. Christopher Pieper and James Ker (Boston: Brill Publishers, 2014), 381.

27. Aristotle, *Aristotle on Rhetoric*, 143–48.

28. Dionysius of Halicarnassus, *On the Ancient Orators*, cited in Kim, "Archaizing and Classicism," 381.

29. Fred Davis, *Yearning for Yesterday: A Sociology of Nostalgia* (New York: Free Press, 1979), 1–2.

30. Clay Routledge, "The Rehabilitation of Old Emotion: a New Science of Nostalgia," *Scientific American, MIND Guest Blog,* July 10, 2013, 5.

31. Ibid., 5.

32. Plutarch, "Life of Demosthenes," 20.

33. Charles Rann Kennedy, "Demosthenes' Use of History," 151.

34. Margaret Miles, cited in Pieper and Ker, "General Introduction: Valuing Antiquity in Antiquity," *Valuing the Past in the Greco-Roman World,* 15.

35. See the map in this text.

36. Pieper and Ker, "General Introduction," 9, 15.

37. MacDowell, *Law in Classical Athens,* 67.

38. John J. Su, *Ethics and Nostalgia in the Contemporary Novel* (Cambridge: Cambridge University Press, 2005), 23.

39. Shawn J. Parry-Giles and Trevor Parry-Giles, "Collective Memory, Political Nostalgia, and the Rhetorical Presidency: Bill Clinton's Commemoration of the March on Washington, August 28, 1998," *Quarterly Journal of Speech* 86, no. 4 (2000), 420.

40. Parry-Giles and Parry-Giles, "Collective Memory," 421.

41. Charles Rann Kennedy, "Demosthenes' Use of History," 156.

42. Simcox and Simcox, *Aeschines and Demosthenes,* xciv.

43. Fiona Hobden, "Imagining Past and Present: A Rhetorical Strategy in Aeschines 3, Against Ctesiphon," *Classical Quarterly* 57 (2007): 491.

44. Pickard, *Demosthenes and the Last Days,* 630.

45. M. M. Austin, trans., sections 132–34, www.livius.org/ajal/alexander/alexander_t13.html.

46. Routledge, "Rehabilitation," 5.

7. ON THE *DEINOS LOGOS* OF *ON THE CROWN*

Jeffrey Walker

> But it is not true, men of Athens! It is not true that you made a mistake
> when you chose to risk your lives to defend the freedom and the safety
> of all—I swear by our forefathers, who met the charge at Marathon, and
> stood shoulder to shoulder at Plataea, and fought in the ships at Salamis
> and Artemisium, and all the rest of the good men who lie in the public
> tombs, all of whom alike, deeming them worthy of this honor, the city
> buried, O Aeschines, not the successful and victorious only. And justly
> so. For what was the work of good men, this they all performed; and what
> fate the god had chosen for them, this they received.
>
> —*On the Crown*, 208

LALIA

The preliminary chat, spoken from the sophist's chair.

It isn't noticeable, probably, and I hardly have improved on the available
translations, but I have spent the last few afternoons attempting to create
my own version of this famous passage from *On the Crown*—one that would
somehow fully render its undeniable *deinótēs*, or "forcefulness," which I
suspect every reader of this text has felt, to some degree, in any translation,
and especially in the Greek. Here it is:

[READS *On the Crown* 208.]

The term *deinótēs*, of course, derives from *deinós*, the original meaning of which is "terrifying." From there it extends to such ideas as "awesome," in the sense of inspiring awe, and with a few more stretches it becomes a rhetorical term that signifies cleverness, genius, impressiveness, virtuosity, masterliness, (rhetorical) power, and "awesome" utterance in general. But it still retains a connection to the root sense of terrified awe. We hear it in Longinus's remark that "No-one is frightened [*phobeitai*] when reading Hyperides."[1] Hyperides is smooth, polished, perfect, and is (Longinus says) the equal of Demosthenes in most respects, except this one. Hyperides lacks the turbulent, impassioned forcefulness of Demosthenes; he does not reach the height (*hypsos*) of eloquence; he is not *scary good*; he is not *deinós*.

This passage from *On the Crown*, however, has *deinótēs*. For most readers it arrives with an abrupt and overwhelming force, like the thunderbolt of "sublimity" famously described by Longinus.[2] It is, arguably, the most forceful passage in the most forceful speech of the most forceful of all Greek orators. So it sets a high mark. And I for several days have tried to render in English an echo of its forcefulness, without notable success. All the translations partly get it, and all of them partly miss.

It is not just a matter of what necessarily gets lost in translation—the subtle nuances of meaning, rhythm, euphony. Rather, much of what makes this passage awesomely *deinós* is not *here*, not *in* the passage, not in the words. Some of it, of course, is here, in the original Greek. The stylistic part: the figures of repetition, the turbulent syntax, the rhythms and cadences, and so on, that are characteristic of *deinótēs*, as discussed in the stylistic treatises of Demetrius, Hermogenes, Pseudo-Hermogenes, and Pseudo-Aristides.[3] But as all these authorities agree, genuine *deinótēs* depends on "thought" (*dianoia, gnōmē*) that in itself is forceful. Ps.-Aristides is unequivocal about it: "*Deinótēs* arises exclusively from the thought, and if anyone thinks otherwise he is greatly mistaken."[4]

Forceful style without forceful thought produces discourse that may *seem* forceful, at least to the naive, but in truth is not forceful at all: a mindless whirl of empty verbiage (as Cicero might say), a froth of pretentious blather (Longinus). And there is, too, forceful thought without an obviously forceful style: a sharp, clear, plain-style simplicity that at first glance seems not forceful, but is awesome when the thought sinks in. Demetrius's main example is the tyrant Dionysius's threat to the besieged city of Locris: "The cicadas will sing to you from the ground" (i.e., we will ravage all your territory, destroy every farm, and cut down every tree).[5] This is forceful (says Demetrius) because it communicates more than it says, as the appalling implications unfold in the listener's or reader's mind (and mind's eye). Indeed one feature of both forcefulness and the sublime is that its "thought" should strike the audience as something they themselves have thought of, in a flash of realization.[6] But best of all is discourse that both seems and is *deinós*: forceful thought presented, performed, in appropriately forceful expression, to an audience that feels that they themselves are saying it, thinking it, feeling it, and are somehow taller, better, and nobler than they were (as Socrates says about his response to state funeral orations.[7] And that is what we have in the famous passage here.

It is, of course, the climactic moment of Demosthenes' argument, the moment when the whole force of that argument, a force built up through the preceding 207 sections, is abruptly brought to bear in a seemingly spontaneous but well-prepared outburst: *But it is not true, men of Athens! It is not true that you made a mistake,* and so on. In this moment Aeschines' case against Ctesiphon and Demosthenes is swept away. All the rest of *On the Crown*—about one-fourth of the speech—is rhetorical mopping up, with Demosthenes speaking to an already-persuaded audience, dispatching the remaining points in the indictment, and pummeling Aeschines, while Aeschines, having already spoken, can only stand by and watch it happen. Aeschines will win less than a fifth of the jury's vote, and in consequence will be heavily fined for frivolous prosecution, will face financial ruin and the loss of citizenship, and will leave Athens in disgrace, to spend the rest of his days (the story goes) teaching rhetoric in Rhodes.

The method of Demosthenes' well-prepared outburst, the method of *deinótēs*—considered as *argumentation*—is what I want to talk about. There are, however, some preliminary matters to get through first.

PROLOGUE

The sophist rises from the chair.

My allotted task is to speak of the *logos* of Demosthenes' speech *On the Crown*. As clear as that assignment may seem, it raises several problems. One is the semantic range and (hence) ambiguity of the word *logos* itself— from *speech, word, utterance, discourse* to *argument, argumentation, calculation, reasoning, logic,* and *rationality* as such. Thus to speak of "the *logos*" of *On the Crown* can involve all or any of those ideas.

Another problem is the Aristotelian triad of *pisteis*—ēthos, *pathos, logos*—which partly organizes this volume. The seeming clarity, completeness, and logicality of that framework give it a certain theoretical appeal, and suggest that it is possible to talk about "the *logos*" of *On the Crown* as distinct from its *pathos* and ēthos (or, for that matter, its style). But that is impossible. The "ethical" and "pathetic" appeals are mediated by *logos*; and *logos* is shot through with affect, as Chaim Perelman long ago observed.[8] Thus we commonly teach beginning students to consider the three *pisteis* as simultaneous dimensions of any argument. More or less all of the rhetorical handbooks (*technai*) surviving from antiquity just assume that persuasion requires emotively resonant argument (as appropriate) from a speaker thought worthy to be listened to. It is, in short, not possible to discuss ēthos and *pathos* apart from *logos*, or *logos* apart from *pathos* and *ēthos*, and that is certainly the case for an account of what makes Demosthenes' argument, as presented in section 208, so *deinós*.

A third problem is Aristotle's apparent dislike of Demosthenes. Demosthenes was active when Aristotle was writing what became the *Rhetoric* (ca. 355–322 BCE), but Aristotle does not mention him at all.[9] (There is a Demosthenes cited at *Rhetoric* 3.4.3, but context and the antidemocratic sentiment expressed there suggest that it is probably the fifth-century Athenian general named Demosthenes, not the fourth-century orator). The *Rhetoric* does cite some contemporary orators, including the now-obscure Aesion (at 3.10.7), who was an opponent of Demosthenes, and it cites Isocrates repeatedly, especially with reference to style. Demetrius of Phaleron, the only orator of note to come from the Peripatetic school, reportedly considered Demosthenes "vulgar" but also recognized his power.[10]

In fact Demosthenes represents the very sort of rhetoric that Aristotle would like to regulate or ban from what he calls "well-regulated" (*eunomoumenos*) states and civic assemblies.[11] Aristotle prefers relatively small and dignified deliberative bodies where participation is restricted in essence to wealthy, well-educated, experienced men of proven ability and judgment, the prudent (*phronimoi*) and the capable (*dynaminoi*), such as the Council of the Areopagus at Athens. He distrusts the mercurial crowds of common citizens that orators must address in democratic states, those crowds' susceptibilities to rabble-rousing demagogues (*dēmagōgoi*, "leaders of the people"), and the "vulgar" sort of rhetoric required for their "degraded" (*mochthērós*) sensibilities—a point that Aristotle makes twice, in the space of a page.[12]

Yet another problem is the ancient tradition that Aristotle didn't like and wasn't really very interested in rhetoric. We hear it in Cicero's *De Oratore*, in Antonius's declaration that Aristotle "despised rhetoric"; and we hear it as late as the fourteenth century, in Theodore Metochites' acerbic remarks on Aristotle's "intellectual vanity."

> It is obvious that he is a man who wants to appear wise in all fields of education, including [rhetoric]. And what else could one expect, considering that he did not even shrink from prescribing about [*nomothetein*] and compiling [*suntattein*] a book on rhetoric [*technē rhētorikē*], something of which he himself made absolutely no use? . . . But because of his truly enormous intellectual vanity, and because he thinks he is the only person who is able to calculate everything and who knows everything . . . he devotes himself also to this. . . . And it is indeed possible to understand him to be vigorous and highly resourceful in all fields, [including] subjects that he has not studied at all and whose first principles . . . he does not know, and in subjects for which he has . . . no natural ability.[13]

The Stagirite takes up rhetoric only because his theory of everything and his vanity require it, and the result (in Metochites' view) is perfunctory and inadequate.

For such reasons, then, an Aristotelian theoretical framework seems less than simpatico for an account of *On the Crown*, or of its *deinós logos*, its forceful argument. In what follows, then, I will indeed stick to my assigned task, to speak of the *logos*, the "argument," of Demosthenes' *On the Crown*. But I propose to take less of an Aristotelian approach, and more of a sophistic one, in order to explain what makes it *deinós*. It was the sophists, after all, who canonized Demosthenes as the greatest of all orators, and *On the Crown* as the greatest of all orations.

By a "sophistic" approach, however, I mean neither the cynical charlatanism nor the protopoststructuralism often attributed to the early sophists of the fifth century BCE and their successors. Rather, I mean the practical orientation to teaching—to the development of the orator—which is the main activity associated with the later sophists from Isocrates through Hermogenes and others to the end of the Roman world.[14] What this means for my analysis is that, while focusing on the *logos* or "argument" of this speech, I inescapably will be discussing *pathos* and ēthos too. Moreover, seeing that the *technai* generally address arrangement (*oikonomia*, the "management" of a *logos*) under the heading of "subject matter" (the *topos pragmatikos*), that too will need to be addressed.

What, then, I propose to show is that the argument of *On the Crown* needs to be understood as a *process of argumentation* with cumulative effects.

*Narrative/exposition; the sophist paces back
and forth across the platform.*

If an account of the *logos* of *On the Crown* is an exposition of its argument, or of the "thoughts" or subject matter composing it, my task is easy. I can say "See Yunis 2001 7–17 and 2005 28–31," or cite any of a number of perfectly good overviews, and declare myself done. But again, a bare statement of the argument, as if that were the essence of it, cannot explain what makes it *deinós*. I'll begin where the *technai* do, and with some familiar facts.

THE STASIS

As every reader of this speech knows, Aeschines' indictment is aimed not directly at Demosthenes, but at Demosthenes' supporter Ctesiphon, though clearly Demosthenes is the real target. Or, to put it differently, by proposing that Demosthenes be awarded a crown (a civic honor) for his services to the city—"speaking and acting continually for the best interests of the [Athenian] people"—Ctesiphon has provided Aeschines with a pretext for an attack on Demosthenes.[15] Further, Ctesiphon proposes that the crown be awarded in the theater rather than the more-usual Assembly of citizens (the *ekklēsia*), so that the proclamation of Demosthenes' civic virtue can be witnessed by all Greeks. Against this proposal Aeschines brings three charges. Two are narrowly legal: first, awarding the crown in the theater violates the procedure specified by statute law; and second, it is illegal to award a crown to a public official before he has completed his term of office and undergone the required audit (the *euthyna*).

The third charge is more sweeping, and is the real substance of the case: Ctesiphon's proposal violates the law (Aeschines argues) by stating a falsehood, namely that Demosthenes has performed services that make him worthy of a crown. Demosthenes' policy of opposition to Philip of Macedon, after all, has led to the catastrophic Athenian defeat at the battle of Chaeronea and Athens's loss of political independence under Macedonian rule. As Aeschines claims, Demosthenes does not "speak and act for the best interests of the people," but irresponsibly advances his personal interests at their expense. For the city to crown such a bad and unworthy man, such a demagogue, would be shameful. Or so Aeschines argues.

Opinions are divided over the merits of Aeschines' two legalistic charges, but from that very fact it is clear that they were arguable. Firstly, the laws governing the *euthyna* requirement were ambiguous, and secondly, while there were precedents for awarding a crown in the theater, such awards did normally take place in the Assembly. The third and more sweeping charge against Demosthenes' career was likewise arguable. Although Demosthenes had retained much of his popularity—enough to be chosen to deliver the funeral oration for the dead of Chaeronea—the fact remained that his policies had badly failed (despite some initial successes). Furthermore, Aeschines was a formidable opponent, endowed by his earlier career as an actor with an impressive voice and delivery (which Demosthenes mocks as "theatrical" or "tragical"),[16] and he had narrowly defeated Demosthenes' prosecution of him in an earlier trial, winning acquittal by one vote.[17] On the face of it neither Aeschines nor Demosthenes had an open-and-shut case.

There was, then, a *stasis*, an unresolved dispute requiring a trial. It often is noted that, in Athenian legal terms, Aeschines' indictment of Ctesiphon was formally a *graphē paranomōn*, a "writ of illegality." Ctesiphon's proposal was contrary to (*para*) the law (*nomos*). But that is not the precise stasis. As taught in stasis theory from Hermagoras to Quintilian and Hermogenes, the stasis, meaning the specific point in dispute, arises from the defendant's reply to the initial charge—followed, sometimes, by the prosecutor's retort and the defendant's second reply (and so on). So what is Demosthenes' reply to the charge of illegality? An interesting if long-forgotten article[18] notes that Demosthenes' "favorite argument" in *On the Crown*, which reportedly occurs 72 times, is labeled as "*paragraphikon*" in an ancient *scholion* (a marginal note). *Paragraphikon*, also called *metastasis, exceptio,* and other names, is a term for the stasis of "objection" to the indictment or the trial itself, that is, an assertion that the prosecution is legally or procedurally improper and thus should be dismissed or transferred to a different venue. The stasis of objection is often thought of as a fallback position when the defendant's case is weak at the major stases of fact (I didn't do what is alleged), definition (what I did was not "treason"), and quality (what I did was right, or there were mitigating circumstances). Thus Demosthenes, faced with a damaging indictment that he cannot easily defend himself against, discredits the propriety of Aeschines' case 72 times, in different ways, in a sort of sustained and copious, ever-varied *ad hominem* attack meant to invalidate the prosecution itself. (See also chapter 5 by David Mirhady in this volume.)

However, while it is true that Demosthenes showers abuse on Aeschines—his mother was a prostitute, and so on—Demosthenes is not asking for the case to be dismissed or postponed or transferred to another court. He is meeting the charges head-on, promising to "give an account of practically my whole life and my political career" (*Crown* § 8), and asking for a verdict. In fact he calls upon the judges to remove Aeschines from the Athenian public sphere (i.e., by giving him less than a fifth of their votes; § 83).[19] He is, in short, aiming not for dismissal of the charge or cancellation of the trial, but for complete and total victory.

What, then, is Demosthenes' stasis-defining reply? We must go back to "quality," and to the substasis of "counterplea" (*antilēpsis*).[20] Hermogenes treats this stasis in some detail, but its essence is the denial that what one has done is wrong. Demosthenes acknowledges, on the most serious charge against him, that his anti-Macedon policy has failed. There is no denying that the Athenians were defeated on the battlefield and lost their sovereignty. *But what he did was the right thing to do, even if it turned out badly.* Indeed he offers at one point what he calls the "paradoxical" thesis that, even if the Athenians had known in advance that it would fail, they should have pursued that policy anyway, because it was the best and only course of action available to them and worthy of their traditions (*Crown* § 199).

Hermogenes further notes that the prosecution's retort to a defense based on counterplea is typically an objection that, even if the action was right, it was neither right nor legal to do it *in that way.* Such objection gives Aeschines two lines of argument:

1. Demosthenes' policy of opposition to Philip, even if right in principle, was seriously flawed in execution (or corrupt) and could have been conducted more properly (more honorably).
2. Even if it were not objectionable for the Athenians to award Demosthenes a crown for his services, the proposed procedure is improper and illegal.

The first of these objections is handled by Demosthenes' recurrent argument that, if Aeschines was aware that the policy was flawed or badly executed or corrupt when Demosthenes was advocating and pursuing it, why did he say nothing then? This is taken as evidence that the actions proposed and undertaken were the best available at the time, as acknowledged by everyone, even Aeschines; and this argument is further supported by the observation that, in fact, the actions taken under Demosthenes' leadership initially were successful and produced some good results—and even after Chaeroneia their position was better than it otherwise might have been.

The prosecution's objections to the award procedure are likewise met with a version of counterplea, but with more legal argument: it is true that Demosthenes currently holds political office and has not yet undergone his audit (although he has been audited before, and always passed); and it is true, too, that crowns normally were awarded in the Assembly (the crowns awarded in the theater typically were for foreign dignitaries). He acknowledges all that, but claims that, even so, there is ample precedent for what Ctesiphon proposes, including earlier crowns awarded to himself in the theater without any objection from Aeschines (*Crown* §§ 83, 114); moreover, the deeds for which he would be crowned, such as donating his own money to repair the city walls, were not performed as part of his current term of office and are not subject to the *euthyna* (§§ 112–13).

Someone might point out that Hermogenes lived and wrote nearly five hundred years after Demosthenes. Demosthenes was not aware of him, nor of Hermagoras (who was active ca. 150 BCE), nor any of the classical authorities on stasis theory, who all came later. But it is true, too, that Hermogenes' system is based on observation of the argumentation in Demosthenes (and other Attic orators). As Cicero's speakers argue in *De Oratore*, theory follows practice, not the other way around. Thus we find Hermogenes' system in Demosthenes' text: Demosthenes is the paradigm, the grand exemplar, for Hermogenean theory.

There is, however, an embryonic account of stasis in the *Rhetoric to Alexander* (hereafter *Rhet.Alex.*), written probably around 340 BCE, possibly by a follower of Isocrates.[21] It represents (roughly) the sorts of things that Demosthenes could have been taught as a young man, in his schooldays in the 360s. The *Rhet.Alex.* never uses the word *stasis* but does use cognate terms (formed from the ancient Indo-European root -*sta*-) and seems to anticipate the later theory. It says, "The defense speech is constituted [*synistatai*] in three ways": the defendant must show that he did not do what the prosecution alleges; or that what he did was "legal, just, noble, and advantageous to the city"; or that he deserves forgiveness (4). Here are fact, quality, and the mercy plea (which in later theory is a substasis of quality); and quality is described, in essence, as counterplea, the stasis on which Demosthenes takes his stand. His actions and the policies he pursued were legal and just, and for the good of the city—even in failure—and above all noble.

THE METHOD

The *Rhet.Alex.* offers, as well, an additional body of precept useful for the analysis of Demosthenes' argumentation in *On the Crown*: this is its account of exetastic discourse (*exetastikos logos*), and its closely related, distinctly non-Aristotelian treatment of the enthymeme (*enthymēma*) as a figure of argument.[22] Exetastic, which the *Rhet.Alex.* treats as a fourth genre in addition to deliberative, judicial, and epideictic, is basically the discourse of "examination" (*exetasis*). Its method is to focus on contradictions—*enantia*, "opposites"—in an opponent's intentions, words, deeds, and life; or contradictions between the opponent's intentions/words/deeds/life and the just, the legal, the beneficial, the habits of virtuous people, and probability. After examining the contradictions and amplifying his points, the speaker is to conclude with a concise restatement (*pallilogia*) that serves as a "reminder" (*anamnēsis*) of what has been said:[23] that is, a pithy and memorable drawing of the point. This "conclusion" or cap for an exetasis is, in essence, an enthymeme as the *Rhet.Alex.* defines it: "enthymemes [*enthymēmata*] are contradictions [*enantioumena*] not only in words and deeds, but also in anything else"; and they are invented through the methods of exetastic discourse.[24] In sum, the function of an enthymeme *as an argumentative figure* is to cap off an exetasis with an abrupt, compact, memorable, and antithetical restatement of the contradictions, so that the speaker presents his opponent (or the opponent's argument) as unjust, dishonorable, unwise, improbable, and so forth, and himself (or his argument) as the very opposite of those things. That is the basic method of Demosthenes' argumentation: he makes his case at the stasis of counterplea by a fundamentally exetastic procedure, showing the contradictions between Aeschines' words and deeds and the behavior of good citizens—the "good men" buried in the public tombs—while presenting himself, or his actions, as a fulfillment of the high Athenian ideals for which those honored dead gave their lives.

Further, he interweaves his exetastic/enthymematic arguments with a narrative of his career and the events leading up to the present situation. This narrative is broken into four main segments more or less corresponding to Aeschines' account of the stages in Demosthenes' career:[25] first, from the beginning of hostilities with Philip to the Peace of Philocrates in 357 BCE. (*Crown* §§ 17–52); second, from the Peace to renewed hostilities in 339 (§§ 60–94); third, the events leading up to the battle of Chaeroneia in 338 (§§ 132–87); and fourth, the period from Chaeroneia to the present (i.e., 330 [§§ 211–26]).[26] In essence, the segments of narrative provide the data for, and are followed or interrupted by, passages of exetastic argument, which Demosthenes characterizes as "digressions" (e.g., *exebēn*, "I have digressed," at *Crown* § 211).

This procedure has the advantage of permitting a copiously repetitive but varied presentation of Demosthenes' argument in the exetastic "digressions," while sustaining an overall feeling of progression through the narrative. One effect is that the fundamentally repetitive argument seems to unfold progressively, as what Kenneth Burke would call a "qualitative" and essentially climactic sequence.[27] Another effect of this procedure is that it permits what Ps.-Aristides recognizes as a method of *deinótēs*: "It is forceful, too, when one arranges things so as to set up well in advance what will be useful later."[28] And that is, as I have said, what we see in *On the Crown*. Through the repetitive iteration and amplification of his basically exetastic argument, Demosthenes builds, or accretes, a bundle of resonant "thoughts" that come to a head in the climactic, emotive outburst of section 208, which is an enthymematic cap. And yet it somehow comes as a surprise. And that is another characteristic of forcefulness, according to ancient theory: on one hand the audience must feel as if the idea has arisen from themselves, that it is a deeply resonant truth that they have somehow always known; but, on the other hand, they should not quite see it coming. It is not (as Longinus says of the sublime) the product of a syllogistic process leading from premises to logically predictable conclusions—even if it can be restated in that form—but of a repetitive, discontinuous, accumulative procedure that the audience cannot fully predict.

Let's look at the argument more closely. I will start with Demosthenes' prologue (sections 1–17), then take the argument in four main phases: sections 18–59, 60–101, 102–87, and 188–208.

KATASKEUĒ

Elaboration or "confirmation": the sophist returns to the chair, takes a scroll from the book box placed beside it, and turns and unrolls it on a table.[29]

THE PROLOGUE: SECTIONS 1–17

After a mostly conventional opening prayer that the jurors will judge fairly and impartially, according to their oath (1–2), Demosthenes remarks on

Aeschines' advantages in the trial (3–7). It would be, says Demosthenes, more painful for him to lose the esteem of his fellow citizens than it would be for Aeschines to fail in his prosecution; and, since people enjoy hearing scandalous accusations but resent it when people talk about their own achievements—which the nature of the case requires Demosthenes to do—Aeschines can entertain the court while Demosthenes must "irritate nearly everybody" (4). This tension-breaking bit of humor and the declaration of affection that frames it constitute more than a conventional securing of goodwill. First of all it establishes a contrast between the affable, man-of-the-people Demosthenes and Aeschines' schoolmasterish manner in *Against Ctesiphon*.[30] It is also the thin edge of Demosthenes' argumentational wedge, as it sets up a tacit contrast—which will quickly become explicit—between Demosthenes as a good friend of the Athenian people and Aeschines as no friend at all.

In sections 9–16 of the prologue, there is an exetasis on the nature of Aeschines' charges, especially those that go beyond the indictment proper to invectives on Demosthenes' moral turpitude. Demosthenes begins with a "simple and fair" reply: "If you know me to be the type of man he has accused me of being (for I have never lived anywhere but among you), do not tolerate the sound of my voice . . . but stand up and condemn me now" (10). This daring gambit may be, in itself, a micro example of *deinótēs*: the audience is placed, for a moment, in a state of suspended expectation. What will happen? Will anyone stand up? Will *many* stand up? Will Demosthenes' defense collapse right here? There is, in short, a flicker of fear that the bottom might fall out.

But nobody does stand up (apparently), and Aeschines' portrait of Demosthenes' character is thereby rendered *improbable*. According to the *Rhet.Alex.*, a "probability" (*eikos*) is "a statement supported by examples present in the minds of the listeners" (*Rhet.Alex.* 7). Demosthenes' jury, and the audience at the trial more generally, cannot recall examples that support Aeschines' invectives, which in consequence appear to be empty talk (entertaining as they are). Further, the audience-participation gambit ("stand up and condemn me now") strengthens the connection between Demosthenes and the "men of Athens" (*andres Athēnaioi*) who are his judges, while separating them from Aeschines the empty talker, the trash-talking clown, the spewer of clever but improbable insults: their not standing up is both a bodily refusal to endorse Aeschines and an act of solidarity with Demosthenes.

With this opposition (*enantion*) now established, Demosthenes introduces what will be an oft-reiterated argument.

> I have been accused of many crimes, for which the laws provide grave and extreme penalties. But [Aeschines'] purpose in this trial is not that: it is to allow an enemy to heap upon me spite, malice, dirt, and everything of that kind. . . . If he saw me committing crimes against our city which were as enormous as he has just described them in his theatrical style, he had an obligation to use the penalties which the laws provide when the crimes were being committed. . . . If he had ever clearly done this and had taken advantage of such possible measures against me, his accusation now would be consistent with his behavior in the past. As it is, he has stepped off the path of right and justice and avoided investigating my actions at the time they were done: he is playing a stage part, piling up charges and jokes and abuse much after the events. (§§ 12–15)

Aeschines did nothing, and had nothing to say, when Demosthenes supposedly was committing "crimes against our city," so that Aeschines' behavior now is inconsistent with his behavior in the past. Even now he is not indicting Demosthenes but Ctesiphon, and that is a contradiction too: if Demosthenes has committed such crimes as Aeschines alleges, why does Aeschines not indict him? It thus appears that Aeschines is not serious about his charges, and is "playing a stage part . . . in his theatrical style" (§§ 15, 13). Indicting Ctesiphon, who is easier prey, gives Aeschines an opening to smear Demosthenes without having actually to indict him or to formally prove the charges, which suggests that he is not confident about them, and is afraid to confront Demosthenes in court: indeed he has "never [dared] to meet me" on those charges, yet "seeks to deprive another man of his civic rights" merely to score points in a personal vendetta (§§ 15–16). This conduct is both cowardly and, as Demosthenes puts it, "off the path of righteousness and justice" (*exstas tēs orthēs kai dikaias hodou*; § 15).

Thus the exetasis argues that Aeschines' words, deeds, and evident intentions are inconsistent with themselves and with the just, the right, and "the habits of virtuous people," as well as probability. And Demosthenes soon will add inconsistency with the beneficial, in arguments that Aeschines not only had nothing useful to say when the struggle with Philip was developing, but was also positively harmful to the Athenian cause.

The next major segment of the speech deals mainly with Aeschines' role in the events from the outbreak of hostilities with Philip to the Peace of Philocrates (356–46 BCE). During this period Philip improved his strategic position at Athens's expense—extending his power southward into the Greek mainland—while shrewdly manipulating the diplomatic process (two embassies) that ended in the Peace of Philocrates, which more or less ratified all his gains. The Peace was so disastrous for Athens that Philocrates in 346 was indicted for treason (by Hyperides) and fled into exile.

Whereas Aeschines in *Against Ctesiphon* (§§ 58–76) portrays Demosthenes as conspiring with Philocrates (and Philip) to serve the interests of Macedon, Demosthenes reverses the picture by pointing out that he was not yet in politics when hostilities first broke out, and that the first to propose peace with Macedon were associates of Aeschines (*Crown* §§ 18, 22). From here he points up the improbabilities and contradictions in Aeschines' narrative, and constructs a highly probable counternarrative: Aeschines acted as Philip's agent, particularly in the "false embassy," while Demosthenes, once he realized what was happening, did the opposite and continually "made solemn and public forewarnings" (§ 45) about Philip and tried to contain or thwart the Macedonian advance (e.g., §§ 25–33). The exetasis then concludes with an apostrophe (in response to Aeschines' claim to be Alexander's "friend" [*xenos*, foreign guest-friend]): "Before I called you the hireling of Philip, and now [I call you] the hireling of Alexander, as do all of these [judges and spectators] here. If you don't believe me, ask them, or, rather, I will do it for you. Does Aeschines seem to you, men of Athens, to be the hireling or the friend of Alexander? You hear what they say" (§ 52). An improbable legend from the Middle Ages has it that Demosthenes deliberately mispronounced the word "hireling" here (by misplacing the accent),[31] so that the audience shouted out "hireling" to correct him. But it is inconceivable that he would resort to such a transparently cheap trick in the situation that he faced; the judges would have been profoundly offended. It is more probable that, like "stand up and condemn me now," this passage is an audience-participation gambit meant to deepen the relation between Demosthenes and his judges and to further separate them from Aeschines. The "men of Athens" stood up and denounced Aeschines as a "hireling" of the Macedonians.

Along the way to this apostrophic call and response, Demosthenes revisits the inconsistency topos: Aeschines at the time said nothing about the treasonous crimes he now says Demosthenes was committing (§ 23). But here the topos takes a new direction. If Aeschines claims that Demosthenes had both promoted the Peace and opposed it—so that the Athenians accordingly sent a peace embassy to Philip while sending others to the Greek city-states to rally them for war—that is a great slander *against the Athenians*: "For if you [were doing these things], that was an act worthy of Eurybatos, not of a city, nor of honorable men" (§ 24; Eurybatos, a Greek who betrayed the Lydian king Croesus to the Persian Empire in the sixth century BCE, was proverbial for treason). Here Demosthenes indirectly presumes complete identity between himself and the Athenian people, a point that will soon become more explicit. Both he and the Athenians who enacted his policies *could not have acted so dishonorably* as Aeschines claims, in essence *because they are Athenians*, whereas (by the antithetical logic of exetastic argument) the opposite is the case: it is Aeschines, Philip's and Alexander's hireling, who has acted in a dishonorable, un-Athenian, double-dealing way. This is the first appearance of what will become the *deinós logos* of section 208, though here it is introduced very briefly and almost in passing. It is flagged, however, with a nearly identical locution: *"But they are not true, these things, they are not true!"*: the Athenians did nothing wrong, nothing unworthy of their city (24).[32] The basic expression is not unusual, of course, but the repetitive doublets and the turbulent, interrupted syntax of both passages lend emphasis, distinction, emotional force, and memorability to the gesture of denial. The two locutions echo each other. Or, rather, the later one echoes the earlier, and is more elaborate, more resonant. But both announce the heart of Demosthenes' case: what he and the Athenians together did was the right and noble thing for Athenians to do.

At this point, then, when the jurors and spectators at the trial rise and shout "hireling" in section 52, Demosthenes' exetastic procedure already has established his major topoi: Aeschines' inconsistencies in word and deed with himself, with the behavior (the ethics) of decent people (the "good men" of Athens), with probability and truth, and with the best interests of the city—and his treasonous behavior as a "hireling" of the Macedonians and no friend of the Athenian people. Meanwhile Demosthenes has established himself as Aeschines' opposite, has strengthened identification between himself and his judges, and through the appeal to what is worthy of the city he has introduced what will become his *deinós logos*. All of this is accomplished before he turns to the actual indictment (in section 56), approximately one-fifth of the way through the speech, and begins his proper defense.

Demosthenes first promises a "simple and fair defense" that follows the order of the indictment (§§ 56–59)—first the charges against himself, then the legalistic ones. This defense, interwoven with a narrative of the period from the Peace to the outbreak of war with Philip, is the next major segment of the speech.

ARGUMENT PHASE TWO: SECTIONS 60–101

Demosthenes starts by outlining the situation in the late 340s, when Philip was maneuvering aggressively, and in violation of the Peace, to put Athens under increasing threat (§§ 60–61). He then raises the key question: "When all the Greeks were in this [confused and divided] state and ignorant of the growing and gathering danger, you, men of Athens, should consider what was the proper course of action for our city to have chosen . . . Should Athens, Aeschines, denying her pride and her dignity, have taken a position with the Thessalians and Dolopians, [thereby] obtaining the rule of Greece for Philip and nullifying the just and glorious deeds of our forefathers?" (§§ 62–63). What should *Athenians* have done, in such a situation? What should the descendants of the men who gloriously fought at Marathon (and in other battles) have done? Should they have forgotten their traditional role as saviors and defenders of Greek liberty and become Philip's helpers, and thus no different from the insignificant, ignoble Thessalians and Dolopians? Or should they have opposed him? Ostensibly this appeal to the "glorious deeds of our forefathers" is presented with emotional restraint—it is a matter of abstract principle, of civic ideology—but it is hard to overestimate the depth of reverence for the "men of Marathon" in the Athenian psyche, how central that image was to Athenian (male) identity, and how profoundly resonant. Demosthenes here invokes as a matter of deep moral principle his fundamental topos, the "thought" of his *deinós logos* regarding what action, what policy, would have been worthy of the city.

After some observations on the wretched state of most of Philip's "allies" (§§ 64–65), Demosthenes reiterates the question.

What was the right course for Athens, Aeschines, when it saw Philip attempting to gain for himself tyrannical rule over Greece? What was the only policy for a statesman at Athens . . . who knew that our country,

throughout its history, always fought for the first rank in honor and reputation, and had spent more men and money for the honor and benefit of
all than the rest of the Greeks had spent in their own behalf? . . . No one, I
suppose, would have the nerve to say . . . [that] it was proper for you, who
are Athenians, who have before you every day of your lives, in everything
you see and hear, memorials of the courage of your forefathers, to have such
cowardice so as to become volunteers in yielding your freedom to Philip.
Not a single person would say this. (§§ 66–68)

Here the moral principle is presented less abstractly, and with greater
amplification, as Demosthenes invokes the memorials "before you every
day of your lives"—some of which the jurors probably would have passed
on their way to the court[33]—and closes with the quietly emphatic, "Not
a single person would say this." Thus, on the basis of this invocation of
complete unanimity on the moral principle embodied in the "men of Marathon," Demosthenes argues that the only course of action appropriate to
an Athenian was to oppose Philip's aggression. Moreover it was, he says,
the city's choice, with his support: "this course *you* took from the beginning, [while] I proposed [decrees] and [made speeches] in the time of my
political activity" (§ 69; my emphasis).[34] Causality here is almost reversed,
as Demosthenes presents his policy as emanating *from the Athenian people*,
and then being enacted in practical politics through his agency (§ 69).
Demosthenes acts as the voice of the public will, the voice of Athens and
Athenian ideals.

In the rest of this phase of the argument (§§ 69–101), Demosthenes recounts his and the city's actions in constant opposition to the Macedonian threat—and Aeschines' constant failure to say or do anything useful.
Meanwhile the notion of Demosthenes as the voice of the people's will is
frequently reiterated. For example: "Who was it who went to the aid of
the Byzantines and saved them? Who was it who prevented the Hellespont from falling into [Philip's] power at that time? You, men of Athens.
And when I say you, I mean our city. But who was the one who spoke and
proposed and, in a word, devoted himself completely to the situation? It
was I" (§ 88). In this way, through repetition, and through a long list of the
Athenians' noble deeds (and successes) in the struggle with Philip, Demosthenes establishes and reinforces not only the antithesis between himself
and the useless (or harmful) Aeschines, but also a more or less complete
identification between himself, his policies, the Athenian people, the idea

of "Athens" as savior and protector of Greek liberty, and the iconic image of the men who fought at Marathon and elsewhere and were buried in the public tombs and celebrated in memorials. He and his judges all have acted as Athenians should, and can feel proud of themselves as worthy of the city's best traditions; only Aeschines (and his associates) think the Athenians and Demosthenes did wrongly.

This recounting of deeds is interrupted one more time by the topos of Athenian moral principle, with one new element: "Death is the end of every man's life . . . Good men must always involve themselves in every noble course, holding good hope before them as a shield, and bear in a noble spirit whatever the god sends. Your forefathers did this; your elders did this . . ." (§§ 97–98). And so on, in yet another list of noble deeds (through section 101). The key addition is the notion that for "good men" (*agathoi andres*) avoiding death is not the guiding principle of conduct, but doing what is noble (*kalos*) and "bear[ing] in a noble spirit whatever the god sends." The measure of one's deeds is not "what the god sends," whether good fortune or bad, but the nobility of one's purpose. At this point all the elements constituting the *deinós logos* of section 208 are in place. And then it goes away.

ARGUMENT PHASE THREE: SECTIONS 102–87

Here I propose to deal summarily with what are actually several parts of the argument.[35] What is chiefly notable about this material, for my purposes, is that the argument about what action was worthy of the city largely fades into the background, though it is not forgotten. The focus shifts.

First, Demosthenes completes his narrative of the early stages of the war with Philip (§§ 102–9), and then turns to his defense on the legalistic charges (§§ 110–21). I have discussed already that defense, and will pass over it here. At the conclusion of this defense Demosthenes has virtually completed his case, although he has not yet spoken of the events before and after Chaeroneia—the most difficult topic to address. But before he turns to those matters, he pauses for a personal attack against Aeschines: "because of his calumnies, and not because I am fond of abuse . . . I must state some bare facts about him" (§ 126). Aeschines comes from ignoble origins; his father was a slave; his mother was a prostitute; he acted on the stage (a lowly occupation), mostly in minor parts; he only recently became a citizen; his claims to education are a pretense; and so on (§§ 126–28; the story returns with more detail at §§ 257–65). The point of this litany (whose factuality is dubious) is that Aeschines, being ignoble, rose by selling himself and has no moral core, nor any loyalty to Athens or what it stands for. Demosthenes then cites examples of Aeschines' treachery (which he presents as familiar to everyone; §§ 132–37), and concludes with: "It was a fearful thing—Earth and the gods, how could it not have been?—to take Philip's side against our country, even before we were openly at war with him. . . . But [after the war had begun] . . . this evil man, this writer of lampoons, cannot point out anything he did to serve you nor is there any decree in the city's favor, either of large or small importance" (§ 139). But, Demosthenes adds, Aeschines spoke up more than anyone when there was an opportunity to harm the city or discourage it from taking action (§ 140).

Demosthenes then resumes his narrative, addressing the events before Chaeroneia (§§ 141–87). The chief purpose is to amplify the exetastical opposition between the nobility of his (and the Athenian people's) actions and the ignobility and treachery of Aeschines. The deeper argument established already about what constitutes noble action for an Athenian is implicit in all of this, but is not directly stated. The focus, again, is on the contrast between Aeschines and Demosthenes as embodiments (or not) of that ideal. This narrative (and its function) comes to a head in Demosthenes' highly dramatic account of the panicked emergency session of the Assembly after the news arrived that Philip had captured Elateia, and Athens (as well as Thebes) was under direct threat of an invasion. As he portrays it, at dawn, when the Assembly of citizens (numbering at least six thousand) had gathered and the Council had made its report, the herald came forward and asked, "Who wishes to speak?"

> No one came forward. The herald asked the same question again and again, but no one rose, although all the generals were present, all the orators were present, and our country was calling for someone to speak for its security. . . . The crisis of that day, it seems, called not only for the patriotic and wealthy citizen, but also for a man who had closely followed the course of events . . . and who had correctly reasoned why and with what intention Philip was acting. . . . That man, on that day, was I. (§§ 170–73)

Demosthenes, in short, enacts the Athenian ideal: amid the terror and confusion of the moment, as the Assembly sits in frozen silence, he steps forward to meet the danger and propose a plan of action. Aeschines enacts the opposite. As Demosthenes puts it, "You were entirely useless; I did everything the duty of a good citizen required" (§ 180).

And so the Athenians, accepting Demosthenes' proposal, formed an alliance with Thebes (an old enemy) and other cities,[36] took the field against Philip, and met defeat at Chaeroneia. According to ancient reports about 1,000 Athenians were killed and 2,000 captured (out of perhaps 12,000), and their allies suffered comparable losses (Diodorus Siculus 16.86). Demosthenes now approaches the topic that his narratives and digressions have slowly been working up to (and partly avoiding), namely the undeniable fact that, after all, the course of action he proposed ended in catastrophe. This fact is the ultimate ground of any retort that Aeschines might have left against Demosthenes' counterplea: even if one grants that fighting Philip was the right thing to do, it was not right to do it *in that way*, that is, to lose. Indeed there were legal penalties for the authors of policies that turned out to be harmful to the city (though Aeschines has not formally indicted Demosthenes for that).

At this point Demosthenes already has been speaking for about two hours (at a rough estimate). He has established, repeated, and augmented the argument about what policy was worthy of the city, invoked the glorious ancestors, and kept that idea reverberating (if submerged) through the copious reiteration of the antithesis between himself and Aeschines, so as to strengthen identification in the jurors' minds between themselves, Demosthenes, and the idea of Athens, and to separate them from Aeschines the un-Athenian, the hireling, the sycophant,[37] the second-rate actor, the ignoble babbler of vicious slanders, the useless caviler. There is considerable (and building) tension here, insofar as the audience is primed to accept these identifications and divisions *but* cannot get past the brute, humiliating fact of the disaster.

Demosthenes begins by (re-)asserting that no one, then or later, even in hindsight, could think of a better course of action than the one he chose (§§ 188–91), that there is no point in caviling about the outcome if no better policy was available, and that the intention and not the outcome should be the criterion of judgment: "For the final result of all actions depends on the will of heaven, but the choice itself reveals the mind of the statesman. Don't blame me for a crime, if it turned out that Philip was victorious in battle; the result here rested with the gods, not with me" (§§ 192–93). Here Demosthenes' *deinós logos*, or a part of it, begins to reappear: the policy was noble, and worthy of the city, regardless of its success or failure. In fact (according to Diodorus Siculus 16.85–86) the battle hung in the balance for a long time and could have gone either way, but eventually things fell apart for the Athenians and their allies. In the chaos and fog of war, much depends on "the will of heaven" and outcomes are unpredictable. "Good men" pursue the noble course of action and bear what the gods decide.

This point is reiterated several times, as is the portrait of Aeschines as a caviler who had nothing useful to say at the time, or even now, but blames Demosthenes for the outcome of his policy (§§ 194–98). Finally, the argument about quality of intention rather than outcome as the criterion of judgment brings Demosthenes to the "paradoxical" argument that I have mentioned before: "Since he concentrates his charges on the outcome of these events, I wish to make a rather paradoxical assertion. . . . If the outcome was entirely clear, and everyone knew about it beforehand, and you were predicting it, Aeschines, shouting at the top of your voice—you who did not utter a word—not even in those circumstances should the city have backed off from its course, if in fact it was concerned for its reputation or its forefathers or the future" (§ 199). The rationale for this "paradox" rehearses the civic ideology that has been rehearsed before, and is laid out in the solemn, balanced, epideictic manner of an *epitaphios* (a funeral or memorial speech) in praise of the Athenian progenitors who risked all to fight the invading Persians at Salamis.

> For Athenians [to voluntarily accept subjection] was not something they had learned from their ancestors, nor [was it] morally tolerable nor natural . . . No one has ever been able to persuade our city to attach herself to those who are strong, but act unjustly, and live the secure life of slavery; rather, Athens has continually fought for and taken risks for first place in honor and reputation throughout [all] time. . . . The Athenians of that day were not looking for an advisor or general who would lead them to become happy slaves, [and] did not even think it right to go on living if they could not live in freedom. (§§ 203–5)

That is, the Athenians of that day chose the noble course—defending their liberty, and that of all Greeks—even when it appeared that they had no chance. Their glory lies in the heroic nobility of their choice rather than, or more than, the miraculous victory they achieved. By implication, the rightness of the policy that led to Chaeroneia was of a piece with that nobility, though the gods decreed a different outcome.

That argument brings Demosthenes to his *deinós logos*.

I am showing you [judges and spectators] that this was your own choice, and I am pointing out that the city had this spirit before me, but I do say that I contributed some service in each of the actions you took, and that Aeschines here . . . hungers to deprive me of this [crown] and is robbing you of the praise you deserve for all future time. If you will condemn Ctesiphon on the grounds that my policies were not for the best, you will be thought to have made a mistake, and you will make it appear that the results you suffered were not due to the harshness of fate. *But it is not true, men of Athens! It is not true . . .*

And so on (§§ 206–8). Demosthenes has adroitly shifted the issue to whether the Athenians were wrong (*hēmartēthen*, were mistaken) in choosing the policies he proposed, or whether they "deserve praise for all future time." In response to that final question Demosthenes delivers his *deinós logos* as a passionate outburst that gathers force from all the identifications (and disidentifications) established and amplified in the earlier phases of his argument, and their emotional resonance, which is further intensified here by style (cadences, rhythms, etc.) and by the iconic images of the heroes "who met the charge at Marathon, and stood shoulder to shoulder at Plataea, and fought in the ships at Salamis and Artemisium, and all the rest of the good men who lie in the public tombs" (208, using my own translation).[38] Significantly *all* of these heroes are portrayed as buried in the public tombs (which contained the bones of those who had fallen in battle), and all alike in honor whether they succeeded or failed. Thus the identification established between Demosthenes, the "men of Athens" on the jury and in the crowd, and the image of Athenian greatness is complete. The men who chose to fight Philip at Chaeroneia are worthy of and consubstantial with the "good men" buried in the public tombs and celebrated in the memorials that one might pass by every day, though Aeschines would deny their greatness and deprive them of their praise. But it cannot be, it cannot be that they did wrong. This argument has overwhelming force for its audience of Athenians, and even audiences today. Aeschines' best and last retort is swept away.

And all the rest, as I have said, is rhetorical cleanup. Demosthenes presents the last part of his narrative (from Chaeroneia to the present), losing no opportunity to reiterate and amplify the antithesis between Aeschines and himself, the bad Athenian and the good, or to engage in invectives even more colorful than before (§§ 258–62). But my water clock has run out, and it is time to conclude.

EPILOGUE

The sophist comes to the front of the platform.

I will make just two short observations.

First: in his essay on "Psychology and Form," Kenneth Burke illustrates the principle of arousal and fulfillment of expectation (or "desire") with an example from Shakespeare's *Hamlet*. Someone has reported that a ghost is haunting the battlements of the castle, and Prince Hamlet joins the night watch to see if it will appear. So the audience is primed for a ghost encounter. Time passes. Hamlet and his companions fall into conversation about the drinking habits of their countrymen. More time passes. The ghost is almost forgotten. Then it appears. Burke argues that this delayed fulfillment of expectation increases the impact of that fulfillment when it arrives.

The example, and the principle, may seem rather simple. But something like it occurs in the argumentation of *On the Crown*. Demosthenes sets up a powerful argument about what an Athenian should have done—what would have been worthy of the city—and then submerges it through sections 102–87, in order to bring it back as a "forceful" outburst in section 208. It returns abruptly, as if in response to a particular point, when the audience has mostly stopped thinking explicitly about it and don't quite see it coming; but it carries with it the conviction and resonance already established. It comes back to the audience as their own thought, cathartically, as something they have somehow always known and that ennobles them and makes them worthy of their ancestors. In short, the delay (or submersion) of the *deinós logos* enhances its *deinótēs* when it suddenly reappears. Perhaps that is what Ps.-Aristides means when he says that setting up early on what will be useful later is a method of forcefulness.

On the second point I will be even briefer. In the *Poetics* (14) Aristotle says that a bare statement of a tragedy's plot should be sufficient to produce the tragic effect (a catharsis of fear and pity). Few, I think, consider that statement plausible. Surely the complete drama produces that effect much more powerfully and completely. We find, however, something similar in the notion that the *logos* of a text can be adequately analyzed by reducing it to a set of propositions, a "rhetorical syllogism" (whether in syllogistic or Toulminian form). Obviously something can be gained that way, especially for beginners, but it seems clear that a full account of an argument *and its impact* requires considering that argument as a *process of argumentation*. "The argument" is not the skeletal substructure of propositions that a text can be reduced to, but the surface that the audience encounters, in all its fine-grained detail, minute by minute. The *deinós logos* that appears at section 208 of *On the Crown* can be considered an enthymematic cap as discussed in the *Rhetoric to Alexander*, but what it caps—and directs into a particular stance—is the accumulated potential of all the arguments, examples, exetases and so on that lead up to it.

This "surface" process is, on the one hand, extremely simple. But on the other hand, it is extraordinarily complex in its operation, and difficult to describe precisely. (Perhaps the best explanation would be a *performance* of the text, an oral interpretation, or a translation.) I think my effort at describing the *deinós logos* of *On the Crown*, like my effort to translate the climactic outburst, necessarily has fallen short. *Deinótēs*, like sublimity, exceeds what can be reduced to rule: sublime and forceful rhetors are seldom perfect, and perfect rhetors (like Hyperides) are seldom forceful or sublime. But I hope that I have at least arrived at a moderately persuasive understanding of Demosthenes' awesome argument.

But now it is time for me to entertain your questions and replies.

The sophist returns to the chair.

Who wishes to speak?

NOTES

The translation of the epigraph is mine; elsewhere I follow the Keaney translation reproduced in this volume. All other translations of Greek sources are mine unless otherwise stated.

1. Longinus, *On the Sublime* 34.4.

2. Longinus 1.3–4. Keep in mind that Longinus's treatise is titled *Peri hypsous*, "On the highest" [eloquence]; the translation of *hypsos* as "the sublime" (and all that that entails) is a modern phenomenon.

3. See Demetrius, *On Style*; Hermogenes, *On Types [of Style]*; Pseudo-Hermogenes, *On the Method of Forcefulness*; and Pseudo-Aristides, *Rhetoric*, books 1–2. Of these four texts, all but Ps.-Aristides are available in English translation; for Ps.-Aristides in French, see Michel Patillon, ed. and trans., *Pseudo-Aelius Aristides, Arts Rhétoriques* (Paris: Les Belles Lettres, 2002).

4. Ps.-Aristides, 1.124.

5. Demetrius, *On Style* 243.

6. Demetrius 240–43; Longinus 7.2–3.

7. Plato, *Menexenus* 235a-b.

8. Chaim Perelman and Lucie Olbrechts-Tyteca, *The New Rhetoric: A Treatise on Argumentation* (Notre Dame, IN: University of Notre Dame, 1969): 140.

9. J. C. Trevett, "Aristotle's Knowledge of Athenian Oratory," *Classical Quarterly* 46, no. 2 (1996): 371–79.

10. Plutarch, *Demosthenes* 9, 11; on Demetrius of Phaleron see Diogenes Laertius 5.5. I discuss this point a little more fully in *"Pathos* and *Katharsis* in 'Aristotelian' Rhetoric: Some Implications," in *Rereading Aristotle's Rhetoric*, ed. Alan Gross and Arthur Walzer (2000).

11. Aristotle, *Rhetoric* 1.1.4–5.

12. Aristotle, *Rhetoric* 1.1.3–6, 3.1.4–5, and 3.7.

13. Metochites, *Sententious Observations* 5.4 in Karin Hult, ed. and trans., *Theodore Metochites on Ancient Authors and* Philosophy (Göteborg, Sweden: Acta Universitatis Gotoborgensis, 2002), 64–65. Thanks to Vessela Valiavitcharska, who pointed out this passage.

14. See Jeffrey Walker, *The Genuine Teachers of This Art: Rhetorical Education in Antiquity* (Columbia, SC: University of South Carolina Press, 2011).

15. The text of Ctesiphon's proposal has not survived but appears to be echoed in the language used by Aeschines and Demosthenes: see *Ctesiphon* 49 and *Crown* 57, which both look like direct quotation.

16. Demosthenes says Aeschines has *etragōidei kai diexēiei* his supposed crimes (13), which Keaney renders as "described in his theatrical style." Harvey Yunis offers "recount[ed] in that tragic voice of his," which I think better. See Harvey Yunis, trans., *Demosthenes: Speeches 18 and 19* (Austin: University of Texas Press, 2005). A more literal (and barbaric) rendering would be "tragedized and described."

17. See Demosthenes' *On the False Embassy* and Aeschines' defense-speech *On the Embassy*, in Yunis, *Speeches*, and Chris Carey, trans., *Aeschines* (Austin: University of Texas Press, 2000).

18. Francis P. Donnelly, "The Argument Used 72 Times in the Crown Speech of Demosthenes," *Classical Weekly* 28.20 (1935): 153–56.

19. From here I will be using in-text parenthetical citations for *On the Crown*, e.g., "(*Crown* § 208)," since they will be frequent and essential to my discussion, and flipping back and forth to the endnotes would be cumbersome.

20. Malcolm Heath, *Hermogenes On Issues* (Oxford: Oxford University Press, 1995), whose translations of the terminology I am following.

21. Pierre Chiron, ed. and trans., Pseudo-Aristote: Rhétorique à Alexandre (Paris: Belles Lettres, 2002), and "The *Rhetoric to Alexander*," in Worthington, ed., *A Companion to Greek Rhetoric* (Oxford: Blackwell, 2007): 90–106. See also Walker, *Genuine Teachers*.

22. *Rhet.Alex.* 5, 10, and 37.

23. *Rhet.Alex.* 37.

24. *Rhet.Alex.* 10.

25. Aeschines, *Against Ctesiphon* 163–64ff.

26. Yunis, *Speeches*, 30–31; Carey, *Aeschines*, 163–64.

27. Kenneth Burke, *A Rhetoric of Motives* (1931; Berkeley: University of California Press, 1968).

28. Ps.-Aristides 1.124.

29. This "book box" is a *capsa*, the ancient equivalent of the briefcase—a hat-box-shaped affair used for transporting books (papyrus scrolls) and other documents.

30. For example: "You are well aware, men of Athens, that there are three kinds of constitution in the whole world . . . With this firmly in mind, you should hate people who draft illegal decrees . . . Another thing you should bear in mind is . . ." (*Against Ctesiphon* 6, 7, 8).

31. *Místhōtós* for (the correct) *misthōtós*, which probably got into the manuscripts originally as a transcription error.

32. Translation masks the similarity of these two locutions. Compare: *all' ouk esti tauta, ouk esti* (24) vs. *all' ouk estin, ouk estin hopōs hēmartet, andres Athēnaioi* (208). (The dropping of the *n* from *estin* is determined by phonetic context.) Keaney translates this locution in section 24 with the lackluster "it simply is not so."

33. For example, the "Painted Stoa" (*stoa poikilē*), which was decorated with paintings of battle scenes from Marathon and Troy, was situated just off the northern edge of the Agora, and thus close to the jury courts.

34. Keaney's translation of this sentence, while correct, is not completely satisfactory; I present an edited version here.

35. See Yunis, *Speeches*, 31.

36. As Yunis, *Speeches*, 24, points out, the Theban alliance was a brilliant "diplomatic coup" for Demosthenes.

37. The term "sycophant" (*sykophantēs*) typically signified hired gun (or bribed) accusers and orators who acted as front men for others who wanted their enemies dragged into court, or proposals that served their interests moved in the Assembly, without having to reveal themselves or to personally risk the dangers of a trial. Demosthenes at one point (189) describes Aeschines as a sycophant.

38. In particular the *sound and rhythm* of the gesture of swearing by the ancestors has, in the Greek, considerable intensity: *mā tous Marathōni prokinduneúsantas tōn progónōn . . .*

8. DEMOSTHENES' STYLE: *LEXIS* IN *ON THE CROWN*

Richard Leo Enos

> The specific activity of the philologist is contextualizing conceptually
> distant texts. For many philologists in the past that was the only goal,
> an annotated edition of a written or oral text. . . . Notice that language,
> in these instances and always, communicates on at least two levels, the
> actual surface content of the message (the proposition being asserted, re-
> quested, questioned, etc.) and the relational statements that are conveyed
> simultaneously, more often by intonation, posture, facial expression, and
> the like, than by direct statement.
> —A. L. Becker, *Beyond Translation: Essays toward a Modern Philology*

Demosthenes' fame as a Greek orator is largely attributed to his mastery of style. His ability in the rhetorical canon of style transcended his own time and culture. Although many of Demosthenes' orations have been preserved and translated, his *On the Crown* is widely acknowledged to be his stylistic masterpiece. Dionysius of Halicarnassus considered Demosthenes' speech to be the finest example of style in all of Greek oratory.[1] No less an orator than Marcus Tullius Cicero considered Demosthenes' ability and range of style to be a model for Roman rhetoric, as it had been for the Greek rhetoric that preceded him.[2] In fact, Cicero even attempted to translate *On the Crown* into Latin so that his Roman readers could appreciate Demosthenes' eloquence.[3] Modern efforts to study Demosthenes' style have emphasized

174

the philological nuances of his Attic prose by isolating and examining his use of figures and the cadence of his prose rhythm. Only within the last several decades, however, have scholars of rhetoric come to realize that an understanding of Demosthenes' style requires moving beyond the aesthetic features printed on paper. Capturing the fullness of Demosthenes' style in *On the Crown* requires a reconstruction of the rhetorical context within which Demosthenes performed his oration for Athenian listeners. Sensitivity to the political climate and social situation that prompted Demosthenes' oratory provides a more accurate, thorough, and representative accounting of his style than merely examining words in a vacuum. In addition, another critical challenge, one of shared importance to sensitivity to the actual utterance of *On the Crown*, is the task of capturing his style for readers of English. However, if we only restrict our examination of style to a listing of philological features of Greek grammar when examining the English translation, we will find ourselves not only self-constraining our appreciation of Demosthenes' style at the moment of utterance, but also find ourselves saying more about the skill of the translator than the stylistic artistry of Demosthenes. This chapter seeks to complement philological studies of the style of Demosthenes' *On the Crown* with a rhetorical analysis of the contextual and extralinguistic features not readily apparent from a strictly literary analysis of his Attic Greek but nonetheless indispensible in understanding the full range and impact of his style.

WHAT REVEREND KING TEACHES US ABOUT DEMOSTHENES

One of the commonplaces of design is that "form follows function." That is, the shape that an object takes is in large part determined by the task that it is constructed to perform. In many ways, this commonplace of design is helpful in understanding the style of Demosthenes' *On the Crown*. That is, we can better understand the style of Demosthenes if we first understand the context of his oration. In short, just as function is to design, so also in oratory does the "function" (the rhetorical context) influence the "form" (the style) of the address. Rhetorical context here means not only the immediate moment of utterance but also the larger social and political temper of Demosthenes' tumultuous times. Part of this larger sense of context also includes the mentality of Demosthenes and his fellow Athenians.[4]

Oratory was viewed as a source of power in antiquity and essential for effective leadership. For classical rhetoricians such as Isocrates, and later for Cicero, the potential "to harness wisdom with eloquence" (*prudentiam cum eloquentia iungere*) was a valuable and essential feature of rhetoric.[5] At various times our own country has heard great orations, speeches that served to guide by uniting wisdom and eloquence.[6] In this respect, what we have learned from the life of Rev. Martin Luther King Jr. and his *I Have a Dream* speech teaches us much about appreciating and approaching the style of Demosthenes and *On the Crown*.

To fully appreciate masterpieces of eloquence we must recognize the way Demosthenes' listeners viewed the world and their own people. For example, when Martin Luther King Jr. gave his famous *I Have a Dream* speech at the steps of the Lincoln Memorial in Washington, D.C., on August 28, 1963, America was a nation torn apart with civil unrest, devastated by blatant racial prejudice, and lacking a clear vision of procedure and resolution. King's eloquence provided a view that revealed both a vision and a path on how to attain what he later called the journey of racial equality to the "Promised Land." Over a half-century later, King's speech still resonates with wisdom and eloquence, in large part because his oration was not only sensitive to the mentality of his listeners, but also demonstrates that Rev. King was acutely aware of the shared values that united Americans and the need to ease the tension of the times within which he spoke. Equally, *I Have a Dream* was effective because of the style of King's presentation. Although racial equality in America was seen as a civil rights issue, King articulated his vision in the style of an epideictic oration that was sermonic in tone. The values that he preached transcended his cause from a civil to a moral issue. King was an effective preacher, and we can appreciate his style best by understanding that he not only transformed the March on Washington from a civil rights demonstration to a religious gathering, but also because he transformed his civic speech into a sermon by employing a homiletic style that turned his listeners into believers. Words on the page alone do not capture King's sermonic style and, to that degree, limiting our notion of style to a printed text only barely reveals the power of his oratorical style as a persuasive force.

If we recognize such factors that we see in King's speech when Demosthenes presented his *On the Crown* we will be able to appreciate in a much more sensitive way the power of his style. Our understanding will go beyond what could be realized from a direct reading of the Greek, what goes beyond a traditional literary analysis that concentrates only on isolating and enumerating the aesthetic features as a way of revealing his mastery of Greek grammar. Rather, we will be able to appreciate the style of Demosthenes in a rhetorical sense. That is, we will see the style of Demosthenes as a force that engaged the reasoning and sentiments of his fellow Athenians; the sense, feeling, tone, and intention of his utterance literally provided a voice for what he felt was the vision of Athens. This rhetorical sense of style, the understanding of style as a persuasive and motivating force, is essential if we are to more fully appreciate the effectiveness of Demosthenes' presentation. To do so, however, we must—as indicated above—reconstruct the moment and environment within which *On the Crown* was delivered.

GREEK EARS AND ENGLISH EYES: THE DIALECT OF DEMOSTHENES AND THE PROBLEM OF STYLE IN TRANSLATION

EMIC/ETIC FUNCTIONS AND STYLE

One of the difficulties in capturing the (oral) style of Demosthenes' *On the Crown* is that we are moving from an emic (first-language) mode of Greek expression to an etic (second-language) mode of English expression. This transfer difficulty is further challenged because we are moving from orality to literacy. An accomplished logographer, or writer of speeches, Demosthenes was meticulous in his preparation of speeches by writing out his orations beforehand.[7] That is, Demosthenes' practice was to compose his speech by writing it out (a mode of secondary rhetoric) in order to then present it orally (primary rhetoric). Our understanding of some of the basic components of style—sense, feeling, tone, and intention—are thus qualified by the uniqueness of this phenomenon. That is, we lose some of the dynamics of his oral style when we (silently) read his speech in English and in isolation. For example, a stylistic figure such as *paromoiosis* requires the sound between the words of two Greek clauses to be parallel for rhetorical effect. Finding the best English words for capturing this tonal symmetry would be a challenging task for the translator, such as in this passage from *On the Crown* with the repetition of the Greek preposition *anti* that is translated here as "instead of":

(§ 229).... Instead of the Thebans joining Philip in an invasion of our land, as all expected, my policy, which Aeschines attacks, caused the Thebans to line up with you to check Philip; (§ 230) instead of the war being fought in Attica, it was fought eighty miles from the city at the farther boarders of Boeotia; instead of pirates from Euboea plundering and pillaging, the side of Attica on the sea enjoyed peace throughout the war; instead of Philip seizing Byzantium and holding the Hellespont, the Byzantines fought with us against him.

However, *paronomasia*, or wordplay, would be less challenging for a translator to capture, but would still require an awareness of Athenian public knowledge in order to ensure that the etymology of a word's meaning would be understood by Demosthenes' listeners. This wordplay is evident when Demosthenes claims that Aeschines tries to confuse or deceive listeners by calling Demosthenes a "sophist, and similar epithets" (*"sophisten kai ta toiaut onomazon"*) when these are the very qualities that Aeschines himself exhibits (§ 276). In short, reading sentences silently, and without a contextual knowledge of the audience's mentality, provides few cues as to how Demosthenes emphasized his words in his oral performance and what effect the particular meaning of those words had on his listeners. That said, understanding the context can help us to provide an index of meanings, ranging from sincerity to irony.

DELIVERY WEDDED TO STYLE IN ORALITY

Another feature that is difficult to capture in English translation is Demosthenes' tone, the "topography" of his style. Just by tone, a speaker can imply meanings that range from irony to outrage.[8] Reading *On the Crown* silently only allows one sense, sight, to appreciate the style of Demosthenes—the viewing of translated words on a printed page. If we could have had the luxury of hearing and seeing *On the Crown* as originally performed by Demosthenes, we could better appreciate his tone, his vocal emphasis, his pacing, his volume. We would also have a direct experience in observing the listeners' reactions to his speech and have a better sense of how they received his style. Further, because of the very nature of his Greek, Demosthenes was able to use pitch to stress his tone. In fact, as Richard Upsher Smith Jr. explains, the term "accent" in Greek "means the spoken pitch of a particular syllable in a word."[9] For all practical purposes, we English speakers have no systematic use of pitch in prose in the Greek sense of the term that compares with Demosthenes' Attic Greek because in Latin and English accent means stress and is determined by the length of the penult; that is, when the penult is long, it will receive the stress in the word.

Pitch, in the Greek sense and use of the term, was clearly a force in Demosthenes' style that is difficult to capture in an English translation. For example, in Aristophanes' *The Birds* (*Aves*), Aristophanes has his characters use pitch to "chirp" their lines.[10] Audiences hear not only the words but have another range of meaning from the vocal tone that is possible with the ancient Greek. Christopher Lyle Johnston has done acoustical studies of the sound constraints at the Athenian Pnyx.[11] His research, done directly at the archaeological site, makes it clear that effective style was bound with delivery, for an orator such as Demosthenes—without the aid of any technology beyond the topography of the setting—had to have the pitch to carry the force of his style to large audiences without screaming or shrieking. Delivery, in a word, is wedded to style in orality but difficult to capture when accessed only through literacy. For example, the Greek term for "baritone" (Gr. *barutonos* or "deep-sounding") would have been an acoustical feature of style, but we lack the resources and technology to retrieve this feature of Demosthenes' performance.[12] Demosthenes himself considered delivery (*hypokrisis*) to be the most important factor in oratory.[13] Merely reading his words silently on the page does not capture this important dimension of Demosthenes' speech. Dionysius of Halicarnassus recognized this problem and encouraged his readers not merely to read Demosthenes but to try to deliver his speeches in the way that they believed they would have been spoken.[14]

DIALECT TO GRAPHOLECT

There are other factors of orality and literacy that also must be considered in order to have a sense of Demosthenes' effective style. A native Athenian, Demosthenes spoke in the Attic-Ionic dialect of his region. His dialect would be a point of identification for his Athenian listeners and readers. There are five major dialects (that we know of) in ancient Greece: Arcado-Cyprian, Aeolic, Attic-Ionic, North West Greek, and Doric.[15] Demosthenes' *On the Crown* was delivered in some form of the Attic-Ionic dialect. The Attic-Ionic dialect would have been, in short, the native (emic) style of his fellow Athenians; they would have heard ideas expressed in a manner, in a cadence, and with terms that they would have recognized as "Athenian" at heart. The importance of speaking in a native dialect should not be minimized. Antebellum orators, for example, identified with their listeners of the Old South by sharing a dialect that was alien to northern ears but harmonious with the tonal quality of southern culture. Demosthenes' (oral) dialect was not only the one used in Athens but also was synonymous with the best stylistic form of expression for formal address and (written) literature or grapholect. Thus, when this speech became "literature"—when it was removed from the rhetorical situation and recorded in order to be preserved for posterity—the same Attic-Ionic style would also have been the style of choice for the best of Greek literature. This selection of *a* dialect becoming *the* grapholect is the same as Italy selecting the Tuscan dialect of Florence as *the* grapholect for "proper" literature and making the Tuscan dialect the national language of Italy; that is, the dialect of Florence was selected to be the national "Italian" language. Just as King's *I Have a Dream* speech moved from an oration delivered at and for a particular event to become universalized, enduring literature, so also did Demosthenes' *On the Crown* move from oral rhetoric to literature. In the spirit of Father Walter Ong's discussion of orality and literacy, both masterpieces moved from their respective dialects to enduring grapholects—*On the Crown* and *I Have a Dream*—forever preserved by being expressed in the proper (literate) style.[16]

PROSE RHYTHM AND ORAL STYLE

There are features of style in Greek rhetoric that are nearly impossible to "translate" into English, one of which is prose rhythm, a concept of style in oratory that Jebb believed Isocrates perfected to the point that "in forming the literary rhetoric of Attica, Isokrates [*sic*] founded that of all literatures."[17] Ancient rhythm uses ◡ as a short syllable and a — for a syllable twice as long. Thus, the dactyl is —◡◡ or 2:2, the iambic is ◡— or 1:2, and the paean is ◡◡◡— or —◡◡◡ or 3:2/2:3. However, there is a range and interplay to such schemes, if we understand that ◡◡ equals —, so that the two can be substituted for variety. As A. D. Leeman points out, the longness and shortness of syllables precludes the "flow" (*ruthmos*) of the rhythm and the quality of the style.[18] There also is a definite, conventional prose rhythm for each level of style in classical rhetoric: iambic (◡—) for the plain style; dactylic rhythm (—◡◡) for grand style; and the paean (◡◡◡— or —◡◡◡) for the middle style.[19] Demosthenes was an expert in prose rhythm, his composition of long and short syllables provided a lyrical quality that enhanced his arguments with his Attic listeners. Just as we would admire the poetry of Homer for not only the epic story but also for its dactylic hexameter verse, so also was Demosthenes admired for the cadence of his periodic structure and its rhetorical force in persuasion. Cicero commented in his *Orator* that "those lightning bolts of his [Demosthenes] that vibrated so intensely would not have been hurled so vehemently, if they had not been carried by prose rhythm."[20] W. H. Shewring argues that Demosthenes' favorite rhythm clause is —◡◡—◡.[21] Interestingly, Cicero's own preferred rhythm clause of —◡—◡ is amazingly similar to Demosthenes.[22] As Harvey Yunis explains, however, Demosthenes had no consistent pattern of prose rhythm but uses a variety of metrical devices throughout *On the Crown.*[23] Ancient rhetoricians, such as Aristotle, believed that different types of prose rhythm were appropriate to different levels of style.[24] *On the Crown* varies in plain, middle, grand, and even (at times) forceful styles.[25] In fact, Dionysius of Halicarnassus believed that one of the greatest strengths of Demosthenes' style was his range and his judgment on how to adapt his style to different audiences.[26] Part of the genius of Demosthenes' style is his interweaving of a variety of styles with the appropriate prose rhythm in order to maximize rhetorical effect.[27] This range and variety of prose rhythm and different levels of style would have been a force influencing Athenians hearing his oration, but that feature of style is lost in the translation for English eyes that are limited only to reading his address in another (but now silent) "tongue."

THE RHETORICAL CLIMATE: THE SOCIAL CONTEXT OF 338–330 BCE

It is important to know the rhetorical climate in which Demosthenes lived in order to appreciate the context of his argument. The Battle of Chaeronea was a confrontation in 338 BCE between the Macedonian army of King Philip, and his son Alexander, against Athens and other Greek city-states.[28] Philip was victorious while Demosthenes, who strongly advocated and pushed for the confrontation, was criticized for his policies and allegedly (and probably unfairly) for his lack of valor during the fighting. About two years after the Battle of Chaeronea Philip was assassinated and Alexander assumed the Macedonian kingship. Many saw this moment of change as an opportunity to counter Macedonian hegemony. Thebes tried and tested the young Macedonian king; they were overwhelmed by Alexander. Through his stunning victory, Alexander served notice not only to Thebes, but also to Athens and the rest of the Greek world, that the power wielded by his father Philip would continue with Alexander. In short, the rhetorical climate created and stimulated by Philip's threat of domination was continued under the reign of Alexander.

It is this rhetorical climate that provided the exigency calling Demosthenes to trial. In one sense, Demosthenes' *On the Crown* was six years in the making; 336 BCE was the charge—the same year that Philip was assassinated and Alexander assumed the kingship of Macedonia—and 330 BCE was the trial. Such a period of time is an index of its importance and place. There was a pro-Macedonian contingent in Athens—important citizens who, if not happily allied with Macedonia, clearly saw the advantages of

Panhellenic unity. One such proponent was Aeschines. During this period, however, Alexander turned his attention and energy away from the wrangling of Greek city-states. Alexander's interest in the East, in conquering Persia and expanding his empire into India, gave Athenians such as Demosthenes hope, a hope fired by the belief that Alexander could never defeat the Persians on their home soil. Athenian hopes were dashed by Alexander's stunning victory at the Battle of Issus in 333 BCE and his subsequent conquests. Yet, as reports came back to Athens that Alexander was going eastward, the chances of his surviving and returning west were diminished.

These factors reached a head in 330 BCE, about eight years after the Battle of Chaeronea. Cteisphon's proposal to award Demosthenes a crown for his public service to Athens would be taken as a civic endorsement of Demosthenes' position against Alexander. In short, the defense of Ctesiphon came to issue at the instigation of the Athenian pro-Macedonian party in order to crush the political power of Aeschines' hated rival, Demosthenes, but also to solidify the pro-Macedonian party's power in Athens. Clearly, there was more at issue than Demosthenes receiving the crown. The real issue on trial was foreign policy; specifically, the direction that Athens would take in respect to Alexander and who would lead them in that direction (§ 52). Rival political views made the vision of Athens an unstable one and it is these larger issues that Demosthenes' faced in *On the Crown* and that help to explain the magnitude and severity of his style. In essence, public knowledge was uncertain, for rival views were being considered, and Demosthenes felt that anything other than Athenian democratic hegemony was a threat to his city. His rhetoric in *On the Crown* was not just about his own vindication, but the endorsement of his policies and programs, a reaffirmation of the sort of public knowledge that would do nothing less than (again) send Athens into battle against Alexander, if need be, in order to ensure the best interests of Athens.

THE RHETORICAL SITUATION

"THE WOLF IS AT THE DOOR!": MENTALITY, URGENCY, AND STYLE

What do these factors tell us about the rhetorical climate, the rhetorical situation, and how they bear on Demosthenes' style in *On the Crown*? Historians of this speech reveal that this rhetorical situation is unique and is a factor in understanding Demosthenes' style. On the one hand, Demosthenes was brought to trial approximately six years after the initial charges.

The motives for the delay by Aeschines and his colleagues are a point of speculation, but (as we have seen) it is clear that events that unfolded over those six years, and reached a head shortly before the speech, were meant to serve as a way of undermining Demosthenes' anti-Macedonian sentiment and to discredit his power and leadership in Athens. Thus, although the events spanned several years, Demosthenes' style grows out of a sense of urgency. The issues that Demosthenes addressed in *On the Crown* are urgent because of his belief in the imminent threat of battle with Alexander. In fact, Plutarch wrote that Demosthenes considered Alexander the "Macedonian lead-wolf" (*Makedóna monólukon*).[29] To borrow a Roman expression, Alexander was the wolf "at the door!" who was poised to attack. This exigency doubtlessly influenced the severity of his style and the engagement of his listeners.

Style is meaningful when stakes are high and issues are highly contested. There was much at stake here in Demosthenes' defense, *On the Crown*. This serious situation fitted the normal style of Demosthenes: serious, intense, emphatic. Demosthenes' situation, and the eloquence of his style, is a response of importance in the same respect that Abraham Lincoln responded to the Civil War with his *Gettysburg Address*, that Winston Churchill responded to the Nazi threat to the British in his *Blood, Toil, Tears and Sweat* address, and that Rev. Martin Luther King Jr. responded to racial inequality in the United States with his *I Have a Dream* speech. Each responded well to the seriousness of the situation with a style that matched the importance of the event. While the situation or event does not control the style, we can see that eloquence is achieved when the orator selects a style that is in such harmony with the problem that the context for the speech transcends the moment and endures as a lesson to recall when similar moments of crisis occur.

RHETORICAL IMMINENCE AND DEMOSTHENES' SEVERE STYLE

On the Crown is devoted to a serious subject, and Demosthenes addressed these issues in the oration seriously. He had a clear, fixed view of Athens and was convinced that his vision was the proper course to take at a time when the very existence of Athens was threatened. By all accounts, Demosthenes was zealous in his love of Athens, often to the point of being accused of being a "frenzied patriot" whose jingoistic "jeremiads" "raised paranoia to an art form."[30] Although his views on Athenian democracy were highly contested, Demosthenes spoke sincerely and from a fixed point of view. He was secure in his principles and motives for what he believed to be best for Athens. That is, the starting point of his oration presumes fixed values on the importance of preserving the sovereignty of Athens, the value of freedom, and the hegemony of the city-state, and opposition to all forms of threat and control by Alexander. The personal conviction and self-assurance of his views gave stability to the premises of his arguments. In one respect, this view is akin to the one that Richard Weaver argued for in understanding the eloquence of the Old South.[31] Weaver believed that southerners shared a view of the Southland and therefore orators did not need to "win" over the audience to their premises; that is, orators presumed that the values of all that the South meant to antebellum listeners were secure in their history and legacy. This stability of shared values between orator and audience left southern orators free to launch ideas into higher levels resulting in eloquence. In brief, Demosthenes' high style came from a secure, fixed belief in his values, and that starting point allowed him to launch into eloquence. Style is much more than the isolation and identification of literary techniques but the belief in shared values between rhetor and audience.

DEMOSTHENES' STYLE IN RELIEF:
CONTRASTING STYLES WITH AESCHINES

In order to appreciate fully Demosthenes' *On the Crown*, we must first understand that his oration was a response to Aeschines' *Against Ctesiphon*. From this perspective, examining only the oration of Demosthenes gives us only half of the rhetorical dynamic. No small portion of Demosthenes' *On the Crown* is devoted to counterattacking the claims, credibility, and character of his arch-rival orator, Aeschines.[32] Aeschines was older, an actor of fame, a rhetorician, and a political opponent of Demosthenes. Some of Aeschines' speeches survive today, and we are especially fortunate that one of the surviving orations is *Against Ctesiphon*, the speech that argued against Demosthenes being awarded a crown for public service. It was this address by Aeschines that brought the rhetorical situation to a head and prompted Demosthenes' reply, *On the Crown*. Although it is not our place here to analyze Aeschines' oration or his style, it is nonetheless important to see to what charges Demosthenes was responding. Essentially, Aeschines' argument against Demosthenes being awarded a crown clashed on three major points of *stases* or issues. First, Aeschines argues that the awarding of a crown to Demosthenes violates many technical requirements of both protocol and procedure. Second, Aeschines argues that as a candidate, Demosthenes is unworthy of receiving this honor. Third, Aeschines claims that awarding Demosthenes a crown would not only be detrimental for the first two reasons but also would have immediate and long-range political consequences that are not in the best interests of either Athens or Greece as a whole.

One of the factors necessary for an oratorical masterpiece is that the issue be of direct, immediate, and enduring importance, that the point of dispute has real consequences. As Donovan J. Ochs has argued, Demosthenes considered Aeschines' challenge as a personal attack and *On the Crown* is best understood, from that perspective, as an apologia.[33] As we have seen from our understanding of both the rhetorical climate and the rhetorical situation, the Athenian audience was well aware that the "problem" was much more than Demosthenes being publicly recognized for service to the city. Demosthenes had been awarded crowns in the past.[34] The awarding of a crown was, in fact, not an uncommon event, and there were protocols in place for such ceremonies at the Theater of Dionysius. In fact, Demosthenes even tells us that the location for his receiving the crown was the theater [§ 120], which we may take to be the Theater of Dionysius, located immediately next to the Agora. The real issue was that recognizing Demosthenes would have been seen as an endorsement not only of his public service but also of his public policies. Such an endorsement would include Demosthenes' opposition to the growing hegemony of Alexander, a factor that could upset the delicate balance of policies and position of negotiation that Athens had with Macedonia and other city-states.

Aeschines' policies and style contrast greatly with those of Demosthenes in tone and perspective. Aeschines was one of the ten Attic Orators of classical Athens. Known to rhetoricians chiefly as a respected actor who became an eloquent spokesperson on Athenian civic policy, Aeschines was often chosen to be one of Athens' ambassadors or *presbyters* and sent on embassies to be a spokesperson for Athens.[35] On such embassies, Aeschines would accompany other prominent *rhetores*, such as Demosthenes, and articulate his and the city's political position to powerful leaders such as Philip and Alexander. Similar to Isocrates, Aeschines often pled for peace. Unlike Isocrates, Aeschines argued for a peace that would not *de facto* subordinate Athens to Macedonia. Aeschines' primary opposition came from Demosthenes, who viewed both Philip and Alexander as distrusted enemies who could only be stopped by war. In stark contrast to Demosthenes' reactionary "Athens first" view, Aeschines had a conservative but moderate style to accompany his conciliatory foreign policy. Aeschines was much more inclined toward a Panhellenic, pro-Macedonian view, believing that working with King Philip and (at the time of his speech against Demosthenes) his son Alexander was the best route for Athens to take for long-term security.

From the perspective of Aeschines' *Against Ctesiphon* we can better appreciate how well Demosthenes directly and forcefully challenged the points made by Aeschines. That is, Demosthenes' *On the Crown*—in broad terms—is also divided into three major sections. In the first part of the oration, Demosthenes seeks to refute the assertions that he should not be awarded the crown on technical grounds. In the next major part of the speech, Demosthenes defends his ethos by discussing his personal integrity, courage, and abilities through his service and steadfast devotion to Athens. Moreover, Demosthenes seizes the opportunity to heighten his own merits by contrasting his ethos with Aeschines to the point of ad hominem attack. Third, Demosthenes devotes much of the latter part of his oration arguing that the consequences of his view will not mean the demise of Athens, but rather a response that is in harmony with Athens' venerable history of meeting challenges to the city's freedom with the same sort of heroic courage and conviction as did their ancestors. One of the factors that makes *On the Crown* such a stylistic masterpiece is that Demosthenes and Aeschines were in direct, clear opposition to one another. Just as with the maxim of Greek theater—"no conflict, no drama"—so also did the conflict between Aeschines and Demosthenes produce great (real-life) drama. They dramatically differed in all the major points and directly clashed in all the major issues or points of *stases*. Thus, we can appreciate the merits of Demosthenes' *On the Crown* not only for its intrinsic features but also by seeing it in contrast with Aeschines' views.

Demosthenes structured his oration to promote the contrasting styles between himself and Aeschines. As mentioned, Aeschines was not only an accomplished orator but also a renowned actor. The Greek word for actor is similar to our term "hypocrite" or "pretender" (*hupokrités*). Demosthenes exploits this meaning to stress the sincerity of his own beliefs with what he characterized as the insincere manipulation of the pragmatist Aeschines who is "like an actor in a tragedy" (*tragoidíai*, § 127). In fact, later in the oration, Demosthenes refers to Aeschines in hostile terms, calling him a "bit-actor of tragedies" (*etritagonísteis*, § 265). Demosthenes' intensity provides an indirect message of his sincerity and, in contrast, he hoped to heighten the credibility of his message by portraying Aeschines as a smooth-talking, expedient manipulator and opportunistic sycophant. In fact, Demosthenes makes note of this very issue in *On the Crown* by claiming that Aeschines wants this case to be reduced to a mere sophistic "contest of eloquence and declamation" (§ 276–80). Demosthenes urges his listeners not to judge differences between Aeschines and himself as an oratorical contest but rather on the issues at stake.

There is good reason to ask why Demosthenes' attack on the character of Aeschines is so vitriolic, why his outrage seems to know no limits. Could Aeschines really have been as despicable as Demosthenes portrays him to be in *On the Crown*? Ochs offers a cogent explanation for Demosthenes' scathing style of address toward Aeschines. Ochs characterizes his agonistic, forensic rhetoric as akin to the *pankration*, a no-holds-barred Olympic event where victory often came at the near-death submission of the opponent.[36] There is little doubt that the audience was well aware that Demosthenes was engaging in *hyperbole* and *amplificatio*, that his exaggeration was done only to ignite the emotions of listeners in the way that today's professional wrestlers will bait the crowd in order to whip them into a frenzy. One of Demosthenes' greatest talents of style, Ochs points out, was his "superior command of portraiture," and Demosthenes was a master at painting his opponent, Aeschines, in the darkest of colors.[37]

As is well known, there was an agreement that the loser of this decision had to leave Athens. After Aeschines lost, he went to Rhodes and established a school of rhetoric.[38] One of the stories, however, is that the students of Aeschines heard him repeat his oration and praised their teacher for his eloquence. Aeschines is said to have replied that if they thought well of his own oration they should have been present to hear Demosthenes speak![39]

A SYNOPTIC VIEW OF DEMOSTHENES' STYLISTIC STRATEGIES

Demosthenes begins *On the Crown* in a quasi-religious tone by evoking the gods (§ 1). The sense of seriousness immediately induces a feeling of the weight and importance of the *kairos* or rhetorical situation of the moment. On trial is not only the justification for his receiving a crown for public service to Athens, but that such acts signal public approval for the political policies that Demosthenes advocates. Demosthenes also establishes for his audience the burden he carries on the defense and its inherent nobility over the unjustified accusations of the prosecution.[40] "Good men," he asserts, "must always involve themselves in every noble course" (§ 97). Demosthenes meticulously challenges the technicalities and veracity of Aeschines' accusations. In fact, much of the early and middle sections of *On the Crown* are devoted to presenting various forms of nondiscursive evidence to counter the charges of Aeschines.

The major stylistic strategy of Demosthenes throughout the oration is to contrast and thereby distance himself from Aeschines. Refuting the technicalities of Aeschines' charges, and especially Aeschines' claim of the inappropriateness of the awarding of the crown to Demosthenes, is addressed early and in a matter-of-fact style. However, the inherent strategy of Demosthenes' style is in attacking Aeschines' motive, intent, and character. Demosthenes calls Aeschines "the hireling of Philip, and now, the hireling of Alexander" (§ 52). Conversely, Demosthenes portrays himself as acting in the best interests of Athens as a patriot (e.g., §§ 57, 86, 321) while Aeschines takes Philip's and Alexander's side (e.g., §§ 139, 143).

In addition to challenging and contesting Aeschines' motives and intent, Demosthenes contrasts his own ethos with Aeschines. That is, Demosthenes' style is to present his character as being the opposite of Aeschines. For Demosthenes, as mentioned earlier, Aeschines has the character of a hypocrite (§§ 282–83). Demosthenes uses ad hominem attacks in order to contrast his character with the ignoble sycophant Aeschines. Virtually every aspect of Aeschines' life is mocked by Demosthenes. In one of the earlier parts of *On the Crown* (§§ 126–36), Aeschines' lineage, education, and integrity are disparaged mercilessly. At the same time, Demosthenes contrasts his own social status, education, service to Athens, and sincerity. These character attacks are repeated with the same detail in the latter parts of the oration (e.g., §§ 282–84).

Demosthenes had a reputation for using antithesis as an oratorical style.[41] By contrasting his own ethos with Aeschines' character, Demosthenes sought to destroy any credibility of Aeschines as a trustworthy source. This "betrayal" is heightened beyond the validity of Aeschines' accusations of Demosthenes to a larger issue for Athens: one of patriotic zeal versus inherent injustice (§ 286). Through such stylistic contrasts, Aeschines stands for nothing less than the "betrayal of the foundation of Greece" (§ 297). By such contrasts, Demosthenes coexists with the long-distinguished heroes of Athenian democracy and Aeschines with their opposites. Demosthenes is explicit in inviting such comparisons of his character with Aeschines (§ 315) and his other contemporaries who doubtlessly would have been familiar to his listeners (§§ 315–19). Through such antithetical structuring of stylistic opposites, Demosthenes hopes to make imminent the *krisis* or central point of issue between himself and Aeschines: the dangerous situation of Athens in the climate of his times (§ 220, 248). The strong emotive appeals that dominate the later portions of *On the Crown* are intended to intensify the worth and urgency of the contrasts that have been stylistically composed throughout the speech. Such a strategy should have not only attracted listeners to Demosthenes as one who stands for only the best for Athens but also repulsed listeners away from Aeschines to his opposite, Demosthenes, since Aeschines' policies, motives, intent, and character are all presented as a betrayal of Athens and a mockery to Athens's long-fought-for history of freedom from tyranny.

THE TECHNICAL FEATURES OF DEMOSTHENES' RHETORICAL STYLE: MACROSCOPIC AND MICROSCOPIC STYLE

FORENSIC IN FORM, EPIDEICTIC IN STYLE

Harvey Yunis has edited a volume of the Greek text of *On the Crown*, and his detailed scholarship provides a thorough, excellent analysis and commentary of the text and a philological analysis of Demosthenes' Attic Greek.[42] Our task is to examine the English translation offered in this volume in a manner that reveals the power of Demosthenes' style. In this respect, we treat style not in terms of its literary aesthetics but rather as a persuasive force of Demosthenes' rhetoric. That is, we examine Demosthenes' style in order to better understand how he moved his listeners and secured their agreement over Aeschines.

In a literal, technical sense, Demosthenes' speech was situated in the genre of forensic rhetoric; Demosthenes, and all he stood for, was on trial. Much of *On the Crown*—particularly the first part of the oration—is devoted to answering and refuting the technical charges brought against his being awarded a crown for distinguished service to Athens. Yet, in its performative style, *On the Crown* is much like an epideictic oration.[43] Yunis argues that Demosthenes' speech is "agonistic rather than epideictic."[44] However, for reasons expressed throughout this chapter, the claim is made that *On the Crown* is forensic only in appearance and form but epideictic in reality and performance. In fact, Yunis even acknowledges that while "Athenian forensic speeches seldom open with a prayer," Demosthenes begins by evoking the gods in order to provide "a weighty communal enterprise."[45] Such a beginning is clearly epideictic in spirit. Demosthenes even reminds his listeners of his "solemn prayer" later in the oration (§ 142). Demosthenes treats the issues not only as a specific charge against him but also as a ceremonial occasion to make moral judgments by praising his own virtue and condemning Aeschines' vice.

Treating this forensic oration as an epideictic oration permits a forceful and, particularly in the latter parts of the oration, a histrionic style to be much more appropriate and compatible with the mode of his address than would be an appropriate level of style for a forensic oration. As mentioned earlier, we have seen such transformations in style occur in American oratory. For example, those who have seen *and* heard Martin Luther King Jr.'s *I Have a Dream Speech* will witness how his speech begins as a public civic address but evolves into a highly charged emotional sermon.[46] Just as King's speech evolved into a sermonic style that highly engaged his listeners, so also did Demosthenes transform his oration from a forensic into an epideictic mode that warranted his highly emotive style. The latter part of his oration is an intense emotional plea that is predicated on securing his listeners' agreement of the earlier parts of *On the Crown*.[47]

THE DUNAMIS AND ENERGIA OF DEMOSTHENES' STYLE

It is important to remember that we likely could find the name for a stylistic figure in every sentence of Demosthenes' *On the Crown*. Listing and identifying specific figures will reveal the command that Demosthenes had for his control of Attic Greek, but it will not give us a complete understanding of why these techniques of style were so full of rhetorical force. In Book 1 of his *Rhetoric*, Aristotle described the capacity of rhetoric as a *dunamis*, as a potential power that could be energized into discourse; in fact, the term that Aristotle used to show how this potential *dunamis* was unleashed is *energia*.[48] These concepts are critical to understanding the force of Demosthenes' style. Demosthenes' metaphors, similes, and all the other specific stylistic techniques were energized by the force of his character. That is, *On the Crown* is constructed to reveal the character of Demosthenes: his sincerity, his conviction, his love of Athens. This persona energizes his stylistic techniques and gives them meaning. Demosthenes was very sensitive to the fact that the audience, his Athenian listeners, were the ones who judged the validity of his argument (§ 196).[49] His style would fall flat if his listeners believed that he was duplicitous, a hypocrite, if he was insincere. "Who would not have killed me," Demosthenes questions, "if I had attempted, even with words, to bring shame upon any of the noble traditions of our city" (§ 101)? It is for this reason that much of the early parts of *On the Crown* are case-building efforts to warrant his patriotism, his love of Athens, his obligations as a citizen. Securing this ethos gives his stylistic techniques credibility; they justify his forceful, passionate style, which dominates much of the later part of the oration.

One factor that helps to grasp the style of Demosthenes is stichometry. Traditionally, we think of stichometry as the study of the "rows" (*stichoi*) of lines in the scroll that composed (in this case) the speech that Demosthenes wrote out. This numbering of rows was functionally important for the scribe to log the length of the scroll. Of course, the length was an approximation because no two writers wrote the same length of line. In our case, however, we can see stichometry in a more rhetorical sense. That is, by looking at the oration in units, we can discern patterns that will help to review the style of Demosthenes. These clusters are not so much units of rows but rather clusters of thought-patterns that show how Demosthenes structured his meaning. In a larger, more macroscopic sense, we would think of this feature of style as falling under *taxis* or arrangement, where larger portions of the oration are placed in rubrics in order to follow the line of argument. Here units are more microscopic and observed so that we can focus on how ideas are expressed in discrete chunks that help to explain the momentum of style that Demosthenes builds as he nears the ending of his oration. Cicero recognized this aspect of Demosthenes' style in his *Orator* when he observed how *On the Crown* started in a very subdued (*pressius*) style but intensified in emotion as the oration developed.[50]

It is important not to merely list the stylistic features of *On the Crown* but rather to understand their sequencing and interplay. The overarching stylistic feature of *On the Crown* is called here "chiastic contrasting." That is, Demosthenes' intent was to show that he was the antithesis of Aeschines, the very opposite of all that Aeschines stood for, and to secure the agreement of the audience in the process. Demosthenes uses all three classical appeals in *On the Crown*: ethos, logos and pathos. In the earlier part of the speech Demosthenes concentrates on logos by countering the technicalities of the charges against his being awarded the crown for his distinguished service to Athens. He also sought to magnify his ethos by contrasting his character with Aeschines. These two appeals are done to secure a justification for his righteous indignation and an unleashing of his emotive appeals of pathos. This orchestration is called "reasoned action" or justification based on good reasons to warrant the strong emotional appeals inherent within the issues.[51] In short, every stylistic device used in *On the Crown* is done for the instrumental effect of chiastic contrasting. All stylistic devices were done to praise Demosthenes and his cause and to condemn Aeschines and his cause.

CHIASTIC CONTRASTING

In Demosthenes' use of antithesis we can see style in two respects. One, as mentioned earlier, is an overarching, macroscopic style called chiastic contrasting. Chiasmus (Greek, *chiasmos*) is a Greek rhetorical figure of style. The term *chiastic contrasting* comes from the twenty-second letter of the Greek alphabet (*chi*) and is written as X. In oratorical style, *chiasmus* is the structuring of discourse in contrasting parallelism; that is, terms or phrases are uttered in reverse order. In Greek style parallelism, the structure of oratory was a prominent feature and falls under the general label of *Gorgianic figures*.[52] The general balancing of the parts of a sentence—called *isocolon* and *parisosis*—occurs when the clauses are balanced evenly. These and other features of style were attributed to the sophist Gorgias of Leontini, who perfected this art in rhetorical discourse.[53] One of the most important rhetorical functions of figures of speech, according to Dionysius of Halicarnassus, is that they help to elicit emotion, and one of the most important of these figures is antithesis.[54]

The rhetorical intent of *chiasmus* is to establish polar-opposite contrasting meaning. Terms often appear as model/antimodel opposites so that listeners—in this instance—come to see one concept as the direct opposite of another. Normally, one concept is seen as valued and the other as its opposite vice. Christians, for example, are taught to believe through chiastic contrasting that the opposite of God is the Devil, that the opposite of heaven is hell, that the opposite of grace is sin, etc. The intended rhetorical effect of chiastic contrasting is that it not only associates concepts as being in direct opposition, but it also encourages listeners to be repulsed from the lack of value of one concept and to be moved toward what they are encouraged to believe to be its direct, highly valued opposite. For example, Christian preachers give sermons of "fire and brimstone"—such as Jonathan Edwards's *Sinners in the Hands of an Angry God*—in order to have believers so terrified of Satan that they are repulsed away from Satan and moved toward the opposite, God, by "having the hell scared out of them."

Chiastic contrasting is, as stated earlier, the dominant, overarching feature of style in Demosthenes' *On the Crown*. All other stylistic techniques and figures are used to illustrate, heighten, and intensify the view that Aeschines and his cause are the direct opposite of Demosthenes and his cause. In this sense, the intersection of the *chi* (X) is the *stasis* or central point at issue of the case and Demosthenes' efforts are to move his Athenian listeners from that point to his side of the argument. We can see the orchestration of chiastic contrasting in the following passage (§ 265): "Compare the kind of lives each of us lived, calmly, Aeschines, not bitterly. Then ask these jurors whose luck each of them would choose. You taught school, I attended school. You initiated people, I was an initiate. You were a minor clerk, I was a member of the Assembly. You were a minor actor, I was a spectator. You were hissed off the stage, I joined in the hissing. Your policies supported our enemy, mine, our country." Demosthenes' major effort of style is to contrast himself with Aeschines. This dissociation is done to create polar opposites. All that Demosthenes is and stands for is the best for Athens. All that Aeschines is and stands for is the worst for Athens. Secure in his justification and agreement with the audience, Demosthenes can then unleash emotional tirades (e.g., § 123) because his discourse has established a view of reality where his listeners are encouraged to believe every positive value to be associated with his cause.

EXAMPLES OF STYLISTIC TECHNIQUES AND FIGURES USED TO FOSTER ANTITHESIS

THE SCAFFOLDING OF DEMOSTHENES' STYLE

Demosthenes uses a variety of techniques of chiastic contrasting to create antithesis in *On the Crown*. The three most common are: (1) metaphor and simile; (2) ridicule in the form of ad hominem attack and invective; and (3) the juxtaposition of concepts through prose-rhythm. These techniques are the scaffolding upon which Demosthenes constructs his style. In metaphor and simile, Demosthenes presents a common point of understanding, one that would be widely recognized by his listeners (e.g., §§ 194, 243, 299, 300, 308). He then draws from that public knowledge features that he wishes to compare and contrast either with his own acts or those of Aeschines. Demosthenes also constructs arguments based on ad hominem attack in an effort to undermine the credibility of Aeschines and, by contrast, enhance his own ethos (e.g., § 284). We should note, also, that Aeschines was not above using ad hominem attack, for Demosthenes indicates his resentment toward Aeschines for calling him "Battalos," which may have been meant to imply a lack of courage and decisiveness in the conflict against Philip and Alexander, or, as Yunis maintains, may have been a reference to Demosthenes' early tendency to stammer when he spoke (§ 180).[55] Finally, Demosthenes will, as discussed earlier, juxtapose ideas and highlight distinctions through the tone of his prose rhythm. The variety of the cadence of his prose rhythm allowed him to compose arguments that contrast in plain, middle, grand and even a forceful style. Demosthenes builds on such scaffolding through the use of rhetorical figures, and the principle ones are offered below.

REPETITION AND REDUNDANCY

Demosthenes' *On the Crown* uses repetition and redundancy to highlight chiastic contrasting. There are many forms and variations of repetition and redundancy in Greek that are done for rhetorical effect. Demosthenes will, for example, repeat a word or phrase (*anadiplosis*) with the intent of highlighting the coexistence of ideas or of dissociating the appearance from the reality of acts, such as when (as discussed earlier) he describes himself as a sincere citizen in contrast to Aeschines who is portrayed by Demosthenes as merely an actor or "pretender." On occasion, Demosthenes will repeat concepts at the beginning of a word or phrase (*anaphora*) or when beginning one idea by repeating a key word or phrase that was the last word of the preceding sentence (*anastrophe*) as is evident in this passage through the extended use of metaphor and rhetorical questions.

(§ 301). . . . Was it not to gain Euboea for Attica as a shield against attack from the sea, to gain Boeotia against attack from the plains, to gain the states on our southwestern boarders against attack from places in the Peloponnese? Was it not to ensure that provisions of grain would be shipped along friendly coasts until they reached Peiraios? (§ 302) Was it not to secure some of these areas, Prokonnesos, the Chersonese, Tenedos, by sending troops to help them and by advising and proposing such measures; to make other areas, Byzantium, Abydos, Euboea, dependable friends and allies? Was it not to cut off the principal resources of the enemy and to supply resources which Athens lacked?

As is also evident in the above passage, Demosthenes frequently will repeat the same word, phrase, or clause (*antistrophe*) in order to contrast his views from Aeschines' position (*antithesis*). Finally, Demosthenes will use redundancy (*pleonasm*) not merely to add unnecessary, superfluous verbiage but rather to intensify, or vividly give presence to, the emotional impact and implications of his argument in the way that Renaissance writers would use a conceit to elaborate or embellish a metaphorical point. This redundancy, like *asyndenton*, is done by duplicating correlative phrases or clauses with coordinating conjunctions (e.g., §§ 241, 304). When done to intensify contrasting phrases, a *pleonasm* facilitates the balanced symmetry of chiastic contrasting well. We can see these techniques in use when Demosthenes says (§ 179): "All, together, praised my advice; no one opposed it. I did not speak, but fail to propose measures; I did not propose measures, but fail to serve as ambassador; I did not serve as ambassador, but fail to persuade the Thebans; from beginning to end I preserved and faced, without reserve, the dangers threatening the city."

RHETORICAL ELLIPSES

Although *On the Crown* was meticulously prepared and composed, Demosthenes often will use *ellipses* for rhetorical effect in order to give the appearance of natural, spontaneous discourse. Some forms of *ellipses* employed by Demosthenes for rhetorical effect include phrases where he expresses doubt or shock (*aporia*) about particular acts or occasions, such as when he says to Aeschines (§ 22), "What was the proper word to describe you?" Demosthenes will exhibit shock at his opponent Aeschines by expressing passion that forces Demosthenes to become—for a moment—speechless (*aposiopesis*). Demosthenes will characterize a charge of Aeschines as so absurd that it does not warrant refutation or even merit discussion (*paraleipsis*). Thus, by the silence of omission, Demosthenes counters the assertions of Aeschines by having his listeners infer that no reasonable person would give credence, or even respond, to the absurdities of Aeschines' remarks.

For rhetorical effect, Demosthenes will use *ellipses* by sometimes *not* repeating a critical phrase (*brachylogy*) so that his listeners may fill in (or in this case, repeat) the unstated idea and thus participate with Demosthenes in the completion of the figure by making the meaning themselves. In other words, by intentionally omitting key concepts, he invites listeners to participate by completing the meaning for themselves. Moreover, while such responses appear to be spontaneous, it seems clear that Aeschines spoke first and that Demosthenes must have had knowledge of the specific charges against him beforehand and stylized his "reactions" for rhetorical effect. These planned reactions become apparent when we remember that the details of Ctesiphon's degree served as the basis for Aeschines' prosecution (§ 53).

This feature of Demosthenes' style of *ellipses* is akin to the use of the enthymeme in rhetorical invention where, as Lloyd F. Bitzer has shown, the willful omission of parts of the enthymeme by the rhetor invites listeners to complete the argument in their minds by filling in the missing premises.[56]

Although Demosthenes will omit key concepts, he also will often repeat or anticipate Aeschines' views but recast them in a way that best facilitates his opposition (*hypophora*). In a similar fashion, Demosthenes will also try to draw in his audience through the use of rhetorical questions (e.g., §§ 28, 63, 72, 85, 121). At times he will ask listeners directly, but he will also question Aeschines, such as when he directly challenges Aeschines by saying, "What was the right course for Athens, Aeschines, when it saw Philip attempting to gain for himself tyrannical rule over Greece?" (§ 66). All such stylistic techniques seek to induce engagement for listeners while heightening confrontation with Aeschines.

All such figures—and only some are presented here for the sake of illustration—are done for the instrumental purpose of constructing the overarching, macroscopic style of *On the Crown*: chiastic contrasting. That is, Demosthenes uses stylistic figures to provide a symmetry of opposition, one that intensifies the diametrical opposition between Demosthenes and Aeschines. Demosthenes accomplishes this contrasting antithesis throughout the oration by creating a coexistence that all that Demosthenes does is of virtue and in the best interests of Athens, and all that Aeschines does is of vice and in the worst interests of Athens. Demosthenes' stylistic features are summarized in the table.

In the epigraph to this chapter Alton Becker discussed two dimensions of translation. One is to treat the words on the page and limit our efforts to providing meaning that comes from the text itself. The other dimension that Becker so wisely called our attention to was the effort of the translator to capture all the other factors and features that provide meaning. Becker's insights have guided my analysis of style in Demosthenes' *On the Crown*. We have sought to understand all those other complexities that shape our understanding of style by seeing the mentality and social climate of Demosthenes' times as "rhetorical"; that is, by reconstructing the historical climate and context, we hope to yield a more sensitive understanding of how individuals thought, how they viewed the world, and how they structured the meaning of their thoughts and interactions. An understanding of cognitive and cultural factors helps us to understand how and why Demosthenes

DOMINANT STYLISTIC FEATURES OF
DEMOSTHENES' *ON THE CROWN*

Overarching Stylistic Feature: Chiastic Contrasting

DEMOSTHENES	AESCHINES
Politician	Actor
Sincere	Hypocrite
Justice	Injustice
Appropriate	Inappropriate
Positive Character	Flawed Character
Educated	Trained
Moral	Immoral
Integrity	Expediency
Idealistic	Pragmatic
Athenian Democracy	Macedonian Tyranny

STYLISTIC TECHNIQUES USED TO FOSTER ANTITHESIS

Metaphor and Simile
Ridicule: Ad hominem Attack and Invective
Juxtaposed Prose Rhythm

STYLISTIC FIGURES USED TO FOSTER ANTITHESIS

amplificatio, anadiplosis, anaphora, anastrophe, antistrophe, antithesis, aporia, aposiopesis, asyndenton, brachylogy, ellipsis, homoeoteleuton, hyperbole, hypophora, isocolon, paraleipsis, parisosis, pleonasm

MODE OF ADDRESS

Forensic Rhetoric in Form and Appearance
Epideictic Rhetoric in Display and Performance

STYLISTIC STRATEGY OF REASONED ACTION

Logos Appeal: devoted early part of oration to refuting technical charges of the illegality of the crown

Ethos Appeal: devoted body of oration to establishing credibility, competency, and character as a public servant, and by contrasting his ethos with Aeschines

Pathos Appeal: used established Logos and Ethos Appeals as justification for intensified Pathos Appeal in the latter parts of the oration responded to the particular situation by delivering his *On the Crown* oration. From this perspective it is clear that *On the Crown* was not only a response to the charge made by Aeschines on the appropriateness of Demosthenes being awarded honors for public service, but, more importantly, how the act of such recognition would influence Athenian public policy and the likelihood of another confrontation with Macedonia. When we bring these other dimensions into our analysis we can better understand how his listeners responded and why the oration has endured as a masterpiece of eloquence. *On the Crown* is a masterpiece not only for its aesthetic features but because of the elegant message it delivers by uniting wisdom and eloquence during a time of crisis.

At the conclusion of his commentary on the style of Demosthenes, Dionysius of Halicarnassus claimed that, more than anything else, persuasion requires a mastery of style that will make it possible for a rhetor to elicit emotion, assert morality, and demonstrate force.[57] We have also come to appreciate how closely style is wedded to the other canons of rhetoric. Style, for Demosthenes, was much more than merely "packaging" for the delivery of his arguments. Demosthenes recognized that he had good reasons that warranted his receiving the crown. However, he also recognized that merely listing those reasons would not be sufficient motivation to persuade both the jurors and the public in attendance. Demosthenes sought to have his Athenian listeners share in his view of the reality of his times. To do so, he sought to convince his listeners that he stood in for the heroes of the past, that his way of responding to the crisis of the times was in harmony with those earlier Athenians who made choices and sacrifices for the betterment of the city. Demosthenes wished his listeners to see him as a contemporary manifestation of the best of their past. He wished to have listeners identify with him and his cause because it was congruent with the very heritage and nature of the soul of Athens.

Demosthenes not only used his mastery of style to identify with Athens's past heroes, but also used style to portray Aeschines and his conciliatory view of Macedonia as the diametrical opposite of all that he advocated. That is, Demosthenes' overarching stylistic method of chiastic contrasting was done not only for stylistic effect but also to structure how his view of the political realities of the situation is the polar opposite to Aeschines' position. Demosthenes used a multiplicity of stylistic figures to construct an antithetical view for his listeners. All that he stood for was virtue and all that Aeschines stood for was vice. These methods of style were evident in every form of Demosthenes' classical appeals. His early sections emphasized logos to make the technical accusations for his not receiving a crown appear both trivial and ridiculous. The main body of his oration stressed his ethos in many ways: his civic functions for municipal operations, his justification for the position he took that led to the disastrous consequences in the Battle of Chaeronea, and his invective and unabashed ad hominem attacks by contrasting his own character traits with those of Aeschines. Finally, Demosthenes utilized the last section of his oration through appeals to pathos. Secure in the belief that he had already contrasted his position with that of Aeschines by dismissing the absurdities of the technical charges, and had also established his own ethos as the antithesis of Aeschines' character, Demosthenes concluded with a strongly worded emotive appeal that identified his cause with the best of Athens's past and Aeschines' policies with its destruction.

Why should we consider Demosthenes' *On the Crown* to be a masterpiece of style? Demosthenes seized the opportunity by taking a situation that was intended to discredit him publicly and using that moment of *kairos* to transcend the moment and provide a view of both the soul and vision of Athens. In some ways, *On the Crown* persuaded his listeners to remember Athens. Demosthenes used the rhetorical situation as a paradigm for how to respond to a force that threatened the very identity of Athens. Through his command of style, Demosthenes was able to have his listeners not only share his view of the reality of the situation but his view of Athens's history. Demosthenes needed to be masterful in style for it would not be enough merely to convince his listeners; Demosthenes needed to persuade them to act and, if need be, to fight again for their cause as their forefathers had done.

The greatest *epitaphios* to Demosthenes was written by Werner Jaeger in his essay, "Demosthenes: The Death-Struggle and Transfiguration of the City-State."[58] Jaeger believed that Demosthenes possessed "a profound historical sense of the destiny of Athens and himself, and a profound determination to meet it."[59] The genius of Demosthenes was that, through his passionate style, he was able to raise political oratory—for this was not only a forensic speech but also a political statement—to the height of a literary art.[60] In the beginning of this chapter we saw how Demosthenes, along with Lincoln, Churchill, and King, were capable of using oratory to shape public knowledge, and the very will of their listeners, by expressing ideas so profoundly that the oratory transcended the rhetorical moment and endured. It is no secret, as Jaeger points out, that in times of crisis Demosthenes has been both lauded and vilified. Demosthenes spoke when some of the most influential Athenians—such as Isocrates and Aeschines—wished to move from their history and into an era that signaled the rise of Panhellenism and the death of the city-state. Demosthenes resisted and clung firmly to his city's past glory and independence. What Jaeger termed "spirited nationalism" under Macedonian rule would have meant for Demosthenes compromising the values of his ancestors and submission to live under the tyranny of Philip and Alexander.[61] Like all great oratory of this nature, Demosthenes' passion is motivated by, and grounded in, a sermonic quality. The hierarchy of his values was, he believed, consistent with the heroes of his ancestors, and he was asking his listeners to do nothing less than follow in their footsteps during this crisis in their history. "That," wrote Jaeger, "was the style which expressed the tragedy of his age."[62] To Jaeger's words can be added the idea that style was also the force that made *On the Crown* endure, for tragedies would continue to unfold in history, and many times this masterpiece of eloquence would be reborn to speak again to listeners needing and seeking wisdom united with eloquence in a time of crisis.

NOTES

1. Dionysius of Halicarnassus, *The Critical Essays: On the Style of Demosthenes*, 14.

2. Cicero, *Orator*, 31. 110.

3. Cicero, *De optimo genere oratorum*, esp. 17–18, 20–23.

4. Richard Leo Enos, "Theory, Validity, and the Historiography of Classical Rhetoric: A Discussion of Archaeological Rhetoric," in *Theorizing Histories of Rhetoric*, ed. Michelle Ballif (Carbondale: Southern Illinois University Press, 2013), 8–24.

5. Cicero, *Tusculanae Disputationes*, 1. 4. 7. This theme is inherent in Isocrates, *Antidosis*; Cicero, *De inventione, De oratore*. Richard Leo Enos, *Greek Rhetoric before Aristotle*, rev. ed. (Anderson, SC: Parlor Press, 2012), 171.

6. Donald C. Bryant, "Literature and Politics," in *Rhetoric, Philosophy, and Literature: An Exploration*, ed. Don M. Burks (West Lafayette: Purdue University Press, 1978), 95–107, 114–15.

7. Plutarch, *Moralia: Vitae decem oratorum, Demosthenes* 848C (abbreviated in this work as VDO but also appearing elsewhere as X orat.).

8. Dionysius of Halicarnassus, *On the Style of Demosthenes*, 53–54.

9. Richard Upsher Smith Jr., *A Glossary of Terms in Grammar, Rhetoric, and Prosody for Readers of Greek and Latin* (Mundelein, IL: Bolchazy-Carducci Publishers, 2011), 11; Dionysius of Halicarnassus, *On the Style of Demosthenes*, 48.

10. W. B. Stanford, *The Sound of Greek: Studies in the Greek Theory and Practice of Euphony* (Berkeley: University of California Press, 1967), *passim*.

11. Christopher Lyle Johnstone, "Greek Oratorical Settings and the Problem of the Pnyx: Rethinking the Athenian Political Process," *Theory, Text, Context: Issues in Greek Rhetoric*, ed. Christopher Lyle Johnstone (Albany: State University of New York Press, 1996), 97–127.

12. Smith, *A Glossary of Terms*, 13.

13. Plutarch, *VDO: Demosthenes*, 845B.

14. Dionysius of Halicarnassus, *On the Style of Demosthenes*, 53–54.

15. Enos, *Greek Rhetoric before Aristotle*, 215–28.

16. Walter J. Ong, SJ, *Orality and Literacy: The Technologizing of the Word* (London: Methuen, 1982; rpt., London: Routledge, 1993), *passim*.

17. Richard C. Jebb, *The Attic Orators from Antiphon to Isaeos* (rpt. New York: Russell and Russell, 1962), 2:432.

18. A. D. Leeman, *Orationis Ratio: The Stylistic Theories and Practice of Roman Orators, Historians, and Philosophers* (Amsterdam: Adolph M. Hakkert, 1963), 1:150.

19. Cicero, *Orator*, 57.191–93.

20. Cicero, *Orator*, 70.234.

21. W. H. Shewring, "Prose-Rhythm and the Comparative Method," *Classical Quarterly* 25.1 (1931), 18–19.

22. Shewring, "Prose-Rhythm and the Comparative Method," 19; L. P. Wilkinson, *Golden Latin Artistry* (Cambridge: Cambridge University Press, 1963), 156–57.

23. Harvey Yunis, *Demosthenes: "On the Crown"* (Cambridge: Cambridge University Press, 2001), 24.

24. Aristotle, *Rhetorica* 3.8 (1408b–1409a).

25. For a discussion of the forceful style, see Demetrius, *De Elocutione*, especially 5.240–304.

26. Dionysius of Halicarnassus, *On the Style of Demosthenes*, 8, 14, 15, 33, 44.

27. Dionysius of Halicarnassus, *On the Style of Demosthenes*, 48–50.

28. I was at the battle site at Chaeronea in 1974, and it is an enormous sweeping valley, a plain where one could easily envision two massive armies colliding on a grand scale. Fittingly, the small museum at Chaeronea houses a bust of Plutarch, the biographer of Demosthenes, and the place of Plutarch's birth.

29. Plutarch, *Vitae Parallelae: Demosthenes*, 23.4.

30. Edward M. Harris, *Aeschines and Athenian Politics* (Oxford: Oxford University Press, 1995) 110, 141, 153; see also George A. Kennedy, "The Oratorical Career of Demosthenes," in *Demosthenes' On the Crown: A Critical Study of a Masterpiece of Ancient Oratory*, ed. James J. Murphy (New York: Random House, 1967), 28–47, esp. 45.

31. Richard M. Weaver, "The Spaciousness of Old Rhetoric," in *The Ethics of Rhetoric* (Chicago: Henry Regnery Co., 1953), 164–85.

32. For a thorough account of the long-standing and intense rivalry between Demosthenes and Aeschines, see John Buckler, "Demosthenes and Aeschines," in *Demosthenes: Statesman and Orator*, ed. Ian Worthington (London: Routledge, 2000), 114–58.

33. Donovan J. Ochs, "Demosthenes: Superior Artiste and Victorious Monomachist," in *Theory, Text, Context: Issues in Greek Rhetoric and Oratory*, ed. Christopher Lyle Johnstone (Albany: State University of New York Press, 1996), 129–31 *et passim*.

34. Plutarch, *VDO: Demosthenes* 846A.

35. Plutarch, *VDO: Aeschines* 840B.

36. Ochs, "Demosthenes: Superior Artiste and Victorious Monomachist," 135, 140–43.

37. Ibid., 139.

38. Plutarch, *VDO: Aeschines* 840D; Richard Leo Enos, "The Art of Rhetoric at Rhodes: An Eastern Rival to the Athenian Representation of Classical Rhetoric," in *Rhetoric before and beyond the Greeks*, ed. Carol S. Lipson and Roberta A. Binkley (New York: State University of New York Press, 2004), 183–96. The site of the school is believed to be just on the outskirts of the main city at a place called Rhodini Park. Efforts to find traces of the school itself, other than the literary testimony of Plutarch and other ancient scholars, has been fruitless. Even a visit to the site itself, which I did in 1983, provided no additional evidence.

39. Plutarch, *VDO: Aeschines* 840 D-E; Yunis, *Demosthenes: "On the Crown,"* 13, n. 53.

40. The inherent "nobility" of defense over prosecution became a commonplace for Cicero. In fact, in his *In Verrem*, Cicero even portrayed his prosecution of Gaius Verres as really a defense of the people of Sicily whom Verres had mercilessly exploited while governor of that province: Richard Leo Enos, *The Literate Mode of Cicero's Legal Rhetoric* (Carbondale: Southern Illinois University Press, 1988), 59–77.

41. Plutarch, *Vitae Parallelae: Demosthenes* 9.5; Dionysius of Halicarnassus, *On the Style of Demosthenes* 4, 25.

42. Yunis, *Demosthenes: "On the Crown,"* *passim*; see also Douglas M. MacDowell, *Demosthenes the Orator* (Oxford: Oxford University Press, 2009), 398–407.

43. Dionysius of Halicarnassus, *On the Style of Demosthenes*, 1.

44. Yunis, *Demosthenes: "On the Crown,"* 18.

45. Yunis, *Demosthenes: "On the Crown,"* 105.

46. Students who first only read King's *I Have a Dream* speech are struck by their different impressions of his style and performance after they listen and watch King on film.

47. On Demosthenes' ethical tone, see Dionysius of Halicarnassus, *On the Style of Demosthenes*, 13.

48. Aristotle, *Rhetorica* 1.1.14 (1355b); William M. A. Grimaldi, *SJ, Aristotle: "Rhetoric I": A Commentary* (New York: Fordham University Press, 1980), 5–6; Dionysius of Halicarnassus, *On the Style of Demosthenes*, 21, 22.

49. Yunis, *Demosthenes: "On the Crown,"* 217.

50. Cicero, *Orator*, 26.

51. Daniel J. O'Keefe, *Persuasion: Theory and Research*, 2nd ed. (Thousand Oaks, CA: Sage Publications, 2002), 101–13.

52. Smith, *Glossary of Terms*, 98–99.

53. Dionysius of Halicarnassus, *On the Style of Demosthenes*, 4; Enos, *Greek Rhetoric before Aristotle*, 125–37.

54. Dionysius of Halicarnassus, *On the Style of Demosthenes* 40.

55. Plutarch, *VDO: Demosthenes* 844D–845B; Plutarch, *Vitae Parallelae: Demosthenes* 4. 3–4; cf. Yunis, *Demosthenes: "On the Crown,"* 211.

56. Lloyd F. Bitzer, "Aristotle's Enthymeme Revisited," in *Landmark Essays in Aristotelian Rhetoric*, ed. Richard Leo Enos and Lois Peters Agnew (New York: Routledge, 1999), 179–91.

57. Dionysius of Halicarnassus, *On the Style of Demosthenes* 58.

58. Werner Jaeger, *Paideia: The Ideals of Greek Culture*, trans. Gilbert Highet (New York: Oxford University Press, 1944), 3:263–89.

59. Jaeger, *Paideia*, 3:278.

60. Jaeger, *Paideia*, 3:268.

61. Jaeger, *Paideia*, 3:264–65. Jaeger's research falls under the category of "war-time research"; he characterized Philip "as the Führer of all Greece" (3:282).

62. Jaeger, *Paideia*, 3:280.

EPILOGUE

James J. Murphy

Demosthenes' oration *On the Crown* is evidence of an exception to the rules of the world. That is, it shows that the whole can indeed be greater than all its parts.

The reader of this book can learn that a wide range of elements come together to make this speech a true masterpiece of persuasion. Surely *ethos* and *pathos* and *logos* and *lexis* all play a role in the impressiveness of the oration, as our authors point out so well. No adequate analysis is possible without considering the role of each of these elements. Yet they are not "parts" in the sense that they are like jigsaw puzzle pieces which, when all assembled, create a complete picture. Their simultaneity in Demosthenes speaking to his audience makes possible something beyond their simple presences.

Aristotle at one point defines "soul" as "that which makes a living thing alive." Some modern observers have criticized this statement as a tautology, but in all fairness he was trying to set up a preliminary, tentative locution to enable us readers to begin to think about the nature of "soul."

So, too, in the case of *On the Crown*, how can the reader go beyond the parts and the elements, beyond the strategies of thought and word, to find the soul of this most triumphant oration of the ancient world?

In the introduction to this volume we expressed our intention to make Demosthenes' speech *On the Crown* come alive to modern readers. It is our hope that these essays have helped readers begin a search for the soul of the speech.

SELECT BIBLIOGRAPHY

Included here are four sections: texts and translations of Demosthenes, translations and studies of Aeschines, studies of Demosthenes, and general studies.

TEXTS AND TRANSLATIONS OF DEMOSTHENES

Clemenceau, Georges. Thompson Charles Miner. *Demosthenes.* London: Hodder and Stoughton, 1920.

Demosthenes. *Demosthenes 3–5.* Translated by A. T. Murray. Cambridge: Cambridge University Press, 1936–39.

———. *Demosthenes: Against Meidias; Oration 21.* Translated by Douglas M MacDowell. Oxford: Clarendon Press, 1990.

———. *Demosthenis et Aeschinis Quae Existant Omnia T. 1.* Translated by William Stephen Dobson. London: Dove, 1828.

———. *Demosthenes on the Crown: With Critical and Explanatory Notes, an Historical Sketch, and Essays.* Translated by William Watson Goodwin. Cambridge: Cambridge University Press, 1901.

———. *Demosthenes on the Crown.* Cambridge: Cambridge University Press, 1957.

———. *Demosthenis Orationes 1–4.* Translated by Mervin R. Dilts. Oxford: Oxford University Press, 2008.

———. *Demosthenes: Six Private Speeches.* Norman: University of Oklahoma Press, 1972.

————. *Demosthenes: Speeches 1–17*. Translated by Jeremy Trevett. Austin: University of Texas Press, 2012.

————. *Demosthenes: Speeches 20–22*. Translated by Harris Edward Monroe. Austin: University of Texas Press, 2008.

————. *Demosthenes: Speeches 39–49*. Translated by Adele C. Scafuro. Austin: University of Texas Press, 2011.

————. *Demosthenes with an English Translation*. London: Heinemann, 1926.

————. *The First Philippic and the Olynthiacs of Demosthenes*. Translated by John Edwin Sandys. London: Macmillan Company, 1897.

————. *The First Philippic and the Olynthiacs of Demosthenes*. Translated by John Edwin Sandys. London: Macmillan, 1910.

————. *The First Philippic and the Olynthiacs*. Translated by John Edwin Sandys. London: Macmillan, 1950.

————. *Lettres et Fragments*. Translated by Robert Clavaud. Paris: Belles Lettres, 1987.

————. *The Letters of Demosthenes*. Translated by Jonathan A Goldstein. New York: Columbia University Press, 1968.

————. *On the Crown*. Cambridge: Cambridge University Press, 1904.

————. *On the Crown*. Translated by John J. Keaney. In *Demosthenes' "On the Crown."* Edited by James J. Murphy. Davis, CA: Hermagoras Press, 1983.

————. *On the Crown = (De Corona)*. Translated by Stephen Usher. Warminster, England: Aris and Phillips, 1993.

————. *On the Crown*. Translated by Harvey Yunis. New York: Cambridge University Press, 2001.

————. *On the False Embassy (Oration 19)*. Translated by Douglas M. MacDowell. Oxford: Oxford University Press, 2000.

————. *On the Peace: Second Philippic, on the Chersonesus, and Third Philippic*. Translated by John Edwin Sandys. London: Macmillan, 1953.

————. *Orationes*. Translated by Mervin R. Dilts. New York: Oxford University Press, 2002.

————. *The Orations of Demosthenes*. Translated by Charles Rann Kennedy. New York: American Book, 1898.

————. *Prologues*. Translated by Robert Clavaud. Paris: Les Belles Lettres, 1974.

————. *The Public Orations of Demosthenes*. Translated by Arthur Wallace Pickard. Oxford: Clarendon Press, 1912.

————. *Rede Fur Ktesiphon Uber Den Kranz*. Translated by Hermann Wankel. Heidelberg: Winter-Verlag, 1976.

————. *Select Private Orations of Demosthenes*. Part 1, *Containing Contra Phormionem, Lacritum, Pantaenetum, Boeotum De Nomine, Boeotum De Dote,*

Dionysodorum. Translated by John Edwin Sandys and F. A. Paley. Cambridge: Cambridge University Press, 1898.

———. *Select Private Orations*. Part 2, *Containing Pro Phormione, Contra Stephanum 1, 2, Contra Nicostratum, Cononem, Calliclem*. Translated by John Edwin Sandys and F. A. Paley. Cambridge: Cambridge University Press, 1910.

———. *Selected Private Speeches*. Translated by Christopher Carey and R. A. Reid. Cambridge: Cambridge University Press, 1985.

———. *Speeches 18 and 19*. Translated by Harvey Yunis. Austin: University of Texas Press, 2005.

———. *Speeches 60 and 61, Prologues, Letters*. Translated by Ian Worthington. Austin: University of Texas Press, 2006.

———. *Three Private Speeches of Demosthenes*. Translated by F. C. Doherty. Oxford: Clarendon Press, 1927.

Demosthenes and Aeschines. *Demosthenes and Aeschines*. Translated by A. N. W. Saunders. Baltimore: Penguin, 1975.

TRANSLATIONS AND STUDIES OF AESCHINES

Aeschines. *Aeschines*. Translated by Christopher Carey. Oratory of Classical Greece 3. Austin: University of Texas Press, 2000.

———. *Aeschines, Against Timarchos*. Translated by Nicholas R. Fisher. Oxford: Oxford University Press, 2001.

———. *The Speeches of Aeschines*. Translated by Charles Darwin Adams. Loeb Classical Library. Cambridge: Harvard University Press, 1919.

Cawkwell, George L. "Aeschines and the Peace of Philocrates." *Revue des Etudes Grecques* 73 (1960): 416–38.

Diller, Aubrey. "The Manuscript Tradition of Aeschines' Orations." *Illinois Classical Studies* 4 (1979): 34–64.

Fox, Robin Lane. "Aeschines and the Athenian Democracy." In Osborne and Hornblower.

———. "Aeschines and Athenian Politics." In Osborne and Hornblower, 135–55.

Harris, Edward Monroe. *Aeschines and Athenian Politics*. New York: Oxford University Press, 1995.

———. "When Was Aeschines Born?" *Classical Philology* 83 (1988): 211–14.

Hobden, Fiona. "Imagining Past and Present: A Rhetorical Strategy in Aeschines 3: Against Ctesiphon." *Classical Quarterly* 57 (2007): 490–501.

Kindstrand, Jan Fredrik. *The Stylistic Evaluation of Aeschines in Antiquity*. Uppsala, Sweden: Almqvist and Wiksell International, 1982.

Osborne, Robin, and Simon Hornblower, eds. *Ritual, Finance, Politics: Athenian Democratic Accounts Presented to David Lewis*. Oxford: Oxford University Press, 1994.

Rowe, Galen O. "The Portrait of Aeschines in the Oration *On the Crown*." *Transactions of the American Philological Association* 97 (1996): 397–406.

Ryder, T. T. B. "Ambiguity in Aeschines." *LCM* 2 (1977): 219–23.

Wooten, Cecil W. "Clarity and Obscurity in the Speeches of Aeschines." *American Journal of Philology* 109 (1988): 40–43.

STUDIES OF DEMOSTHENES

Adams, Charles Darwin. *Demosthenes and His Influence: Our Debt to Greece and Rome.* London: Harrap, 1927.

Anderson, Graham. *The Second Sophistic: A Cultural Phenomenon in the Roman Empire.* London: Routledge, 1993.

Antiphon and Andocides. *Antiphon and Andocides.* Translated by Michael Gagarin and Douglas M. MacDowell. Austin: University of Texas Press, 1998.

Badian, E. "Harpalus." *Journal of Hellenic Studies* 81 (1961): 16–43.

Buckler, John. "Demosthenes and Aeschines." In Worthington, *Persuasion*, 114–58.

Burke, Edmund Martin. "Character Denigration in the Attic Orators: With Particular Reference to Demosthenes and Aeschines." PhD Diss., University of Michigan, 1972.

———."The Early Political Speeches of Demosthenes: Elite Bias in the Response to Economic Crisis." *Classical Antiquity* 21 (2002): 165–93.

Calhoun, George Miller. "Oral and Written Pleading in Athenian Courts." *Transactions and Proceedings of the American Philological Association* 50 (1919): 177–93.

———. "A Problem of Authenticity (Demosthenes 29)." *Transactions of the American Philological Association* 65 (1934): 80–102.

Canavero, Mirro. *The Documents in the Attic Orators: Laws and Decrees in the Public Speeches of the Demosthenic Corpus.* Oxford: Oxford University Press, 2013.

Cargill, J. "Demosthenes, Aeschines, and the Crop of Traitors." *Ancient World* 11 (1985): 75–85.

Cartledge, Paul, Paul Millett, and S. C. Todd. *Nomos: Essays in Athenian Law, Politics, and Society.* Cambridge: Cambridge University Press, 1990.

Cawkwell, George L. "The Crowning of Demosthenes." *Classical Quarterly* 19 (1969): 163–80.

———."Demosthenes' Policy after the Peace of Philocrates." *Classical Quarterly* 13 (1963): 200–13.

Chiron, Pierre. "Relative Dating of the *Rhetoric to Alexander* and Aristotle's *Rhetoric*: A Methodology and Hypothesis." *Rhetorica: A Journal of the History of Rhetoric* 29 (2011): 236–62.

Cooper, Craig. "Demosthenes Actor on the Political and Forensic Stage." In *Oral Performance and Its Context*. Edited by C. J. Mackie. Leiden, the Netherlands: Brill, 2004. 145–61.

———. "Philosophers, Politics, Academics: Demosthenes' Rhetorical Reputation in Antiquity." In Worthington, *Persuasion*, 224–43.

Daitz, Stephen G. "The Relationship of the De Chersoneso and the Philippica Quarta of Demosthenes." *Classical Philology* 52 (1957): 145–62.

Didymus. *Didymos on Demosthenes*. Translated by Phillip Harding. Oxford: Clarendon Press, 2006.

Dionysius of Halicarnassus. *On the Style of Demosthenes*. In *Critical Essays*. Vol. 1. Translated by Stephen Usher. Loeb Classical Library. Cambridge MA: Harvard University Press, 1974.

Donnelly, Francis P. "The Argument Used Seventy-Two Times in the Crown Speech of Demosthenes." *Classical Weekly* 28 (1935): 153–56.

Dorjahn, Alfred P. "On Demosthenes' Ability to Speak Extemporaneously." *Transactions and Proceedings of the American Philological Association* 78 (1947): 69–76.

Duncan, Anne. *Performance and Identity in the Classical World*. Cambridge: Cambridge University Press, 2006.

Dyck, Andrew R. "The Function and Persuasive Power of Demosthenes' Portrait of Aeschines in the Speech 'On the Crown.'" *Greece and Rome* 32 (1985): 42–48.

Easterling, Patricia E. "Actors and Voices: Reading between the Lines in Aeschines and Demosthenes." In *Performance Culture and Athenian Democracy*. Edited by Simon Osborne and Robin Goldhill. Cambridge: Cambridge University Press, 1999. 154–65.

Easterling, Patricia E., Edward John Kenney, and Bernard MacGregor Walker Knox. *The Cambridge History of Classical Literature*. Vol. 1, *Greek Literature*. London: Cambridge University Press, 1985.

Gagarin, Michael, and David Cohen. *The Cambridge Companion to Ancient Greek Law*. Cambridge: Cambridge University Press, 2005.

Gibson, Craig A. *Interpreting a Classic: Demosthenes and His Ancient Commentators*. Berkeley: University of California Press, 2002.

Goldhill, Robin, and Simon Osborne. *Performance Culture and Athenian Democracy*. Cambridge: Cambridge University Press, 1999.

Gwatkin, William E. "The Legal Arguments in Aischines' 'Against Ktesiphon' and Demosthenes' 'On the Crown.'" *Hesperia* 26 (1957): 129–41.

Hansen, Mogens Herman. *The Athenian Assembly in the Age of Demosthenes*. Oxford: B. Blackwell, 1987.

Harding, Phillip. "Demosthenes in the Underworld: A Chapter in the Nachleben of a Rhetor." In *Demosthenes: Statesman and Orator*. Edited by Ian Worthington. London: Routledge, 2000. 246–71.

Harris, Edward Monroe. "Demosthenes' Speech against Meidias." *Harvard Studies in Classical Philology* 92 (1989): 117–36.

Hermogenes. *Hermogenes on Types of Style*. Chapel Hill: University of North Carolina Press, 1987.

Holst, Hans. "Demosthenes' Speech-Impediment." *Symbolae Osloenses* 4 (1926): 11–25.

Jackson, Donald F., and Galen O. Rowe, "Demosthenes 1915–1965." *Lustrum* 14 (1969): 5–109.

Jaeger, Werner. *Demosthenes: The Origin and Growth of His Policy*. New York: Octagon Books, 1977.

———. *Demosthenes: Der Staatsmann und Sein Werden*. Berlin: de Gruyter, 1963.

Kennedy, Charles Rann. "Demosthenes' Use of History." In *Demosthenes' "On the Crown."* Edited by James J. Murphy. Davis, CA: Hermagoras Press, 1987. 145–56.

Kennedy, George A. *Progymnasmata: Greek Textbooks of Prose Composition and Rhetoric*. Leiden, the Netherlands: Brill, 2003.

Kirk, William Hamilton. *Demosthenic Style in the Private Orations*. Baltimore: Friedenwald Co., 1985.

Lehmann, Gustav Adolf. *Demosthenes*. Von Athen: Ein Leben Fur Die Freiheit: Biographie. Munich: Beck, 2004.

Leopold, J. W. "Demosthenes on Distrust of Tyrants." *Greek Roman Byzantine Studies* 22 (1981): 227–46.

Luccioni, Jean. *Demosthene et Ie Panhellenisme*. Paris: Presses Universitaires de France, 1961.

MacDowell, Douglas M. *Demosthenes the Orator*. Oxford: Oxford University Press, 2009.

Mader, Gottfried. "Fighting Philip with Decrees: Demosthenes and the Syndrome of Symbolic Action." *American Journal of Philology* 127, no. 3 (2006).

———. "Praise, Blame and Authority: Some Strategies of Persuasion in Demosthenes, Philippic 2." *Hermes* 132 (2004): 56.

Maxwell-Stuart, P. G. "Three Words of Abusive Slang in Aeschines." *American Journal of Philology* 96 (1975): 7–12.

McCabe, Donald F. *The Prose-Rhythm of Demosthenes*. New York: Arno Press, 1981.

Milns, R. D. "Historical Paradigms in Demosthenes." *Electronic Antiquity* 2, no. 5 (1995).

———. "The Public Speeches of Demosthenes." In Worthington, *Persuasion*, 205–23.

Mirhady, David C. "Demosthenes as Advocate: The Private Speeches." In *Demosthenes: Statesman and Orator*. Edited by Ian Worthington. London: Routledge, 2000. 181–201.

Mommsen, Theodor, Paul Jors, Eduard Schwartz, and Richard Reitzenstein. *Festschrift Theodor Mommsen Zum Funfzigjahrigen Doctorjubilaum.* Marburg, Germany: Elwert, 1893.

Montgomery, Hugo. *The Way to Chaeronea: Foreign Policy, Decision-Making, and Political Influence in Demosthenes' Speeches.* Bergen, Norway: Universitetsforlaget, 1983.

Morford, Mark P. O. "Ethopoiia and Character-Assassination in the Canon of Demosthenes." *Mnemosyne* 19 (1966): 241–48.

Mosse, Claude. *Demosthene, ou, les Ambiguotes de la Politique.* Paris: A. Colin, 1994.

Murphy, James J. "Demosthenes." In *Encyclopedia Britannica.* 15th ed. 1974. 4:577–80.

———. *Demosthenes' "On the Crown": A Critical Study of a Masterpiece of Ancient Oratory.* Edited by James Jerome Murphy. Davis, CA: Hermagoras Press, 1983.

Neel, Jasper P. *Aristotle's Voice: Rhetoric, Theory, and Writing in America.* Carbondale: Southern Illinois University Press, 1994.

Ober, J. "Power and Oratory in Democratic Athens: Demosthenes 21, Against Meidias." In Worthington, *Persuasion,* 85–105.

Papillon, Terry L. *Rhetorical Studies in the Aristocratea of Demosthenes.* New York: Peter Lang, 1998.

Pearson, Lionel, and Ignacius Cusack. *The Art of Demosthenes.* Chico, CA: Scholars Press, 1981.

———. *The Art of Demosthenes.* Meisenheim am Glan, Germany: A. Hain, 1976.

———. "The Development of Demosthenes as a Political Orator." *Phoenix* 18 (1964): 95–109.

Pickard-Cambridge, Arthur Wallace. *Demosthenes and the Last Days of Greek Freedom, 384–322 B.C.* New York: G. P. Putnam's Sons, 1914. Rpt. Gorgias Press, 2002.

Pieper, Christopher, and James Ker. *Valuing the Past in the Greco-Roman World.* Boston: Brill, 2014.

Plutarch. *Lives of the Noble Greeks.* Edited by Fuller Edmund. New York: Dell, 1959.

Radicke, Jan. *Die Rede Des Demosthenes Fur Die Freiheit Der Rhodier.* Stuttgart: B. G. Teubner, 1995.

Romilly, Jacqueline de. *A Short History of Greek Literature.* [Translation of Precis de litterature greque.] Chicago: University of Chicago Press, 1985.

Ronnet, Gilberte. *Etude sur le Style de Demosthene dans les Discours Politiques.* Universite de Paris: E. de Boccard, 1951.

Rowe, Galen O. "Demosthenes' First Philippic: The Satiric Mode." *Transactions and Proceedings of the American Philological Association* 99 (1968): 361–74.

———."Demosthenes' Use of Language." In *On the Crown: A Critical Case Study of a Masterpiece of Ancient Oratory.* Edited by James J. Murphy. New York: Random House, 1967.

———. "The Portrait of Aeschines in the Oration on the Crown." *Transactions and Proceedings of the American Philological Association* 97 (1966): 397–406.

Rutherford, Ian. "Hermogenes on Demosthenes." In *Canons of Style in the Antonine Age.* Oxford: Clarendon Press, 1998.

———. "Homer and Demosthenes." In *Canons of Style in the Antonine Age.* Oxford: Clarendon Press, 1998.

Ryan, David Christopher. "Attic Orators: Demosthenes, Aeschines, and Lysias." In *Classical Rhetorics and Rhetoricians: Critical Studies and Sources.* Edited by Michelle Moran and Michael G. Ballif. Westport, CT: Praeger, 2005.

Ryder, T. T. B. "Demosthenes and Philip II." In *Demosthenes: Statesman and Orator.* Edited by Ian Worthington. London: Routledge, 2000. 45–89.

Sandys, John Edwin. *Demosthenes: On the Peace, Second Philippic, On the Chersonesus and Third Philippic.* London: MacMillan, 1900.

Schaefer, Arnold. *Demosthenes und Seine Zeit.* Leipzig: B. G. Teubner, 1856, 1885.

Sealey, Raphael. *Demosthenes and His Time: A Study in Defeat.* New York: Oxford University Press, 1993.

Sipiora, Phillip, and James S. Baumlin. *Rhetoric and Kairos: Essays in History, Theory, and Praxis.* Albany: State University of New York Press, 2002.

Slater, W. J. "The Epiphany of Demosthenes." *Phoenix* 42 (1988): 126–30.

Thomsen, Ole. "The Looting of the Estate of the Elder Demosthenes." *Classica et Mediaevalia–Revue Danoise De Philologie et D'Historie* 49 (1998): 45–66.

Thonssen, Lester, and Albert Craig Baird. *Speech Criticism, the Development of Standards for Rhetorical Appraisal.* New York: Ronald Press Co., 1948.

Todd, S. C. "Law and Oratory at Athens." In *The Cambridge Companion to Greek Law.* Edited by Michael Gagarin and David Cohen. Cambridge: Cambridge University Press, 2005. 97–111.

Too, Yun Lee. *Education in Greek and Roman Antiquity.* Leiden, the Netherlands: Brill, 2001.

———. *The Idea of Ancient Literary Criticism.* New York: Clarendon Press, 1998.

Trevett, Jeremy. "Demosthenes' Speech on Organization (Dem. 13)." *Greek, Roman Byzantine Studies* 35 (1994): 179–93.

———. "Did Demosthenes Publish His Deliberative Speeches?" *Hermes* 124 (1996): 425–41.

Tritle, Lawrence A. *The Greek World in the Fourth Century: From the Fall of the Athenian Empire to the Successors of Alexander.* London: Routledge, 1997.

Tuplin, Christopher. "Demosthenes' 'Olynthiacs' and the Character of the Demegoric Corpus." *Historia: Zeitschrift fur Alte Geschichte* 47 (1998): 276–320.

Wilson, P. J. "Demosthenes 21 (Against Meidias): Democratic Abuse." *Proceedings of the Cambridge Philological Society* 37 (1991): 164–95.

Wohl, Victoria. *Love among the Ruins: The Erotics of Democracy in Classical Athens.* Princeton: Princeton University Press, 2002.

Wolff, Hans Julius. *Demosthenes als Advokat. Funktionen und Methoden des Prozesspraktikers im Klassischen Athen.* Vortrag. Berlin: de Gruyter, 1968.

———. "Demosthenes as Advocate: the Functions and Methods of Legal Consultants in Classical Athens." In *Oxford Readings in the Attic Orators.* Edited by Edwin Carawan. Oxford: Oxford University Press, 2007.

Wooten, Cecil W. "Cicero and Quintilian on the Style of Demosthenes." *Rhetorica* 15 (1997): 177–92.

———. *Cicero's Philippics and Their Demosthenic Model: The Rhetoric of Crisis.* Chapel Hill: University of North Carolina Press, 1983.

———. "Cicero's Reactions to Demosthenes: A Clarification." *Classical Journal* 73 (1977): 37–43.

———. *A Commentary on Demosthenes's Philippic I: With Rhetorical Analyses of Philippics II and III.* New York: Oxford University Press, 2008.

Worman, Nancy. "Insult and Oral Excess in the Disputes between Aeschines and Demosthenes." *American Journal of Philology* 125 (2004): 1–25.

Worthington, Ian. "The Authenticity of Demosthenes' Fourth 'Philippic.'" *Mnemosyne* 44, (1991): 425–28.

———, ed. *The Blackwell Companion to Greek Rhetoric.* Oxford: Blackwell, 2007.

———. "The Chronology of the Harpalus Affair." *Symbolae Osloenses Symbolae Osloenses* 61 (1986): 63–76.

———. *A Companion to Greek Rhetoric.* Oxford: Blackwell, 2006.

———. *Demosthenes: Statesman and Orator.* New York: Routledge, 2000.

———. "The Harpalus Affair and the Greek Response to the Macedonian Hegemony." In *Ventures into Greek History: Essays in Honor of N. G. L. Hammond.* Oxford: Clarendon Press, Oxford University Press, 1994.

———. "Harpalus and the Macedonian Envoys." *Liverpool Classical Monthly* 9 (1984): 47–48.

———. "Oral Performance in the Athenian Assembly and the Demosthenic Prooemia." In *Oral Performance and Its Context.* Edited by C. J. Mackie. Leiden: Brill, 2004. 129–43.

———, ed. *Persuasion: Greek Rhetoric in Action.* London, 1994.

———. "Plutarch Demosthenes 25 and Demosthenes' Cup." *Classical Philology* 80 (1985): 229–33.

———. "Who Is the Demosthenes at the End of Demosthenes 56, 'Against Dionysodorus'? An Exercise in Methodology." *Scholia: Studies in Classical Antiquity* 11 (2002): 18–24.

Yunis, Harvey. "Politics as Literature: Demosthenes and the Burden of the Athenian Past." In *Oxford Readings in the Attic Orators*. Edited by Edwin Carawan. New York: Oxford University Press, 2007.

GENERAL STUDIES

Aristotle. *Nicomachean Ethics*. Translated by H. Rackham. Loeb Classical Library 73. Cambridge: Harvard University Press, 1926.

————. *On Rhetoric: A Theory of Civic Discourse*. Translated by George A. Kennedy. 2nd ed. New York: Oxford University Press, 2006.

Aristotle, Longinus, Demetrius. Aristotle: *Poetics*. Longinus: *On the Sublime*. Demetrius: *On Style*. Translated by Stephen Halliwell, W. Hamilton Fyfe, Doreen C. Innes, and W. Rhys Roberts. Revised by Donald A. Russell. Loeb Classical Library 199. Cambridge: Harvard University Press, 1995.

Athenaeus. *The Deipnosophists*. Translated by Charles Burton Gulick. Cambridge: Harvard University Press, 1950.

Badian, Ernst. "The Road to Prominence." In Worthington *Persuasion*, 9–44.

Barnes, Jonathan. "Rhetoric and Poetics." In *The Cambridge Companion to Aristotle*. Edited by Jonathan Barnes. Cambridge: Cambridge University Press, 1995. 259–85.

Carawan, Edwin, ed. *Oxford Readings in the Attic Orators*. Oxford: Oxford University Press, 2007.

Carey, Christopher. "Rhetorical Means of Persuasion." In Worthington, *Persuasion*, 26–45.

————. "Nomos in Attic Rhetoric and Oratory." *Journal of Hellenic Studies* 116 (1996): 33–46.

Cawkwell, George L. *Philip of Macedon*. London: Faber and Faber, 1978.

Celentano, Maria Silvana, Pierre Chiron, and Noel Marie-Pierre. *Skhema/ Figura; Formes et Figures Chez les Anciens: Rhetorique, Philosophie, Litterature*. Paris: Rue d'Ulm, 2004.

Chiron, Pierre, ed. and trans. *Pseudo-Aristote: Rhetorique a Alexandre*. Paris: Belles Lettres, 2007.

Cole, Thomas. *The Origins of Rhetoric in Ancient Greece*. Baltimore: Johns Hopkins University Press, 1991.

Conley, Thomas. "Topics of Vituperation: Some Commonplaces of 4th-Century Oratory." In *Influences on Peripatetic Rhetoric: Essays in Honor of William W. Fortenbaugh*. Edited by David C. Mirhady. Leiden, the Netherlands: Brill, 2007.

Cook, Brad L. "Swift-Boating in Antiquity: Rhetorical Framing of the Good Citizen in Fourth-Century Athens." *Rhetorica: A Journal of the History of Rhetoric* 30 (2012): 219–51.

Davis, Fred. *Yearning for Yesterday: A Sociology of Nostalgia*. New York: Free Press, 1979.

Dilts, Mervin R., and George A. Kennedy. *Two Greek Rhetorical Treatises from the Roman Empire: Introduction, Text, and Translation of the Arts of Rhetoric, Attributed to Anonymous Seguerianus and to Apsines of Gadara*. Leiden, the Netherlands: Brill, 1997.

Enos, Richard Leo. *Greek Rhetoric before Aristotle*. Revised edition. Anderson, SC: Parlor Press, 2012.

Edwards, Michael. *The Attic Orators*. London: Bristol Classical Press, 1994.

Fortenbaugh, William W. "Aristotle on Persuasion through Character." *Rhetorica: A Journal of the History of Rhetoric* 10 (1992): 207–44.

———. "Aristotle's *Rhetoric* on Emotion." *Archiv fur Geschichte der Philosophie* 52 (1950): 40–70.

———. "Theophrastus on Delivery." *Rutgers University Studies* 2 (1985): 269–88.

Fredal, James. *Rhetorical Action in Ancient Athens: Persuasive Artistry from Solon to Demosthenes*. Carbondale: Southern Illinois University Press, 2006.

Gagarin, Michael. "The Torture of Slaves in Athenian Law." *Classical Philology* 91 (1996): 1–18.

Habinek, Thomas N. *Ancient Rhetoric and Oratory*. Malden, MA: Blackwell, 2005.

Hansen, Mogens Herman. *The Athenian Democracy in the Age of Demosthenes: Structure, Principles, and Ideology*. Oxford: Blackwell, 1993. Rpt. Norman: University of Oklahoma Press, 1999.

Harding, Phillip. "Rhetoric and Politics in Fourth-Century Athens." *Phoenix* 41 (1987): 25–39.

Harris, Edward Monroe. *Democracy and the Rule of Law in Classical Athens: Essays on Law, Society, and Politics*. Cambridge: Cambridge University Press, 2006.

———. "Law and Oratory." In Worthington, *Persuasion*, 130–50.

Hatfield, Elaine and John T. Capiocco and Richard L. Rapson. *Emotional Contagion*. Cambridge: Cambridge University Press, 1994.

Heath, Malcolm. *Hermogenes on Issues: Strategies of Argument in Later Greek Rhetoric*. Oxford: Clarendon Press, 1995.

Hesk, Jon. *Deception and Democracy in Classical Athens*. Cambridge: Cambridge University Press, 2000.

Highet, Gilbert. *The Classical Tradition: Greek and Roman Influences on Western Literature*. New York: Oxford University Press, 1949.

Howatson, M. C., and Paul Harvey. *The Oxford Companion to Classical Literature*. Oxford: Oxford University Press, 1989.

Hult, Karin, ed. and trans. *Theodore Metochites on Ancient Authors and Philosophy*. Studia Gothaburgensia Graeca et Latina, 65. Gothenburg, Sweden: Acta Universitatis Gothoburgensis, 2002.

Hunt, Peter. *War, Peace, and Alliance in Demosthenes' Athens*. Cambridge: Cambridge University Press, 2010.

Johnstone, Christopher Lyle. "Greek Oratorical Settings and the Problem of the Pnyx: Rethinking the Athenian Political Process." In *Theory, Text, Context: Issues in Greek Rhetoric and Oratory*. Edited by Christopher Lyle Johnstone. Albany: State University of New York Press, 1996.

Jebb, Richard C. *The Attic Orators from Antiphon to Isaeos*. London: MacMillan, 1876.

Jones, A. H. M. *The Athens of Demosthenes*. Cambridge: Cambridge University Press, 1952.

Kagan, Donald. *The Peloponnesian War*. New York: Penguin, 2003.

Kennedy, George Alexander. *The Art of Persuasion in Greece*. Princeton: Princeton University Press, 1963.

———. *The Art of Rhetoric in the Roman World, 300 B.C.–A.D. 300*. Princeton: Princeton University Press, 1972.

———. *A New History of Classical Rhetoric*. Princeton: Princeton University Press, 1994.

———. "Oratory." In *The Cambridge History of Classical Literature*. Vol. 1, *Greek Literature*. Edited by P. E. Easterling and Bernard M. W. Knox. Cambridge: Cambridge University Press, 1985.

Lausberg, Heinrich. *A Handbook of Literary Rhetoric: A Foundation for Literary Study*. Edited by David E. Orton and R. Dean Anderson. Leiden, the Netherlands: Brill, 1998.

Lentz, Tony M. *Orality and Literacy in Hellenic Greece*. Carbondale: Southern Illinois University Press, 1989.

MacDowell, Douglas M. *The Law in Classical Athens*. London: Thames and Hudson, 1978.

Marrou, Henri. *A History of Education in Antiquity*. New York: Sheed and Ward, 1956. Rpt. Madison: University of Wisconsin Press, 1982.

May, James, and Jakob Wisse, trans. *Cicero: On the Ideal Orator [De oratore]*. New York: Oxford University Press, 2001.

Mirhady, David C. "Aristotle on the Rhetoric of Law." *GRBS* 31 (1990): 393–410.

———. "Torture and Rhetoric in Athens." *Journal of Hellenic Studies* 116 (1996): 393–410.

Patilion, Michel, ed. *Pseudo-Aelius Aristides*. Paris: Belles Lettres, 2002.

Pfeiffer, Rudolf. *History of Classical Scholarship from the Beginnings to the End of the Hellenistic Age*. Oxford: Clarendon Press, 1968.

Pieper, Christopher and James Ker. *Valuing the Past in the Greco-Roman World*. Leiden: Brill, 2014.

Plutarch. *Moralia*. Translated by Phillip H. De Lacy and Benedict Einarson. Loeb Classical Library 405. Vol. 7. Cambridge: Harvard University Press, 1959.

Roisman, Joseph. *The Rhetoric of Manhood: Masculinity in the Attic Orators*. Berkeley: University of California Press, 2005.

Roisman, Joseph, and Ian Worthington, eds. *Lives of the Attic Orators. Texts from Pseudo-Plutarch, Photius and the Suda*. Translated by Robin Waterfield. Oxford: Oxford University Press, 2015.

Russell, Donald. A. "Ethos in Oratory and Rhetoric." In *Characterization and Individuality in Greek Literature*. Edited by C. B. R. Pelling. Oxford: Clarendon Press; Oxford University Press, 1990.

———. "On Reading Plutarch's *Lives*." *Greece and Rome*. 2nd series. 13 (1966): 139–54.

Schiappa, Edward. *The Beginnings of Rhetorical Theory in Classical Greece*. New Haven: Yale University Press, 1999.

Sundahl, Mark J. "The Rule of Law and the Nature of the Fourth-Century Athenian Democracy." *Classica et Mediaevalia* 54 (2003): 127.

Thur, Gerhard. "Reply to D. C. Mirhady: Torture and Rhetoric in Athens." *Journal of Hellenic Studies* 116 (1996).

Trevett, J. S. "Aristotle's Knowledge of Athenian Oratory." *Classical Quarterly* 46 (1996): 371–79.

Todd, Stephen. "The Use and Abuse of the Attic Orators." *Greece and Rome* 37 (1990): 159–78.

Usher, Stephen. *Greek Oratory: Tradition and Originality*. Oxford: Oxford University Press, 1999.

Vickers, Brian. *In Defence of Rhetoric*. New York: Clarendon Press, 1988.

Walker, Jeffrey. *The Genuine Teachers of This Art: Rhetorical Education in Antiquity*. Columbia, SC: University of South Carolina Press, 2011.

———. "*Pathos* and *Katharsis* in 'Aristotelian' Rhetoric: Some Implications." In *Rereading Aristotle's Rhetoric*. Edited by Alan G. Gross and Arthur E. Walzer. Carbondale: Southern Illinois University Press, 2000. 74–92.

———. *Rhetoric and Poetics in Antiquity*. Oxford: Oxford University Press, 2000.

Werman, David. "Normal and Pathological Nostalgia." *Journal of the American Psychoanalytic Society* 25 (1977): 387–98.

Wooten, Cecil W., and George A. Kennedy. *The Orator in Action and Theory in Greece and Rome*. Leiden: Brill, 2001.

Worthington, Ian. "The Canon of the Ten Attic Orators." In Worthington, *Persuasion*, 244–63.

————."Greek Oratory, Revision of Speeches and the Problem of Historical Reliability." *Classica et Mediaevalia* 42 (1991): 55–74.

————, ed. *Persuasion: Greek Rhetoric in Action*. London: Routledge, 1994.

————. "The Rhetoric of Law in Fourth-Century Athens." In *The Cambridge Companion to Greek Law*. Edited by Michael Gagarin and David Cohen. Cambridge: Cambridge University Press, 2005.

Yatromanolaki, Joanna. *Sympheron, Dikaion and Nomoi in Deliberative Rhetoric: Studies in Aristotle's* Rhetoric *and Demosthenes' Deliberative Speeches*. Athens: Kardamitsa, 1969.

Yunis, Harvey. *Taming Democracy: Models of Political Rhetoric in Classical Athens*. Ithaca: Cornell University Press, 1996.

CONTRIBUTORS

LOIS P. AGNEW is an associate professor of writing and rhetoric at Syracuse University, where she also serves as the chair of the university's writing program. She is the author of *Outward, Visible Propriety: Stoic Philosophy and Eighteenth-Century British Rhetorics* and *Thomas De Quincey: British Rhetoric's Romantic Turn* as well as numerous journal articles and book chapters.

FRANCIS P. DONNELLY, SJ, a prolific writer on education, theology, rhetoric, and literature, was, for many years, a member of the faculty at Fordham University, where he taught courses on rhetoric and literature. His many books include *Cicero's Milo: A Rhetorical Commentary* and *The Oration of Demosthenes on the Crown: A Rhetorical Commentary*.

RICHARD LEO ENOS, a Piper Professor and the Radford Chair of Rhetoric and Composition at Texas Christian University, is a former president and a fellow of the Rhetoric Society of America. He received the TCU Chancellor's Award for Distinguished Achievement as a Creative Teacher and Scholar. He currently serves on the managing committee for the American School of Classical Studies at Athens.

RICHARD A. KATULA, a professor emeritus at Northeastern University, is the author of four books, including *The Eloquence of Edward Everett: America's Greatest Orator*, and is a coauthor of *A Synoptic History of Classical Rhetoric*. He is the former director of a National Endowment for the Humanities program titled "The American Lyceum and Public Culture."

JOHN J. KEANEY was a member of the classics department at Princeton University. His numerous books include *The Composition of Aristotle's "Athenaion Politeia": Observation and Explanation; An Essay on the Life and Poetry of Homer;* and an edition of *Harpocration: "Lexeis" of the Ten Orators.*

DAVID C. MIRHADY, a professor of humanities at Simon Fraser University in Vancouver, Canada, has written several articles and book chapters on Greek law, rhetoric, and the school of Aristotle. He has also published translations of Isocrates and, recently, of the *Rhetoric to Alexander* for the Loeb Classical Library.

JAMES J. MURPHY is a professor emeritus of English and rhetoric and communication at the University of California, Davis. He is the author or editor of numerous books on medieval and Renaissance rhetoric and is a coauthor of *A Synoptic History of Classical Rhetoric.* He is a fellow of the Rhetoric Society of America, a fellow of the Medieval Academy of America, and a Distinguished Scholar in the National Communication Association.

DONOVAN J. OCHS, a former director of the rhetoric program at the University of Iowa, was the author or coauthor of several books on rhetoric and writing, including *Consolatory Rhetoric: Grief, Symbol, and Ritual in the Greco-Roman Era* and *The Tradition of the Classical Doctrine of Rhetorical "Topoi."*

JEFFREY WALKER is a Liberal Arts Foundation Centennial Professor and the chair of rhetoric and writing at the University of Texas at Austin, a fellow of the Rhetoric Society of America, and a recipient of the RSA's Distinguished Service Award. He is the author of *The Genuine Teachers of This Art: Rhetorical Education in Antiquity; Rhetoric and Poetics in Antiquity;* and other books and articles.

INDEX

Landmarks in Rhetoric and Public Address

Also in this series